THE ART OF
EXTRAORDINARY
CONFIDENCE

YOUR ULTIMATE PATH TO
LOVE, WEALTH, AND FREEDOM

B. C. Allen Publishing
1500 SE Hawthorne Blvd.
Portland, OR, 97214
bcallenpublishing@gmail.com

The Center For Social Confidence
4347 NE Sumner St.
Portland, Oregon, 97218
http://SocialConfidenceCenter.com

Cover and interior layout: Olivia Storm

ISBN: 978-0-9889798-5-7

To Christian, Candace, Zaim, and Arman – thank you for teaching me how to do more, love more, and be bigger.

ALSO BY DR. AZIZ GAZIPURA

Books:
The Solution To Social Anxiety

Confidence Training Programs:
The Confidence Unleashed System
The Confidence Code
30 Days To Dating Mastery

E-books:
5 Steps To Unleash Your Inner Confidence
3 Ways To Enjoy Parties (Even If You're Shy)
How To Overcome Your Fear Of Public Speaking
7 Tips To Becoming A Conversation Master
Becoming Irresistible
Rejection-Proof: 5 Ways To Become Unfazed By Rejection

CONTENTS

FOREWORD

Imagine if you could take a magic potion that would cause people to take notice and listen to you more, make the opposite sex immediately more attracted to you, and make more people want to be your friend. This potion would also help you land better job offers, job promotions, and all sort of other opportunities, and allow you to enjoy a better life than you've ever lived so far.

That magic potion is confidence.

Confidence is more attractive than money or good looks. It automatically causes others to feel safer and to trust us more. And it is a powerful tool of influence. If you put two people in a room and have them discuss an issue, the person with more confidence is most likely going to prevail. Confidence is like a super power that gets you what you want out of life.

Most people think that confidence is just something you're born with. They think, "some people are confident, and some people just aren't." But the secret truth is that confidence is something that can be created, and it's something that can be lost. Most people think that if they lose their confidence, then nothing can be done about that either. But there is a system and a science to creating confidence. And once you know this system, and once you learn the keys to creating confidence at will, your whole life can change and get massively better right now.

As a young man, I spent many years of my life with very little confidence around friends and peers. Confidence seemed to come and go depending on the prevailing wind. If something good happened, if I could make people laugh, then I'd think, "I guess I'm good, I'm funny." If something bad happened, or if people didn't like me, I'd think, "I'm so dumb, nobody likes me." I certainly did not grow up with a lot of confidence. I had to learn how to do so, and I'm thankful I did.

With confidence I've been able to influence and inspire others to invest in themselves through my programs. I've been able to step up on stage, lead live events, and reach more people than I ever would have imagined. I've been able to become a multimillionaire and grow my company to over four million dollars per year in revenue.

With confidence I've become peers and friends with highly influential people. I met my wife, who I've been with for 11 years and have three amazing daughters with. Confidence is the key that unlocks the doors and gets you all the things you want in life.

Over the years I've seen there is a difference between being confident and being overly-confident, cocky, or arrogant. With real, pure confidence, people are more likeable. And Dr. Aziz is one of the most likeable people I've ever met.

I've seen how Aziz continually faces his own fears and courageously works through his own insecurities to create more and more confidence in himself. I've seen him use that confidence to inspire others, grow a highly successful business, and become a bestselling author on the topic of confidence. If there's anyone I'd want to learn confidence from, I'd want it to be Aziz.

And this book is loaded with ideas and strategies that you can immediately implement to get more confidence. In fact, just by reading it, you will get more confidence. No matter who you are, this is the book for you. Enjoy.

Christian Mickelsen

San Diego, 2016

PREFACE

Writing this book made me cringe.

Some sections were so uncomfortable to write, they made me squirm in my seat. I wanted to go back and clean them up, polish them until all the raw edges were hidden. I wanted to make myself look better. But I didn't.

Because this book is about being fully yourself. It's about the path to extraordinary confidence, which requires courage, vulnerability, bold action, and heart. And it would be a little ironic if I taught this stuff but was too scared to do it myself.

So in this book you will find the full spectrum of life. You will discover the world's most powerful tools, insights, and strategies for transforming confidence that I've accumulated over the last fourteen years in my relentless quest for ever-increasing levels of confidence and mastery. You will learn from stories, exercises, and games how to apply this transformation in your life immediately, so you can instantly reap the benefits of more self-confidence.

And, most importantly, you will see what confidence *really* looks like. You will see how the path to great confidence is not in becoming invincible, flawless, and seemingly perfect. But rather, it is in embracing your humanity, in all its messy glory and tender vulnerability.

It is my hope that my stories of falling short, failing, and otherwise being far from perfect will help you see the beauty in your own imperfections. I hope you will see that extraordinary confidence is not some distant destination that occurs when you've been expunged of all your flaws, but is something that is available right now, in this very moment. All you need is willingness and heart.

If you are willing to do whatever it takes, then there is no end to the level of confidence, love, wealth, and freedom you can experience in your life. I can't wait to begin this journey with you.

Love,
Aziz

Portland, Oregon
2016

WARNING!

This book will make you uncomfortable...and that's a good thing. Why? Because comfort is killing you. Well, actually it's your quest for comfort that's killing you. Your addiction to comfort is what leads you to avoid anything that makes you feel uncertain, nervous, or scared.

That said, this book is not about comfort. It's about freedom. Expansion. Growth. Income. Purpose. Passion. This book is about getting *uncomfortable*, because the moment you choose to move towards what makes you feel more alive, instead of what makes you feel more comfortable, your entire world will change.

Give it a try. At first you might curse me. *What? Who knew being uncomfortable would be so damn uncomfortable?* But once you get past the initial discomfort of leaving your comfort zone, you will thank me. For giving you this little push. This little love tap.

Ready to begin? Turn the page and your life will never be the same again...

SECOND WARNING!

Look out! This book contains some cursing in it. I sometimes use strong language with clients to emphasize a point or to make them laugh. I found this can interrupt negative patterns of thinking and put people at ease. It can also help them become more relaxed, playful, and flexible as they challenge old beliefs and take new actions. I would like to do the same with you.

So when you come across the occasional curse word, don't be alarmed. My intention is not to offend or be vulgar, but rather to help create a greater impact so you can more rapidly grow towards the extraordinary confidence and freedom you want in your life.

FINAL WARNING!!! (This one's serious)

I don't know about you, but when I purchase a non-fiction book I typically only read or listen to the first three to four chapters. Once in a blue moon I'll listen to the whole thing cover to cover, but that's pretty rare. Of course that means I'm not getting all the good stuff that's in the later chapters of those books, but I'm too excitable and after a few chapters I feel like I get the gist and am ready to move on to the next thing.

I urge you to *not* do that with this book, and here's why: this book is about inspiring you to break through to a higher level of self-confidence than you've ever experienced in your life, then teaching you how to sustain that confidence so it just becomes part of who you are and how you show up in the world; until it becomes part of your identity.

This isn't a fluffy magazine article with a four-point confidence-building check-list and a few tips. It's the most powerful, deep-dive into confidence creation that you may have ever taken in your life. In order to make this book truly transformational, the first several chapters are going to guide you through the layers of excuses, stories, and other muck that's been stopping you from having the confidence you should be living your life with.

Only once those barriers are cleared out of the way will you have a shot at truly living your potential by breaking through fears, eliminating hesitation, becoming rejection-proof, and taking bold action in all areas of your life.

Keeping those potentially life-changing outcomes in mind, if you read Chapters One through Three and then stop, you won't really get much out of this book, let alone the tools needed to create a significant and lasting difference. You'll have some new understanding about what's stopping you from living your best life and what might be sabotaging your confidence. You might even feel inspired to do something about it. But you won't have smashed through the barriers that are holding you back today. You'll still be living in the exact same patterns, getting the exact same results, and feeling the exact same way: stuck, frustrated, and unsatisfied. And, worse still, you may then be carrying with you the new story of, *Oh, I tried that stuff and it doesn't work. So now I am even more certain I'm destined to be this way forever...*

About one out of every five people I coach makes this mistake. And this mistake can be like a mini death. It can lead to a greater sense of hopelessness and frustration. People who make this mistake want to get some intellectual understanding from a safe distance. They want to read the first two chapters of the recent self-help title on the best-seller list and hope this small and painless effort will work some magic in their lives. They don't want to risk taking action, trying something new, and getting hurt or disappointed. And so, ultimately, they don't really want confidence (at least not as much as they want comfort and safety).

Don't be that guy, and if you're a gal, don't be that guy either. Be the one who commits to staying on the boat until we reach the other shore. Be the one who uses this book to change your life forever. Be the one who steps up, takes bold action, and creates a life of extraordinary confidence.

CHAPTER I:

STEP UP

Leaders aren't born, they are forged.

You Are Meant For More

It's true. You are.

I don't care what anyone has told you. What discouraging, disempowering, junky beliefs you've picked up from your family, from society, or from anyone else who told you otherwise.

You. Yes, you.

You are good enough. You are skilled enough. You are intelligent enough. And you have enough heart. You are meant for more.

You are NOT meant to live your life avoiding all major risks, trying to safely make it to your grave. You are not meant to work at a job you hate, or don't like, or that's "not so bad and pays the bills, I guess." You are not meant to stay way longer than you ever wanted to in an industry that sucks your soul dry.

You are not meant to make just enough money to live paycheck to paycheck. You are not meant to live a life where your career dictates every moment of your day and your hourly wage turns out to be thirty-four cents.

You are *not* meant to live a lonely single life because "there's just something wrong with me." You are *not* meant to live in a relationship where the love died years ago but you're staying in it out of fear of never finding someone else, or worse, "for the kids."

You are *not* meant to live a life of fear, stress, self-doubt, and self-criticism. You are not meant to dread social interactions, to second-guess everything you say, and to live in fear of what others think of you. You are not meant to be afraid of others and worried about whether anyone could be upset with you.

You are not meant to live a life where you are held back from doing what you love, making lots of money doing it, and enjoying awesome relationships on top of it. You are not meant to live a life filled with thoughts of "someday," excuses, and postponed dreams.

Now is the time.

It is the time to step up and see what you are really here for. I know that you know you're not on this planet for all the garbage I just listed. I know it because you're reading this book. I know it because you've made it this far. Shit, I know it because you have a beating heart in your chest.

You are here to do something else, perhaps something big. You are here to give something to the world that only you can give. To share your special gifts, your energy, your enthusiasm, your passion, and your light.

I don't know exactly what form that will take, but I can promise you one thing: you do. Once we clear out the excuses, the false stories, and the fear, and replace them with pure boldness and extraordinary confidence, your passion and your purpose will explode out of you. You won't be able to help yourself. You won't be able to stop.

And other people will see this and be drawn to you. They will show up to support you in your mission. To align with you. To love and encourage you along the way. To cheer you on.

Yours may be a Grand Purpose that touches thousands or millions of people across the earth. It may be a Noble Purpose that deeply impacts those closest to you: your partner, your children, your friends and family. Neither is better or worse. It's just more or less you. More or less what you're here to do. That's what this book is all about. To get you to do what you're here to do. And confidence is the golden key.

Dare To Dream

What do you want?

What do you *really* want?

Take a second to think about this. You may have done so in the past, or when you started your new job or created your business, or on December 31st of the last year. But do it again now. Right in this moment, if you could get anything you wanted out of your business, your finances, your health, your time, your emotions, your love life, your relationships, your friendships... What would it be?

Before you sigh, roll your eyes, or flip the page, hold on for a second. Most of us have been conditioned not to dream. At least not very big. But small goals merit small outcomes, modest incomes, and "good enough" results. Most of us ask for just enough to show that we're good enough, but not too great. We fear being perceived as too big headed, grand, greedy, or offensive to anyone, so we don't risk much in terms of goal-setting.

Or we've bought into the bullshit beliefs in our heads (and many other peoples') that we can't pull it off. It's impossible. We don't have the skills, intelligence, money, connections, education, or credentials. We're not attractive, charming, desirable, or worthwhile enough to achieve our wildest dreams, so we don't even allow ourselves to dream them.

Don't worry about those scary and depressing stories you've been telling yourself. Over the next few chapters we'll eliminate all that nonsense so you can freely flow towards whatever makes you feel alive and full of energy. But before we do that, we have to identify what it is you actually want.

In fact, put down this book for a few minutes and really think about what that is. You could even set a timer on your phone for four minutes, then close your eyes, and imagine. If you could have anything, do anything, be anything... if you had unlimited confidence in yourself, what would you create in your life? If you knew that you could not fail, what would you go after?

Do that now, and I'll see you in four minutes.

Hold Nothing Back

Welcome back. What did you come up with? Was it a short list or a long list? Was it easy to come up with ideas, or did it feel challenging and uncomfortable?

Did you hold back? Were there some things that you wanted that sounded "better" than others? Did you leave some things off because they made you look silly, foolish, greedy, or otherwise "bad"?

Forget about sounding good, looking good, or pleasing others. Forget about being a "good person" or being spiritual, or anything that takes you further away from your authentic self. Because guess what? Everything you desire is good. Even if it's for "less noble" motivations like impressing others, feeling good enough, or getting even to "show that son of a bitch he was wrong."

All of your desires are good because they drive you. Your desire drives you to step up, to be big, and to break through the fears and doubts that are holding you back. It gives you energy, fuel, motivation, and power. Your desire gives you purpose.

The beauty of it all is that as you grow, your motives will become more expansive, more universally beneficial for yourself as well as for others. You'll be driven by things like love, variety, and wanting to make a contribution to the world.

So don't worry about how noble or admirable your desires are currently. Start where you're at by simply acknowledging what you actually want in this moment. Be honest. If you can't be honest with yourself, then you're in for a long, confusing road through life.

Let's start with the big stuff that almost everyone wants: love, money, and freedom. Do you want more love in your life? Do you want to feel free and confident to put yourself out there, enjoy dating, and attract an amazing partner? Do you want to find the love of your life and create a life together? I started that journey with my wife, Candace, about five years ago and -- wow! It's more awesome than I could have ever imagined.

Maybe you're in a relationship and it's not going that well. What do you want from it right now? More love, more time together, more sex, more close feelings of connection and joy? Or are you on the other end of the spectrum and wanting to leave your relationship? Have you been planning your escape for two years? Are you holding on to a piece of driftwood because you're scared that if you let go you'll never make it to that tropical island paradise?

Here's a taboo that we often gloss over: what about sex? Do you want to feel more confident sexually? More attractive, powerful, desirable, and lovable? Do you want to feel more free to flirt, touch, and enjoy sex without self-consciousness, fear, or shame?

Really imagine what you want in your love life. Hold nothing back.

Let's keep the taboos rolling—what about money? How much money do you want to be earning per month? How about per year? How big do you want your business to be? How many people do you want on your team? If you work for a corporation, what level of management do you want to be at? Department manager? Senior VP? COO? CEO? Where do you want to live? What kind of house do you want to live in?

Does this sound too materialistic? Too greedy? Are you telling yourself these goals are impossible for someone like you anyway, so why even imagine them?

Whatever doubts or insecurities are popping up in your mind right now, don't worry about them. In fact, try not to even pay attention to them. We'll deal with all the self-doubt and fears and negative beliefs plaguing you, as we get into this book. For now, focus back on the dream, the vision. Focus on whatever makes you feel excited, maybe even a little nervous. What if I *could* earn this much? Whoa. That's right. Focus on that.

What else do you want from life? A deeper relationship with your children? More close friends? More time? A stronger sense of freedom to do what you want with your time? Do you want to only do what you love and be freed up from working just to pay the bills? Do you dream of creating your role in your business or company so that you do only what you enjoy doing and outsource the rest?

Perhaps regularly feeling a sense of peace and relaxed confidence is something you want. What if your new normal meant feeling confident and comfortable in your own skin, regardless of who you spoke with or what you did. Meeting new people, dealing with customer service representatives, making sales, giving a presentation to a large group - what if you experienced all of those moments with a sense of peace, excitement, and purpose? What if you didn't doubt yourself, criticize yourself, or second-guess every decision you made? What if you believed in yourself and trusted that you could handle whatever life sent your way?

Now, wait a second. Before you start with that "impossible" stuff again, stick with me. We're not in the implementation phase yet. We're still in the dreaming phase. Don't shut anything down. You, like all of us, are terrible at determining what is really possible or impossible for yourself. The reality is that you have no idea what you can actually do. So let your mind explore these dreams and be guided by that excited, expansive feeling in your chest. That's your heart coming alive.

In fact, let's go bigger.

GO BIGGER

After having talked to thousands of people about this kind of stuff, it seems pretty clear to me that most people do not let themselves dream very big. The average person seems to dream at fifty percent capacity, at most. Some people dream at an even lower capacity, dreaming at five or ten percent of what makes them feel excited and alive. That's only five to ten percent of what they could do, experience, give, and be in this life. Even the big, bold people who've done this kind of stuff a lot are still usually maxing out at fifty or sixty percent of what they could truly ask for and achieve.

I think this is because on some level we were all fed a hefty dose of "Who do you think *you* are?" as kids. Whether it was from our teachers, peers, siblings, or sadly, our parents, many of us got the message to not stand out, to not be extraordinary. This kind of message made it uncomfortable for us to see ourselves as big, special, and powerful. In fact, it makes most people feel squeamish and uncomfortable, even as adults. It makes them feel warm, tingly, and a little sweaty.

You might be thinking, but wait, what about the guy who says, "I want to be a billionaire." Isn't he going closer to 100 percent of his financial potential at least? Yes, there's always a guy (or girl) in the crowd who is going for the big B. As we did this exercise, you might have discovered that you are that guy. And that's cool. What I've found though, is that usually that person is just trying it on to see how it feels. It's kind of risky, significant, and exciting to say you want to be a billionaire. It might even make you feel better than others for a moment. You might get a sense of satisfaction in thinking, *My goals are bigger than your goals.*

But I've found very few people who actually truly want that and have a deep desire to contribute enough to the world to receive that much in return. And that's because in order to earn a billion dollars, you have to deliver astronomical value to the world first. If that's part of your purpose and your mission, then you'll do it.

My point here is that we all dream much smaller than we could. We all perceive our potential as much, much lower than it really is. To be clear, dreaming big is not necessarily about size or a number. Going big isn't about getting tons more. It's about the impact your dreams will make.

Going big for you can be about being an incredible parent who so profoundly loves and guides your children that they are set on a course to be all they can be. It can be about earning a decent living while doing what you truly love and having lots of free time to enjoy your family, friends, and hobbies. It can be about mastering your confidence in dating so that you have a deep sense of trust in your ability to attract the perfect partner for you into your life. Going big can be about exploding your business, skyrocketing your income and having a massive impact on the world.

So what does dreaming big mean for you?

Power Questions

Here are a handful of powerful questions you can ask yourself to break through the invisible ceiling that's keeping you from dreaming bigger. Read each one and then pause for a few moments. Put the book down. Close your eyes, take a few deep breaths, and really think about how you'd answer it.

- If you had all the confidence in the world, what would you do?
- If you knew you could not fail, what would you try?
- If all work paid the same, how would you most want to spend your day?
- If you could design your ideal day, what would you do? How would you start the day? What activities would you fill it with?

- How much time do you want to spend with your family? Your spouse? Your friends? By yourself?
- How much money do you want to earn?

Whatever you came up with for that last one, try doubling it. Does that make you nervous? Excited? Uncomfortable? Does it seem far-fetched, unrealistic, bad, wrong, or greedy? Good! That means you are dreaming outside of your comfort zone and part of you is getting scared, so it's coming up with stories, excuses and judgments.

IS IT REALLY POSSIBLE?

Yes. Yes it is. Next chapter.

Oh, ok, I'll spend more time talking about this. *Is this possible?* is a question our minds ask all too often. More often, in fact, our minds don't even ask a question like that, they just say, *That's not possible for me.* We spend a lot of time categorizing our desires and dreams into two camps: possible or impossible, with most of the really good stuff ending up in the impossible camp.

The strange thing is, these decisions are totally arbitrary. They are made up. Our mind is a terrible future-prediction machine. There have been dozens, if not hundreds of moments when my mind has told me in no uncertain terms, *You cannot do that. It absolutely will not happen.*

Here are just a few items on the long list of the "impossible" my mind has predicted in the past:

- It's impossible for the women you find really attractive to want to be with you.
- You cannot sustain a lasting, loving relationship with an amazing woman
- No one will buy your book.
- No one will invest in your training programs.

- No one will pay you for coaching/training.
- That group coaching program will never fill.

…and on and on. And guess what?

Every single one of those predictions above was completely false. Instead of believing them, I took action towards what I wanted and the exact opposite of what my doubtful mind said would happen, happened.

Have you ever done the "impossible"? Have you ever achieved or experienced something that your mind told you would never happen, or that you couldn't do?

Of course you have. Unless you've lived a life of total restriction and fear and never challenged the edge of your comfort zone. If that's the case, good God I'm glad you are reading this book. Life can be 1,000 times better than it's been for you so far.

You have to stop believing your mind when it says something is impossible. It's not an accurate statement. That is just fear talking. Your mind is terrified by the uncertainty of life outside of your comfort zone. It will say whatever it can to get you safely back into that comfort zone, with the covers pulled up over your head. You will learn all about this (and how to break free from this habit) in Chapter Four.

But let's go back to this question for a second: *Is it really possible?*

My answer is yes, if you are committed to the following two things. If you do these (and this book will show you how), then your success is inevitable:

1. Be willing to do whatever it takes.
2. Do whatever it takes.

That's it. When you are in the process of doing these two things, you can achieve the impossible. And you can do so rapidly. The only thing that stops you from doing whatever it takes is fear. Once you have that handled and you've made friends with your fear so it no longer holds you back, you can make rapid progress towards your dreams. Even the big, "impossible, that will never happen" dreams. Those are the best ones.

My Story: Sub-Average to Super Confident

How dare I claim "super confidence"?? That phrase makes me smile because it reminds me of an old Looney Tunes cartoon with Bugs Bunny and Wile E. Coyote. Wile E. decides he's done trying to catch the Road Runner and turns his sights towards Bugs. He formally informs Bug Bunny that he is now going to outsmart him, catch him, and eat him (which of course he never does). Throughout the episode he keeps referring to himself as "Wile E. Coyote: Super-Genius."

I'd say that just by stating that I'm super confident demonstrates that I do in fact have a lot confidence. But I didn't always. And that's important to know for many reasons. One, it can help you realize that I understand where you are coming from. I've been there, too. I know every aspect of social anxiety, shyness, and low confidence. I know the feelings of inferiority, insecurity, constant comparison, self-loathing, and fear. Ugh.

I'm not speaking from the detached place of someone who's always been naturally confident. No, no, no. I had to claw my way there. And I learned a great deal along each step of the journey, and continue to do so to this day.

Based on my own transformation, and the ones I've seen in hundreds of clients, no matter where you are right now, I can say with complete certainty that you can greatly increase your confidence in yourself. There is no doubt in my mind.

I'd say I started at Sub-Average. In this stage, I was riddled with social anxiety, I was uncomfortable talking to people I didn't know, I constantly compared myself to other people and found myself to be inferior, and I didn't believe in my capacity to pursue a career I liked or earn the kind of money I wanted to earn. Oh, and I also thought I was horribly unattractive and that no woman who had her life together would want to be in a relationship with me (let alone date, or even talk to me).

I played a lot of video games, smoked a fair amount of pot, and hung out with my several guy friends (playing video games and smoking pot). That part was pretty fun. If I hadn't been so depressed about my career and dating prospects, it would have been great.

I existed within my comfort zone. If something scared me, I completely avoided it. I lacked so much confidence that I didn't even actively avoid things, I just never allowed myself the option to do things that may have scared me. It's not like I considered whether or not I would approach that attractive woman or speak up in a group of people. Those actions were foreign to me and completely off my map: I didn't even consider them. I didn't like myself that much, so I used to criticize others a ton, just to feel temporarily better about myself. Never to their face of course, I was too terrified and non-confrontational to do that. No, it was always in my head or with one of my guy friends. That's how I'd describe sub-average.

Then, I had a moment when my life changed forever.

Having just worked up the courage over a period of months to ask a woman out, only to receive a polite no, I sat in my room, discouraged and hopeless. To make matters worse, I could hear the sweet laughter of a woman coming from my housemate's bedroom. He always seemed to have a woman who was interested in him. I was awash in envy, hopelessness, and pain.

I sat there stewing in the land of "never" and "impossible" feeling more and more discouraged. To escape from the negative spiral of pessimism, I decided to flick on my current favorite game at the time: Warcraft III. At least I could defeat some other nerd across the country to temporarily feel better.

But as the game loaded, something happened inside of me, and

I'll never forget it. It was a squeezing right in my solar plexus, in the center of my body. I could feel energy running to my hands, as if I was getting geared up for a soccer game or a fight. Crystal clear and unmistakable, one word flashed into my mind with shocking force: *NO.*

I instantly closed the game's loading screen, opened up my internet browser, and began my search for a solution. My life was never the same again.

Looking back, I know that in that moment, something bigger was calling me to step up to the things that were challenging me in life. The ancient Greeks had a concept of something called a Daemon. It is a spirit or entity that is attached to you when you are born. The Daemon's sole mission is to make sure that you live out your purpose. It knows what you're here to do and it will guide you there. Sometimes the Daemon guides you through pleasant means and encouragement, and sometimes by making you feel terrible when you're not doing what you're on earth to do.

Well, my Daemon gave me a swift kick in the pants that night and got me on the right track. From that moment on, I was no longer dabbling in or just considering solutions to my problems. I was ready to tackle them head on. I didn't even know how to change, or what steps to follow, but I was ready to do whatever it would take to change my circumstances.

Since that night, I have been voraciously studying and applying everything I can learn about maximizing confidence. At the time of writing this book it's been thirteen years since I began this practice, and I don't show any signs of stopping or slowing down.

Through applying what you will learn in this book, I went from a place of feeling uncomfortable and inferior most of the time to feeling excited, inspired, and alive. There are so many things I do on a daily basis now that I never thought I would be able to do.

I interact with people all day long, speak in front of a camera, record my voice, and share what I've written with the world. I engage in daily sales conversations, hear lots of "nos" and get rejected all of the time. I speak in front of groups, large and small. I work with people in positions of power and authority and feel equal to them. I speak with, interview, and am friends with people who I used to think were so much better than I was because they were more confident, more successful, or earned more money.

I am completely comfortable starting conversations with anyone, and I can make people laugh and put them at ease. I can speak up in groups and share stories. I know how to engage, connect, and flirt with women. I have a beautiful, amazing wife who is supportive, loving, wise, and inspiring. And our relationship is full of love, connection, sex (although a little less now with two kids under two years old), and joy.

Now before I get put on a pedestal, I must inform you that I am not perfect. I have bad days. I get stressed out and pissed off. I can feel insecure, take a rejection hard, and sometimes doubt myself and think that I can't do something.

But overall, my center of gravity — where I spend the majority of my time — is in a place of inspired confidence, action, and service. It's pretty awesome. I'm not saying this stuff to brag. I'm sharing this to inspire you to step up and do the same. If you're reading this book, then the same force that's guiding me is guiding you.

There's nothing magical or special about me that is any different than the power that is inside of you. And no matter where you are starting, you can tap into that power to get to the next level. It can give you the confidence to break through any barriers in your way and blast into a whole new level of achievement, income, love, and joy. If I can do it, so can you.

To learn more about my journey and the five simple steps I took to transform my confidence level, go to, http://SocialConfidenceCenter.com

WRITE IT DOWN

Feeling inspired? Great! Capitalize on that. Write those goals and dreams down.

Whatever came to your mind that excited you, that made you feel more alive, write those down. For a few minutes, forget the words unreasonable or impossible. By the end of this book you won't even understand those beliefs in the same way. You'll be ready to take on more than you ever imagined, so you'll want to be going for something that really excites you. Write those ideas down, in specific detail.

I'm sure you're familiar with the classic text, *Think And Grow Rich* by Napoleon Hill, right? I remember listening to an audio version of that many years ago that sounded like it was recorded in the 1950s. The reader had this tone of news anchor mixed with 1950s Tide detergent commercial, which always made me smile. In that book, Hill emphasized that every successful person is very clear on their goals, and reads them out loud every morning, then again before bed.

I sat in my room listening to the Tide detergent man tell me how to transform my life, saying something along the lines of: "Using the powerful principle of auto-suggestion, you can program your sub-conscious mind to carry out your goals by aligning with infinite intelligence."

Harness the power of Infinite Intelligence you say? That sounded pretty good to me. Being the good student, I wrote all of my goals down and read them out loud every morning and every night... for three nights. If you can do it for longer than that, I'm sure that's better and more effective. I can't speak to that. But I do know that I have written down my vision for what I want for myself dozens of times in my life. And the vision for what I want in my life has come true over and over again.

So whether you want to read your goals twice each day, like brushing your teeth, or you want to turn them into a collage and paste them all over your steering wheel, it's up to you. All I know is, write those goals and dreams down. Napoleon Hill says it's good shit.

THE PATH TO GLORY

Now that you have clarity around what you actually want, we can focus the rest of this book on how to get there. A key component of creating these outcomes and living an extraordinary life is confidence. Confidence in yourself, in your ability to relate to others effectively and in your ability to take repeated, decisive action.

The rest of this book is laid out in a specific way that is most effective for achieving rapid breakthroughs and massive progress. First, we will identify and remove the two protective layers that keep ninety five percent of people from boldly stepping up and creating the life they want: Excuses and Stories.

After we've identified the Excuses and Stories we'll dive into the force that really stops us. The root of all hesitation, inaction, self-sabotage, doubt, self-criticism, and anything else that stops us from being fully alive is Fear. In Chapter Four you will learn exactly how to face this beast head on so it never stops you again.

Once you've removed the obstacles in your path and learned how to face fear, we can jump in with both feet. You'll discover the magical secret to getting anything you want in life, from confidence, power and love, to money, success and material abundance: Action. Repeated, unfaltering action. Even though we want all these things in our lives, many of us have some messed up ideas in our heads about having them. From sales and money, to power and love, we'll help you remove the confusion, inner blocks, and insecurities that make getting and keeping these things difficult.

The results of this journey are profound and lead to an extraordinary life. Not just externally, in terms of financial or relationship success, but internally. This journey is one that leads to true internal success: confidence, freedom, love, wealth, joy, and happiness. Because most of us have found that after a moderate amount of external success we quickly realize that's not all that we're after. That it doesn't bring the happiness and joy we seek. That kind of fulfillment comes from facing our fears, breaking through perceived limitations, and doing what we once thought was impossible.

CHAPTER II:

EXCUSES

EXCUSE CITY

Easy for you to say.
You don't know what it's like.
The economy is terrible.
I don't have any marketable skills.
It's too competitive.
Someone else has already done it (better).
It's not fair.
All the good ones are taken.
My parents treated me like crap.
My ex-wife criticized me.
Those lucky bastards were born into successful families.
I was born poor with no connections.

I could go on for thirty pages. Every single one of these excuses is a direct quote I've heard from one of my clients. Do you recognize any of these? What are some of your favorites? Any one of these your go-to refrain? Your chorus? Your mantra?

For me, for many years it was, *someone else has already done it better, so why bother?* And guess what? We haven't even gotten into stories yet. What's the difference between stories and excuses? You'll find out in a few pages. For now, let's talk about excuses.

THOSE LUCKY BASTARDS

I sat there in my office, waiting in silence. I had a strong urge to speak, but I knew better. In my earbuds I could hear the wind blowing on the other end of the line. He had told me he was doing our session during his lunch hour while standing in an open field near his office.

Work had been crushing him and he was desperate to shift his relationships and results in the company. While he was excited about creating his own business, he had stalled out in that process as well. He began the session with half a dozen excuses as to why none of his plans could possibly work out. He couldn't change anything at work because everyone there was selfish and just protecting themselves. He couldn't grow his own business because he didn't have the right connections and nothing he ever did would make any money anyway. After he shared all of these with me, I said, "Wow, it sounds like you feel pretty stuck and hopeless about your current situation. What are you hoping for from our conversation today?"

"I don't know," he replied. "I just want to have a different perspective. I want to find a way out."

We talked for a while about this, but it seemed apparent we weren't getting anywhere, so I said, "It seems like part of you wants to feel more free and excited, and another part of you is angry and wants to blame everyone and everything for your current suffering." I was a little nervous saying it because I always am when I cut through to the heart of things and honestly state my perspective. The "old nice guy" programming in me gets nervous about that. Then there was the silence of my intentional holding back from clarifying, apologizing, or making sure he was ok.

Long pause.

"Yeah. I do want to feel more free. But I just don't see how that's possible. I don't have any family connections in the industry, I wasn't born a director's son. Even if I did create something, it would take five years for it to make any money, if it ever did at all."

I could feel him entrenching himself further into his insecurity as he said this. I could hear the unspoken subtext: *Nope. There is no way out and fuck you if you think you're going to convince me otherwise. I'm staying here.*

What's going on here? He's feeling stuck and frustrated in his life, upset about his work situation, and powerless to do anything about it. He is also reluctant to perceive his situation differently so he can find a way out and transform things.

Have you ever been there? I know I have. Sometimes I still go there late at night after a long day, especially if I haven't gotten enough sleep. I tell myself that life sucks and it's not fair. My wife tries to draw me out, ask me questions, help me see things in a different way. Instead of being grateful, I feel anger. Part of me says, "No! Nothing will work! Everything sucks! How dare you try and talk me out of it?...Wait! Where are you going? Come back! I'm not done complaining yet."

That's what we want when we're in this state. We want someone to listen to us. To hear the entire list of complaints from start to finish. To witness the ways we've been wronged, to see how the world isn't fair, and how things really are impossible and out of our control. And we get angry if our audience doesn't play along.

And that's what happens in a lot of therapy sessions. People go week after week to give their list of excuses, and have the therapist say, "Mmmm, you're right. That sounds really hard. Tell me more."

Back when I was a therapist, when I asked a client why they were there, what they wanted to get out therapy, if they said, "I just want a place to come and vent," I'd shudder inside. And I would not work with them unless their purpose for therapy changed. Because I know venting is not how people create extraordinary lives, let alone change anything about their current situation.

Now, please don't get me wrong. I am not saying it's wrong to feel frustrated, discouraged, confused, or angry about something or someone in your life. And it's important to talk about those frustrations and to explore what's going on in order to heal and move forward. What matters is how we go about doing this. Are we looking for solutions? Are we taking responsibility for our feelings and our lives? In that moment are we taking ownership of our lives or seeing ourselves as the victims of other people and circumstances?

As painful as it is, people sometimes prefer to see themselves as powerless in situations. This phenomenon is called Secondary Gain, and it refers to the benefits we get from remaining the victim in our lives. When we blame others, we get the relief of knowing it's not our responsibility that things didn't work out. We no longer feel like a failure or inadequate in some way. When we are convinced it's hopeless so there is no point in trying to achieve a certain goal, we get to avoid all of the discomfort of taking action and risking potential failure or rejection.

Let's dive in and see what makes us take the exit for Excuse City, and even better, how we can find our way out of this wretched place.

The Victim Stance

The victim stance is a way of relating to the world. We all have the potential to assume this position, and some people do so more than others. Hell, some people spend their entire lives in the victim stance.

What is the victim stance? Summed up in one sentence, it is this: Forces outside of my control determine my destiny. "They" or "it" -

something outside of myself - determines whether I succeed, grow, develop, make money, experience love, feel happiness, or experience anything else I want in my life. I am powerless in this situation.

When we are in this stance, we naturally feel weak, insecure, and afraid. We can also feel pissed off, righteous, and angry. The victim spends his life feeling afraid of what will happen and pissed off at those around him who are "making" him feel however he is feeling. He's also pissed off at the people who are getting the things he wants because they're lucky, immoral, or otherwise wrong.

Let's uncover these elements a little more. This is incredibly important to do, and here's why: There are no people who are permanently victims. It's just a mental stance we can go into—a mindset—and we can all go there now and again. The better you get at identifying that you're in this mindset, the faster you can find your way out of it, which will make your life much, much better.

We'll get into more of that in a moment, but first, let's flesh out the hallmark signs that you're entering Victim Land. Consider these red flags that are there to help you know when you're crossing into the danger zone. Noticing them can help you identify what's happening and then choose to do something different to break the cycle. In that moment you can choose to take care of yourself and give yourself what you need so that you can feel more energized and resourceful.

Signposts of Entering Victim Land

STRONG, PERSISTENT BLAME

When life doesn't go your way—when you fail to reach an outcome, or someone doesn't do what you want them to do—you feel incredibly charged up inside, frustrated, angry, and outraged. You might be thinking, *What the fuck is wrong with that person? How dare they say those things? How could they be so stupid, so ignorant, so lazy, so*

_____ (Insert your favorite outraged insult or choice here)?

Your mind keeps churning it around again and again. You can't think about anything else. You fantasize about revenge, what you'd say to them, how you'd get them back. You carry on an intense and detailed argument with them in your head. Maybe you will actually do or say these things, or maybe you're too scared to and won't doing anything at all. Regardless, you are trapped in a state of inner turmoil and anger all because that person said or did _____ (or didn't say or isn't doing _____).

Oh, and maybe you've "tried everything" and that person still isn't doing ____. And it's their fault and they suck. And you hate them. But you're still going to keep working for them, being their spouse, sleeping with them, or whatever your relationship is with them. Because what else would you do? Leave? That's terrifying and you'd never find anything else that's better. No thank you, instead you'll stay here and blame the shit out of them in order to temporarily feel more powerful.

Which actually brings us to our next signpost: feeling powerless.

POWERLESS

You feel like you are stuck in whatever situation or circumstances you find yourself in. You can't change jobs because the economy is bad and no one is hiring. You can't feel happy because your partner is not doing their fair share around the house and you can't get them to do more.

Regardless of the specific situation, a hallmark feature of being in the victim stance is telling yourself, things can't be different. And, *I can't make them different because some external force won't let me.* It's a discouraging, hopeless, depressing state that leaves you feeling like a frustrated teenager who has to live with strict and uncaring parents.

In fact, that is a good descriptor of the victim stance overall. We still see ourselves as children and the big bad adults aren't giving us what we want. But, I digress. Where was I? Ah, right, powerlessness.

One other factor that makes us feel powerless actually has nothing to do with "them" holding us back. It's actually the endless list of fears and reasons we have about why we're not powerful and capable. Those are your inner stories, and we'll get to those in the next chapter. In fact, underneath all the blame and ranting against external forces, the person in the victim stance deep down fears that they are not good enough; that they don't deserve the happiness they so deeply desire. But that sounds bad and weak and feels terrible, so instead we prefer to sound tough and blame "those lousy illegal immigrants" or whoever else might fit the bill at the time.

When you notice yourself slipping into one of those patterns, congratulate yourself! Being able to identify it and know it is happening is a huge step towards breaking free. It's important to recognize that many people never will break free simply because catching yourself in these comfortable and safe patterns is difficult to do in the moment. These people will remain in a cloud of their victim-thinking and bounce from one painful experience to another, all the while feeling powerless, pissed off, and afraid.

Once you've identified that you're blaming someone else for whatever you don't have, you can acknowledge that you've entered victim land. It's ok. There's no shame in it. We all go there. It's the default place our minds go in response to pain, discomfort, challenge, or adversity. The goal is not to never go to the victim stance, it's knowing how to acknowledge when you're there, then reclaim your power and get back to owning your life.

THE OWNER STANCE

The essence of the Owner Stance is *I am responsible.*

I am responsible for the quality of my life. I am responsible for my feelings, my responses and my results (in the long term). If my life is not going the way I want it to go, I can make different choices and steer it in a different direction. If there is an obstacle standing in my way, I am the one who must find a way around the obstacle in order to progress towards what I want. Rather than being an effect in the world, I am a cause.

If the Victim Stance is like a boat floating at sea, at the mercy of the winds and currents, then the Owner Stance is a boat with sails, oars, and maybe even a motor. Much like sailing, we cannot control the winds or the currents, but we can choose which course to follow, which direction to take, and how to respond to the changing circumstances of events outside of ourselves.

So what does this actually look like in our day-to-day life? First, an owner chooses the direction of his life. What do I want to do? What kind of job do I want to have? What kind of money do I want to earn? Who do I want to spend my time with? Notice the focus on what I *want* to do, rather than what I think I *should* do, or what other people expect of me.

An owner also realizes that people are always at a place of choice. If I don't like my boss, I can choose to relate to him or her differently, or I can choose to quit. If I don't like the way my kid speaks to me, I can choose to respond differently or take new actions to change the pattern. If I don't like my weight, I can change my diet and level of physical activity. If I don't like my economic status, I can take action to increase my income and financial freedom.

The essential belief of the owner is, *I can.* Or at the very least, it's *I must. I am the only one who is going to do it.* And that is absolutely true. No one else is going to take care of your health, make your relationship better, or earn you more money.

Many people exit the owner stance and slip into passive victim stance when they visit a professional. Whether it's a medical doctor or a financial advisor, people will all too quickly give their power and responsibility to the "expert." Just tell me what pills to take and I'll take them. Just tell me where to put my money and I'll do it.

I get it. I have the same desire, too. It can be kind of a relief to let someone who supposedly knows better than I do take over. Ah, whew. I don't need to figure out this complex, ever-changing financial system and learn a bunch of confusing jargon just to make sense of it. I can just talk to this friendly chap here who will ask me some basic questions about my desired level of risk. Then he'll take care of the rest and I won't have to spend the energy on figuring all this stuff out (or face my fears around figuring it all out. More on that in the Money Chapter).

But beware. Whenever we give up our responsibility, we give up ownership of our lives. And while that might be relieving in the short term, it has one fatal flaw: no one is going to care as much about your wellbeing as you do.

I don't mean to make the world sound hostile or uncaring. There are many people that love you deeply and want the best for you. Your spouse or parents might do anything for you. Yet at the same time, they cannot be as absorbed in your wellbeing as their own. At the end of the day, the one who feels the results (good or bad) and cares the most is you. So let's take charge and make shit happen.

Below are the components of a life of ownership. These are beliefs, attitudes, and abilities that people living in an owner stance use to engage in life. See if you can notice one theme that links all of them together. The one thing that is required in order to live this way. I'll share at the end of the list, but see if you can pick it up along the way

Owner Stance Components

1. ASSERTIVENESS: SAY WHAT NEEDS TO BE SAID

An essential tool in the owner's arsenal is being able to speak up. It requires boldness and courage to do this as a way of life. The pull towards fear-based people-pleasing and conflict avoidance is strong in most of us. As a result, we hold back, bite our tongues, and keep our thoughts to ourselves. We often do *not* say what needs to be said in the moment. And then we suffer.

However, when we are taking ownership of our lives, we know that we are responsible for our relationships with others. I don't mean some kind of weird over-responsibility where you need to take care of someone else's feelings and make all their decisions for them. I simply mean that you are responsible for your own experience. Let me paint a picture for you.

Imagine that you are pissed off with someone after spending time with them. Most likely you didn't say what you *really* wanted to say to them in the moment. Instead, you decided to go vent to a friend and maybe you even get them to agree that your boss, or your dad, or whoever else is an inconsiderate jerk, but this does nothing to solve the problem with this person in your life. You still feel angry at them—perhaps validated for why you're angry—but the anger hasn't gone away. And the person you're mad at still doesn't even know what they've done to upset you. Your anger remains pent up inside you, unproductive and harming only your own mental state.

The only way to solve this problem is to step up and be bolder. Say what needs to be said to the person who needs to hear it.

Of course there is a skill to doing this. If you storm into your boss's office and say, "Listen here you fat, miserable loser. I'm here to say what needs to be said!" then results will be questionable. Although, you might be better off than years of passive, resentment-building submission. But I digress…

Instead, you pay attention to what is really going on, and ask yourself, what it is you're really upset about. What boundary did this person cross? What did they do that you would have preferred they didn't? Anger is just a sign that you are internally saying "no" to something, so what is it that they did, that you need to say "no" to? Did they give you unsolicited advice? Did they keep interrupting you or talk over you in a meeting? Did they tease or poke fun at you in a way that felt critical or malicious?

As you make a study of this and gain more clarity, you can start speaking up for yourself more often. Ideally in the moment, but you can always go back to something. "I want to talk with you for a second about yesterday's meeting…"

It's even better to do this right in the moment. As soon as Jimmy Bob starts to interrupt you, raise the volume of your voice about 25% and say, "Hold on, hold on a second Jimmy Bob, let me finish." You can even casually put your hand up. Then keep talking. Don't wait for his approval or acknowledgement. Own it.

If someone pokes fun at you, fire something back. It doesn't have to be the wittiest response in the world. It doesn't even have to make a lot of sense. The key is to just blurt something back fast. If you struggle to respond to criticism or bullying at your workplace or in life, I recommend listening to this episode of my internet radio show – Shrink For The Shy Guy. It provides clear strategies and examples on how to defend yourself and speak up with confidence. http://shrinkfortheshyguy.com/dealing-with-critics-haters-and-bullies/

The key here is to realize that you are responsible for the relationships in your life. If you don't like them, then speak up to change them. If that doesn't work because the person is not open to it, or is too defensive or stubborn, then stop interacting with that person. Leave that company and go to a different one. Move to a different department. Fire them. Break up with them. Stop being friends with them. Don't see that family member or talk to them (except when forced to once a year at Thanksgiving or something).

You get my point? You don't *have* to spend time with anyone. It's a choice. I'm not saying your first course of action is to leave every place where you have a challenging interaction with someone. That's a last resort. You'll be amazed how much you can transform the relationships in your life just by being bold. Take a deep breath. Have the sweaty, uncomfortable five-minute-long conversation you've been needing to have. Step up and say what needs to be said. Life gets a whole lot better when you do.

2.   AGREEMENTS: GET CLARITY ON YOUR EXPECTATIONS

I pressed the "send" button on my email and sat back in satisfaction. There, I'd done it. I'd finally stopped doing all of the video editing myself and took the necessary steps to start outsourcing the work. I'd found Levente, my newfound friend in Romania who would take care of all of my problems.

The next day I checked my email. No response. Huh, not super awesome, but let's see what happens. Nothing the next day as well. At this point I was pissed. *Seriously? Two days go by and not even a nod of receiving the files? No "I got these and will have them back to you by next Thursday"? Nothing?? I'm gonna fire his ass and find someone new!*

Then I remembered something I learned from Steve Chandler about agreements versus expectations. Expectations are all of the ideas you have in your head about how everything and everyone *should* be. I have expectations about how a contractor or employee *should* respond to me. I have expectations about how long things *should* take, how responsive people *should* be. And guess what? It's all bogus.

Not because clarity on what I want is bad. Neither is having a desire for responsiveness and quick results. In fact, that's what I want on my team. But it's all bogus because it's just in my head. I haven't actually talked about it with anyone. I've just been holding onto these expectations without letting others know I had them, or without having the courage to speak up and create mutual agreements with those I interact with.

I see this in every area of life. Whenever a client is having a challenge with a spouse, co-worker, employee, supervisor, or boss, the first thing I get curious about is: what are the unspoken expectations here?

In fact, that's usually what I'll ask my client right off the bat. Then we'll explore them together. Nine times out of ten, the expectations have not been discussed. The two parties didn't share what they wanted from one another and come to a mutual understanding and agreement.

I remember one client who initially took offense to this notion. He was the COO of a moderately large tech startup and had many people reporting to him. "I shouldn't have to do that. People should understand my expectations and make things happen. That's what I'm paying them for," he complained.

"Makes sense," I replied. "You can keep that stance as long as you like. It may actually be true too. What I'm curious about is how effective it is. You have high turn-around and are chronically frustrated with the people you work with. It doesn't seem like your approach is working effectively. Perhaps it's sub-optimal."

I love that word. I learned it from Brian Johnson, who is the founder of enTheos and is a walking encyclopedia. It's a great way to highlight something that isn't working well without making anyone sound bad or wrong. It's not stupid, it's just sub-optimal.

Do you know what was behind his resistance? It's the same thing behind both my resistance and yours around this topic. It's fear.

Fear of direct conversations. Of sharing what we want. Of hearing what other people want and need. Fear of being real, vulnerable, and honest. Fear of direct contact with other humans. Yep, even the big tough COO had this fear. We all do on some level.

So we all have a choice. We can remain cowardly and cling to our unspoken expectations. This allows us to feel frustrated and self-righteous about how everyone else is letting us down. Or we can choose to act with courage, speak directly and early on about what we would like. We can find out if what we want seems reasonable to those we are making decisions with. Find out what they think about it, and come to an agreement.

People have a deep evolutionary need to keep the agreements they set themselves. It goes back to reciprocity and all kinds of wiring from our distant tribal relatives. Once we make an agreement with someone else, we generally have a desire to fulfill it, and we experience discomfort around breaking it. However, people do *not* have any need to meet all of your expectations. Especially ones you didn't explicitly share or ones you just impose on them against their will. Doing so creates resistance, resentment, and subtle rebellion. And nobody likes those things.

So the next time you're pissed off at someone, find out what expectation of yours they are breaking. Ask yourself, *What agreement would I like to make with this person? How can I talk about it with them to see if we're on the same page?*

Then go have the conversation.

3. *Responsibility: I Am 100% Responsible For My Feelings*

Every person who is emotionally successful in life - that is they feel good much of the time, have great relationships, and regularly enjoy feeling fulfilled, inspired, energized, and grateful - takes 100% responsibility for their own feelings.

They are not happier and more resilient because their life circumstances are vastly superior to others, or because they are rich or lucky. There are thousands of very wealthy people who are emotionally very unsuccessful. They feel upset, angry, impatient, stressed, worried, and dissatisfied much of the time. They are hurting inside. I don't know about your definition, but in my book that isn't success, no matter how much money you have.

What does it mean to take 100% responsibility for our feelings? It means we don't blame outside circumstances and other people for how we feel. We stop believing we feel a negative emotion because someone didn't do something we wanted. We stop saying things like, "You made me feel angry."

Instead we know that our feelings are our own to deal with. My upset, hurt, and fear are my problem to solve. And yet, it's amazing how easy it is to immediately blame something outside of ourselves for our uncomfortable feelings.

He shouldn't have said that. She's too much of this or not enough that. He's too noisy. She's too bossy. It should have gone this way. My tire shouldn't be flat. It goes on and on.

The unspoken assumption here is: *if _____ were different, I would not feel this way.* This is based on an old emotional formula that most of us carry around inside our heads. It goes like this (Warning! Math alert! Math alert!):

If X happens, I will feel Y.

X can be anything that anyone says or does. It can also be events that happen in life like making a sale, getting a job, getting fired, or traffic on the freeway.

- If there is traffic on the freeway, I will feel impatient and agitated.
- If he says no when I ask for the sale, I will feel discouraged, frutstrated, and hopeless.
- If I get the job I want, I will feel happy, excited, and relieved.
- If I get fired, I wil feel scared, hurt, and like a failure.

Perfectly natural, perfectly normal, right? Everyone would agree with you if you said any of these things.

"Hey, how's it going today?"

"I'm frustrated and agitated."

"Really? How come?"

"So much traffic on the freeway today. It was nuts. And it's raining."

"I hear ya!"

No one would bat an eye at this conversation. But it reflects a massive flaw in the system that will lead to years of emotional pain and suffering. It reveals that both of these people will probably never feel emotionally successful or happy for very long. Because guess what? Traffic doesn't seem to be going away. And it's always going to rain (hopefully, unless we're headed for a Mad Max style mega-drought apocalypse).

Taking 100% responsibility for your feelings will set you free. Because it will help you see that X does not cause Y. In reality, Y is a feeling that is looking for a way to come out. And X is the perfect opportunity to let it out. *What?? This guy's talking crazy.* I know it seems backwards, but hear me out.

Let's say Y is frustration and anger. We have a lot of that inside of our bodies. We have all these desires and needs that go unmet and tension builds inside of us. Some of these we are aware of, and some we don't even consciously know about. Maybe I'm hurting about something someone said to me. Maybe I'm feeling pressure from life's demands. Maybe my heart is aching because I miss a friend or a former lover. Then I hit traffic. *What the fuck it this? Look at all these stupid people cutting over from the left lane? What the hell is wrong with them? Idiots.*

All that emotional energy now has a little outlet. A pipe for all that steam to flow out through. Well, maybe not all of it, but some of it. Best of all, I don't have to acknowledge and feel all those uncomfortable feelings, like desire, grief, or heartache. I just feel angry at random people on the road.

Emotion gets pent up inside of us in response to life, and how we interpret what happens to us. If we take 100% responsibility, then we take time each day to just feel those feelings, without resisting, blaming, or fighting them. Just let them burn through us like a prairie fire. We also pay attention the stories and interpretations we tell ourselves. We notice how easy it is to blame someone else instead of feeling those raw, uncomfortable feelings directly. Then we go back to feeling the feelings. If you are curious what this means and how to do it, keep reading. You are going to discover how to relate to your emotions, including fear, in a completely new way that will set you free.

In the meantime, just remember this: X does not cause Y. I'm sure you can see moments from your own life where this is true. Have you ever hit traffic and been totally relaxed? Perhaps you were listening to an audiobook and didn't really care about how quickly you would get to your destination. Maybe you had a busy, full day and hitting some traffic gave you some time alone to just sit and think, and you felt peaceful, relaxed, and grateful to have some quiet solitude. So you can experience X, and instead of feeling Y, you might experience Z, or A, or B. Maybe even a combination of all three.

Circumstances and other people do not cause my feelings. It's how I interpret and relate to those circumstances and people. It's how I relate to the emotions and discomfort inside of me. These are the beliefs of an owner, and these are the beliefs that lead to emotional success, happiness, and lasting fulfillment.

There are some people who take this philosophy and turn it into a strangely cold and uncompassionate dogma. They demand Vulcan-like control of their emotions because after all, if it's just their perception, then they will change it in order to stop feeling pain. I know I've done this. I once read that "Happiness is a choice, so just choose to feel differently." It sounds good and feels empowering to read it, but is much harder to apply in practice. The result is an ever-increasing loop of demanding that I feel differently and then hating myself for not being good enough to "just get over it." This is not what I mean.

Let me share one more example so you can easily get this and apply it in your life. At the time of writing this, I have two sons: a two-year-old toddler and a one-month-old baby. The toddler does what toddlers do. Runs around like a maniac, tries to take his diaper off, and wants to see what happens when he climbs on the table after dad says, "Please don't climb on the table." The newborn does what newborns do - he nurses, poops, and sleeps. And cries like a banshee if he is uncomfortable or one of his needs isn't being met fast enough. Lots of irritating stimulus for mom and dad. Oh, and lots of night waking and greatly reduced sleep.

Now with all that going on, when I am up at 4am with my newborn son and he's screaming as I am screwing the nipple onto a bottle of breast milk, it is quite natural to feel frustrated and angry. I'm angry *because* he's crying so loudly in my ear and I'm trying to get him the milk he wants. If he stopped crying, I wouldn't feel angry.

But what's really going on here? If I take 100% responsibility, then my anger and frustration is my own to deal with. It is not happening because my son "made me" feel that way. And it's certainly not the case that I have to feel angry when he cries and can only feel peaceful when he stops. If that were the case, I would be a victim of circumstance. But I am not the victim of my life, I am the owner, so I looked for a better way. Truth be told, I only looked for a better way after many nights of being the victim and feeling depressed and miserable. Might as well try something else...

So, instead of looking outward, I looked in. I focused on what happened inside of me that made me react to the crying with frustration and anger. What ideas did I have that created this anger? What feelings did I not want to feel? As I slowed down, breathed, and just felt the hot sensation of anger in my chest without resisting it or trying to get away from it, answers emerged.

First, I felt frustration at not being able to calm him immediately. I wanted to be more effective, to have more control. Then I noticed massive tension in my body around the idea that my wife would hear our son crying and think, "My husband sucks at being a dad. If he was a better dad he could soothe our baby." Wow, fear of disapproval. That's a good one. I went even deeper into the burning sensation in my heart and felt the pain and discomfort directly, without trying to analyze it or solve it. I just breathed and surrendered to it. There I found deep aching in my heart about re-homing my cat, whom I lived with for twelve years. With the two babies he was not thriving and we had given him away to live with a dear friend. I missed him. Part of me was screaming inside, "I don't want this! I want him back!"

Underneath anger there is always pain. Always fear or grief. Fear of losing something, pain about not having things go the way we want them to, unmet needs, or hurt feelings. We just have to slow down, get out of our blame, take 100% responsibility to face our own feelings, and we will find it. And when we do, we set ourselves free.

4. ACTION: I CREATE MY DESTINY

The owner is not waiting for some force outside of himself to come save him. A substantial majority of people are unconsciously waiting for something to come and make their lives better. Whether it's their boss, their spouse, or God, their destiny is placed in the hands of another.

When we take ownership of our lives, we decide to take action. We figure out what we want in a given situation and ask this question: "What can I do?"

Not "Who can I blame?" or "How come nothing ever works out for me?" or "Why is life so hard and unfair?" These questions suck. They dig us deeper into the victim stance and strip us of our power.

Instead, take charge. Figure out what you can do to make the situation more favorable. See what fears might be getting in the way and stopping you from taking those actions. Then, face those fears, and take those actions.

Overcoming fear and taking bold action are so important for a life of confidence that they each have their own chapter in this book. You will discover much more about how to blast through fear and take decisive action later on.

For now, notice whenever you fall into a victim stance where you are stuck because "they" aren't cooperating. Decide to see it differently. Even if they truly aren't cooperating, complaining about it in your head is *not* going to change anything. God is not going to come down and make them different because you lamented it wasn't fair.

If that person is taking too long on their end of the project, ask them about it. Did you set up clear agreements? If this is a pattern and they keep doing this, find a way around it. Can you work with someone different? Can you fire them and hire someone else? Can you do the task yourself?

If your boss is criticizing you in meetings and you feel deflated and ashamed at work, ask yourself the question - "what can I do?" First, you can maintain your self-respect and internally challenge all his critical garbage. Second, can you speak up in the meetings? Can you tactfully question or challenge your boss? He may respect you more for it. Or, why not leave? Yes, you can find another job. No, you don't need to work there.

Do you see what it's like to approach the world from an action-oriented ownership stance? The more you do it, the less frustration and resentment you feel, and the freer you become.

Notice how the owner takes responsibility for his life, even when outside circumstances don't go his way. Even when shit happens. He operates from a Utilization Mindset. This simply means you can use anything that life throws your way and work with it. Instead of viewing it as some bad, terrible situation that *shouldn't* be happening, you view it as an unexpected turn that requires more flexibility on your part.

The truth is we can use anything in our lives to benefit us. Even the most challenging situations or painful experiences can end up serving us greatly if we let them. Events that seem tragic in the moment, as if life has "gone wrong," such as losing a job or experiencing a breakup, are actually of tremendous benefit if we let them be. They deepen us, strengthen us, and sculpt our souls. They are also stepping stones on our path and are guiding us in ways we don't even realize until years later.

WHERE DO YOU LIVE?

Where do you spend most of your time? Do you live more as a victim of circumstance or do you see yourself as an owner of your life? Sometimes people call someone "a victim" as if it were an inborn personality trait. The truth is no one is born an owner or victim. These are merely ways of being in the world: mindsets, and styles of response. Sometimes we choose ownership. Sometimes we choose a more disempowered stance.

As you read this, you might conclude that from here on out and forevermore, you will choose the owner stance. That sounds nice and logically seems like the "best" thing to do, but it's damn near impossible to simply become an owner and stay that way. The best thing we can do is to commit to becoming more aware. To notice when we're giving our power away, blaming others, feeling like we don't have a choice, and feeling resentful and powerless. The more we notice this, the more we can choose differently, and find ourselves operating from a place of ownership more and more often.

You may also begin to notice that you tend to approach some areas of your life more consistently from a place of ownership than others. Perhaps in your health and fitness you show up as an owner, take responsibility for what you eat and when you work out. You don't let work or a long day stop you from taking care of your body.

But then when your partner asks you for something you always feel obligated to say yes, even if you don't want to. Saying no makes you feel guilty and selfish so you avoid that messiness by always consenting. Then you feel resentful about doing some of the things you said you would do, because she's "making" you do them.

This example is purely hypothetical of course, and I have no idea about such things because I would never stoop so low as to do that with my wife.

Look, we don't have to take this choice so seriously and make it a big deal. Bring your playful awareness to the topic and view it like a game. Whenever you catch yourself in the victim stance, smile and say, "Oh, me.. There I go again." Take a deep breath in. Remember you made choices that got you here. Try saying in your mind, *I am 100% responsible.* Feel the power of that statement. Sense the expansive freedom it provides. I can choose. Everything is a choice. Everything.

Now is the time to choose differently.

For detailed training videos on how to identify your personal excuses and stories, go to, http://SocialConfidenceCenter.com and sign up for my newsletter.

Grab The Helm

For those of you who are not as high-class as me and don't have vast nautical knowledge, the helm is the steering wheel of a ship. (I actually had to Google that to make sure that's what it meant).

It's time to grab the helm! I just like saying that. It makes me feel strong and adventurous, like a Greek hero. You may be ready and excited to take charge of your confidence, your life, and your destiny. If so, awesome! You are in the right place. After you apply what you learn in this book, your life will never be the same again. However, there are two things that get in the way and can stop us from taking charge. One is fear, which we will help you completely obliterate in Chapter Four.

The other is something a bit more subtle. More insidious. It sneaks in like a cloud of smoke or vapor that you inhale over time without knowing it. Yet it has the power to stop you dead in your tracks. Curious what this sneaky, almost undetectable hurdle is?

Let me show you what it is, then we'll talk about it. Imagine, for a moment, taking ownership of one area of your life. Maybe it's your relationship with your partner, your career, or your finances. What would it look like if you approached that area from a place of complete and total ownership? Where you knew you were a powerful force in the world who could make whatever you wanted to happen, and it was only a matter of time before it all came to fruition.

What kind of relationship would you create? Would you have a deeply loving relationship with a spouse? A relationship where your partner was the most important thing in the world, you loved spending time with him or her, you felt deeply grateful to be with them and couldn't possibly want anything else in life?

What kind of business or career would you have? Would you be running your own business? Growing your current business geometrically? Would you be only doing what you loved? Would you be earning more money than ever before and enjoying the lifestyle and contribution that can come from being wealthy?

Take a moment to really imagine what a life of ownership would look like for you…

Now, let me ask you this. What's happening inside of you? How do you feel? Excited? Hopeful?

Discouraged? Skeptical?

For the vast majority of people, what happens when we remove excuses and really start to take ownership of our lives, is that we bump into the second protective layer: Stories

Without further ado, let's take a trip into Story Land…

CHAPTER III:

STORIES

"The only thing that stops you from having what you want in life is the story you keep telling yourself about why you can't have it."
- Anthony Robbins

I can't.
I don't know how to.
I don't know enough yet.
I'm not smart enough.
I don't have enough education.
Of course she wouldn't find me attractive.
I'm ugly.
I'm not capable.
I'm not good enough.
There's something wrong with me.
No one would want me there.
I'm a loser.
I'm a failure.

Ugh. Just reading that list makes me feel depressed. These are just a few of the hundreds of stories we tell ourselves on a daily basis. Sometimes they are obvious and blaring in our minds. Other times they are subconscious: operating in the background like computer viruses. Not overt, but with just enough influence to stall us out or sabotage our success.

What's the difference between stories and excuses? Stories are deeper than excuses. In order to gain the confidence you need to create the life you want, you will first have to push past your layer of excuses about why the outside world won't give you want. Then you'll start bumping into your stories.

Stories are how we interpret the world, others, and ourselves. Our beliefs, opinions, and the meaning we give events are all part of these stories. Most importantly, our stories determine how we see ourselves. They make up our identity.

Stories tell you what you are capable of and not capable of. Whether you are attractive or unattractive. Desirable or undesirable. Intelligent or dumb. Wealthy or poor. Destined for greatness and a life of adventurous fulfillment or doomed to perpetual struggle and never quite "making it."

There are two major kinds of stories: identity stories and ability stories. Both are about who you are and what you are capable of. Both can be inspiring and empowering or discouraging and highly limiting. Let's explore each kind so you can see what's holding you back, and ultimately be free of it.

IDENTITY STORIES

Right now, in this very moment that you are reading this text, you have a complex network of ideas, beliefs, thought impulses and neurological connections operating beneath your awareness. They are guiding your choices, decisions, and actions throughout the day, all without you even thinking about it. They make up your sense of who you are. They determine what you do and do not do.

I am this. I am not that.

Let me show you what I mean. Read the sentence below:

I am a man.

As you read that, it instantly seemed true or not true, right? And it happened incredibly fast, didn't it? You didn't have to spend much conscious time and attention determining if that was true about you. Your mind instantly concluded, *Yep.* Or *Nope, I'm a woman.* (Of course if you're transgender or gender queer your internal response may be more complex.)

Simple enough, right? But what if we apply the same test to the following statement:

I am intelligent, charismatic, and a powerful leader.

What happened when you read that one? Did it register as true? Not true? Sorta, kinda, maybe true-ish, with lots of qualifications and exceptions? If you could assign it a percentage of truth, where 100 would mean it felt completely true and 0 would mean it felt completely false, how does your gut response rank this statement?

Interesting, huh?

Now let me ask you this: If you had two people and everything about them was equal, except that Person A believes, *I am an intelligent, charismatic, and powerful leader* 95% and Person B believes it 5%, who would have better results in business, their career, their relationships, and in life?

What if instead of being an intelligent, charismatic, powerful leader, Person B believed deep down that they were not intelligent, not good enough, and had somehow fooled everyone into thinking they knew a thing or two? That's right, they would be stressed and anxious about being "found out," feel constant pressure to perform and prove themselves (which would never be enough by the way), and ultimately they would self-sabotage by severely limiting their success or flushing it down the drain entirely.

Scary? Damn right. Those identity stories have tremendous power over us and over the quality of our lives. We definitely want to be aware of the toxic ones that are holding us back. So which identity stories are serving you and which ones are holding you back?

Identity Game

Let's find out with a little game. Remember that these beliefs often reside in our unconscious. We are usually not fully aware of them. In fact, our conscious mind sometimes does not want us to be aware of them because we think it might make us look bad, to ourselves or others. Or worse, we may start seeing right through these stories and have to face what we're really scared of (more on that in the next chapter).

So our game has to access your unconscious mind. That's where it gets fun and that's why I call this a game. Because it's fun. Ready?

Step 1. Grab a sheet of paper (or open up a blank document on your computer, phone, tablet, smart watch, retina imprint, or cyborg brain implant) - just find something to write on.

Step 2. Wait for everyone else to complete Step 1. If you haven't done Step 1, it's you we're all waiting on. Come on. Don't be a boring old dude. Play this game with us. Great.

Step 3. Write out the words "I AM..." and then write whatever comes to your mind afterwards. Don't filter it, question it, or hesitate for any reason. That's your conscious mind trying to play goalie and prevent you from scoring. Just let it fly. No one in the world other than you will read it (unless you want them to). Do this twenty times. Yes, twenty. Just for fun. It's okay if you repeat yourself or if they are similar (they often are). It's okay if they're positive, negative, happy, or sad. Whatever you write, it's all perfect.

In fact, I'll play with you. Go ahead and make your list. I'll do the same and then we can compare. Ready? Begin now.

My list:

I am bold.
I am intelligent.
I am capable.
I am rich.
I am anxious.
I am a homeowner.
I am Aziz.
I am intelligent.
I am capable.
I am driven.
I am abundant.
I am nervous.
I am bold.
I am toaster.
I am a husband and a father.
I am Candace's husband.
I am a great husband.
I am a great dad.
I am not present enough with Zaim.
I am cool.
I am good looking.
I am loved.
I am loving.
I am taken care of.

I am healthy.

I am strong.

I am powerful.

I am intelligent.

I am funny.

I am too future-oriented.

I am Aziz.

I am Arabic.

I am Pakistani.

I am American.

I am powerful.

I am bold.

I am great at talking to people.

I am fun to talk to.

I am able to talk to anyone.

I am great with women.

I am an awesome and dynamic speaker.

I am authentic, real, and honest.

I am kind and patient.

I am loving.

I am incredibly easy to talk to.

I am a powerful healer.

I'm an extraordinary coach.

I am dedicated to helping people.

I'm not a good enough coach.

I'm not desirable enough as a coach.

I am powerful and effective at helping people.

I am loved.

I am aware and conscious.

I am dedicated to learning.

Ok, that was way more than 20, but I got on a roll. I find that game fascinating and fun because I never know what's going to come out. I'm mean, "I am a toaster"? Seriously, what the fuck? But as I was writing that sentence I thought of our toaster and it's what came from my subconscious so I didn't filter it. I can also see where I have a really solid identity (around being a good husband/father) and where I have conflicting beliefs (being a great coach and a not a desirable enough coach).

This list is very different than it would have been fifteen years ago, five years ago, or even one year ago. Over a decade ago my list would have been mostly made up of my shortcomings and flaws. How I wasn't attractive, social, bold, or skilled. Five years ago it would have included tons about my inability to be in romantic relationships because I was somehow messed up or defective. My list is a lot better now. If you are open to constantly growing, then your identity can transform dramatically and rapidly.

Questions for you: what was it like creating your list? Did you discover anything interesting about your subconscious beliefs? Was it more positive than you realized? More negative? Whatever you discovered is okay. It's great, actually. Because these beliefs are already there, operating beneath the surface. If you're not aware of them, they will control you and the negative ones will severely limit you. Once we bring them to the surface, we can break free of them and reach a whole new level of personal and professional liberation, freedom, and peace. That's what the second half of this book is all about, once we've removed all these obstacles.

Identity Sculpting

So what do we do with this list? I'll share this in a moment, but before I do I want you realize how powerful this list is. Most people will never create something like this in their entire lives. They believe that their identity is fixed, that their beliefs about themselves are true, and that's just "who they are."

- I'm not a social person
- I'm not good at presentations.
- I don't like being the center of attention.
- I'm not comfortable telling people what to do.
- I prefer to follow rather than lead.
- I'm not good at sales.

People say stuff like this all the time, both out loud and in their heads. And it's all made up. They are all stories. It's not who you are. It's not fixed into concrete like a carved Roman numeral. You are fluid. You are dynamic. You are a living, breathing, constantly changing organism. Alan Watts, an incredibly illuminating philosopher of the last century, said we are like a whirlpool in a river. If you come back tomorrow, the whirlpool will still be there, but all the water will be completely different. In fact, it is different in each moment. You are just like that.

You can change your identity to something that suits you more. As one of my coaches, Steve Chandler says, you can reinvent yourself. You can do the things that scare you and eventually they will no longer scare you. Hell, do them enough, and they will become an everyday part of your life. From talking to people, to delegating, to selling, to doubling your profits, to approaching an attractive stranger, to being an incredible parent and partner. No big deal. It's just who you are and what you do.

As Steve likes to point out, you are not a noun, you are a verb. Instead of seeing yourself as a fixed object that is set in one particular way, you can see yourself as a constantly evolving, fluid process.

Are you starting to see the power of identity here? My boy Tony Robbins says, "The most powerful force in the human personality is to remain consistent with our identity." (Two Tony quotes in one chapter?? What can I say, the man has a lot of good stuff to offer).

So how do we do that? How do we change our identity to something more powerful, more helpful? To one that serves us more and makes us feel better about ourselves throughout the day?

Drugs. And lots of them.

No I'm kidding (partially).[1]

Let's talk about how to transform your identity. And exactly what you should be doing with that dang list.

First off, go back and note all of the beliefs that inspire, support, and empower you. Put stars next to those. Or circle them. Or do whatever you like to make them stand out. Those are your stallions. Those are the ones that will take you where you want to go in life.

You'll want to start by reinforcing those beliefs. Say them out loud. Repeat them in your head when you're in line at Jamba Juice. Write them down a lot. Say them before you step into a big meeting, or do anything else that makes you nervous. Jump up and down on a rebounder, pump your arms in the air and shout them out. (I'm serious, that shit works).

Not enough of them? Come up with more. Ask yourself this question - what beliefs would I need to have to get to where I want to go? To achieve what I want to achieve? To experience what I want to experience?

Better yet, look at someone who's done what you want to do. Someone who lives the way you want to live. Who is an inspiring, badass hero of yours? Then ask yourself, what does she believe about herself? What identity beliefs must he have? Don't just fabricate them out of thin air (although that's a good start). Research them a little. Read about them. Watch videos where they share their ideas. Read an interview with them. If you know them personally, holy shit you

1 Psychoactive medicines such as the African Iboga root, South American Aya-huasca, and good old fashion psilocybin mushrooms have all been shown in legit-imate studies from major institutions to produce powerful and lasting effects on life choices, addiction recovery, and spiritual growth. If done in the right context, with the right intention and the right people, those medicines can produce deep, positive, and life-long changes in identity. For more information about this re-search, visit: http://www.maps.org.

are in luck. Take him to lunch and find out what he believes about himself. Say, "You are doing some really cool stuff in the world and I want to follow in your footsteps. Can I ask you a few questions?"

Then ask your role models how they see themselves? How do they approach sales conversations? What do they believe about finances? Failure? Rejection? How do they deal with setbacks? In a fifteen minute conversation you can uncover the most powerful map to get to where you want to go. And best of all, they'll love sharing with you because it makes them feel honored, appreciated and significant. Win-win.

Once you have some good beliefs, integrate them into your list. Repeat them. Say them out loud. Even if they don't feel true yet, that's fine. They're just unfamiliar. They're the new kids. You just don't know them well enough yet. Soon they'll fit right in and you'll forget who was new and who was original.

For example, let's say you came up with: *I am a powerful and persuasive presenter.* Perhaps you decided this would help you grow your business, get new customers, increase your sales, be more effective in meetings, and take your career and income to the next level. Good stuff. I agree with you.

But Aziz, you might be thinking, *I'm not a powerful and persuasive presenter. I avoid presentations. I hate them. And I don't think I'm very good at them.*

Well, at least we know our starting point. This may be true in your past experience. I'm not saying you're supposed to pretend or close your eyes and use magical positive thinking to instantly transform your life. All we're talking about here is changing your story. Because once we do that, doors will start to open up. As soon as you say the new identity statement, things start to heat up inside. Immediately your mind says, *Oh no you didn't. Stop saying that. It's false.*

And check this out. If that belief were true, how would you show up to work? How would you approach presentations? Would you schedule a lot of them? Seek them out? Probably. And how do you feel if you imagine doing that? Dread? Fear?

Awesome. That's exactly what we want. You are stepping out of the comfortable safe-zone of the old toxic story and stepping into life. You're getting out onto the field. And it can be terrifying at first. You'll understand more about how this is a good thing in the next chapter about fear. Then you'll learn how to transform your new story into something that really is true for you. No endless affirmations, no weird hypnosis, just a healthy dose of action and boldness. (Ok, and maybe a little weird hypnosis).

In order to change your identity, and fundamentally alter the way you see yourself for the better, you will need to first change the story you keep telling yourself about who you are. This is like hacking away the vines, bushes, and heavy undergrowth that prevent you from moving forward towards your goals. Then you must take action; you must do the very things that are outside your old identity. You'll seek out presentations, seek out challenges, seek out risks and opportunities. You'll consistently take different actions and as a result become a different person with a different identity. This habit of massive action is like building the superhighway where the undergrowth used to be. Now your path towards your goals is faster than you imagined (and just might have fourteen lanes if you're in Los Angeles).

What about the identity statements on your list that suck? The ones that seem really negative, toxic, or limiting? Ones like:

- I am a loser.
- I am a failure,
- I'm not good enough.
- I'm mean.
- I'm bad.
- I'm ugly.
- I'm fat.
- I'm weak.
- I'm boring
- I'm awkward.
- I'm weird.

Here's the thing. After doing this for over a decade I've discovered the following fact: If you have more than three of these kinds of identity statements in your list, you're screwed. There's no hope for you. You are doomed.

Ok, in a moment we'll be moving on to our next chapter...

I'm kidding! Seriously, you're fine. Reading the first list I ever wrote was like reading a hate letter from my worst heckler. It was terrible. I had a bunch of garbage on there. No matter how bad your list looks, it's a good list. Trust me. Awareness in this process is your friend. In fact, it's your most powerful ally.

Now that you are aware of these beliefs, what can you actually do with them? These negative pieces of our identity fall into two camps. One category is highlighting where we are out of alignment, or not living our values. For example, if I had an identity statement that said, "I'm a bad father," it's worth checking out to see if I'm being, well, a shitty dad.

Am I gone all the time, drinking in bars instead of coming home at night? Do I make lots of promises and break them, forget my son's birthday and not show up to any of his sporting games? If so, then maybe that statement is alerting me to being off course. If so, we can work with it. We will have to remove the self-hatred though because that never helped anyone change for the better, ever. We also have to look at our standards and expectations for ourselves because they may be way too high. More on this in Chapter Seven, the love chapter. Oh yes, this book has it all.

While realizing we are out of alignment happens sometimes, the vast majority of these negative identity statements fall into the second camp: good old fashion self-hate. Instead of pointing towards something valuable to work on, these statements are just a form of self-criticism and harsh judgment. They do not help us grow, make us "better people" or really serve us in any useful way.

So why do we hold these beliefs? Why is virtually everyone dealing with some level of inner monster who pounces on them and tells them they're shit when they do something wrong? I've had deep, personal conversations with thousands of people over the years, and trust me, *everyone* is wrestling with this. Everyone.

What the heck? Why on earth would we have a bunch of our identity made up with self-hating statements? Well, I'll tell you. It just so happens that while these criticisms are not helpful, they do serve a purpose. There is a reason they exist. And there is a reason why we keep saying them to ourselves and have a hard time letting them go. Do you know what it is?

Safety.

Self-hate serves one function - to keep us safe. Because as long as you believe, *I'm an ugly loser that no one would want to be with,* guess what you don't have to do? Talk to people! Ask them out! Take risks and get your ass rejected. You get to avoid all of that. These criticisms are like a barbed-wire fence that keeps you safely inside of the walls of your comfort zone. Sure it's confining, depressing, and only half of a life. But at least it's safe, dammit!

In a moment, we'll get to Ability Stories, which can also stop us from stepping up and taking bold, confident action in the world. But first, let's take a moment to get to know your Safety Police. They are pretty important characters in our internal drama, so it's worth bringing them to your awareness.

Safety Police

So far in this chapter we've been talking about stories. The stories we tell ourselves, that stop us in our tracks and prevent us from taking action. I wonder if, as you're reading this chapter, you are starting to identify some of your personal stories that hold you back and are beginning to realize that they aren't as rigid or permanent as you once thought.

But thus far I haven't been entirely clear about exactly *who* is telling you these stories. I've been saying "you" just for ease, but actually it's not all of you, just a part of you. Because "you" are not just one set of beliefs, thoughts, ideas, and feelings; you are made up of many parts. There is a part of you that might want to order the kale salad for lunch and get up at 5am to go for a run. And then there's the part of you that wants to order the bacon cheeseburger, fries, and Dr. Pepper and binge watch Futurama on Netflix. Dang, that actually sounds really fun. I guess I know which part is most active in me right now. Mmm, cheeseburger.

And that's just the thing. We have all of these parts, and your actions depend on which one is in charge at a given moment. Which one is driving the bus. If you always let Cheeseburger man drive the bus, then you will have the quality of life he determines (hedonistic pleasure combined with obesity and other health problems).

Just like with health and exercises choices, we have parts of us that want to chose immediate gratification and we have other parts that carefully determine our level of risk, uncertainty, and the possible discomfort we could experience in any given moment.

This overly- cautious bunch is what I like to call the Safety Police.

(Insert MacGyver-esque theme music here. If you don't know who MacGyver is, stop reading this and go Google him now. Prepare to have your mind blown. In fact, disregard what I said about binge-watching Netflix earlier, and go binge-watch MacGyver on Netflix now. He is just that important).

Now that you've filled the MacGyver-shaped-hole in your heart, let's move on. Your Safety Police is your own personal squad of "protectors" whose sole job is to keep you safe, in this moment right now. No matter the reason, and no matter the cost. Safety first, safety always.

And what's deemed "safe" is what is known, what is familiar, and what is predictable. Anything that is outside the ordinary, unknown, or new is "unsafe." Anything that involves risk, potential loss (of money or esteem in the eyes of others) is definitely not safe. Potential rejection, failure, setback, humiliation, embarrassment, and anything else that makes you feel vulnerable is to be avoided at all costs.

This is the Safety Police imperative.

How do they carry out their mission? There are several main characters on the squad. There's usually a primary one that you rely on quite a bit, as well as a few of his buddies. Here are a few of the common ones:

THE REASONABLE COP

This guy likes to calmly and clearly tell you how things are. His tone is sensible, convincing, and often has a ring of "I hate to break it to you, but this is just how things are," to it. *I hate to break it to you, but you just aren't good enough for her. Someone like her will never want to be with someone like you. That's just how it is.* (This is the Identity Story)

Listen man, there's no way they would hire you for that job. You wouldn't be able to lead all those people. You can't do that sort of thing. (This one is the Ability Story)

You can't earn that much money. No one will pay you that. Come now...

If the edge of your comfort zone is surrounded by a fence, Reasonable Cop gets to you long before you ever reach it. If you think about walking towards the fence because you're curious about what's on the other side, he'll calmly step up beside you, put his arm over your shoulder and turn you back towards the center of your comfort zone. His advice always encourages you not to take those risks because whatever your goal is, it won't work out anyway. His voice is very matter of fact, direct, damn convincing, and above all certain. This guy is absolutely sure of himself, which can cause you to doubt yourself.

You turn back around, slowly starting to nod your head. *I guess he's right. What was I thinking? Change my career? Invest in training myself to create my own business? Ha! Silly. Back to the salt mines for me.*

The Terrified Cop

This guy is my favorite. He's been a major player in my Safety Police for years. He's like the expendable character in a movie who is convinced he's going to die.

"We can't go out there! The place is crawling with them! We're not going to make it. We're toast. Oh God, oh God! I should never have come here. What are we going to do? There are so many of them, and so few of us. We're all going to die!"

As he talks, he works himself up into more and more of a frenzy, sweating and wide-eyed. In day-to-day life, it may look something like this:

You can't do that presentation! You are going to fuck it all up. You're going to forget what to say and freeze like a stone statue up there and everyone is going to stare at you and you won't be able to recover and it will be the most horrible, awkward, terrible, unbearably painful thing you've ever experienced and you'll never forget it and neither will anyone else and they'll all talk about it behind your back for forever and ever and ever!

Or something along those lines. His advice is always some version of the terrible, bad, unbearable things that will happen if you were to do _____ (insert a healthy risk of your choice here).

This guy is extremely effective at telling us Future Stories (which we'll get to in a moment) that spook us into procrastination, indecision and confusion.

The Old Cynical Cop

This weathered battle-axe comes out when your dreams, hopes, and aspirations start to lead you out towards the edge of your comfort zone (aka the "safe zone"). You start cooking up some dream in your mind — doubling the size of your business, finding an amazing person to spend the rest of your life with, writing a best-selling book — and just then, he comes into the room with a sneer on his face.

"You? Write a book? Ha, right. I'm sure it will be an amazing work of art. Your stories in third grade were especially good, so now I'll bet they're even better. Ha! Pathetic."

"Yeah, he's going to want to date you. Ms. Lumpy. And then you'll live happily ever after, right? Fat chance."

This one is a little different than the reasonable cop because he's not gently talking you out of something and pretending to be your friend. He's just rolling his eyes at how pathetic you are and at how it's even more pathetic that you don't see how pathetic you are. And that you think you, of all people, could do something worthwhile or amazing? That's the most pathetic part of all.

Boy, this guy is a real jerk. But he's just doing his job. He's got to do whatever it takes to keep you safe.

THE ANGRY RAGER

This is the "bad cop." This is the one who kicks in the door of the interrogation room after the good cop has been nicely asking the perp questions for fifteen minutes without getting the answers he wants. He slams a baseball bat on the table and says, "Listen you little shit. You are going to do what we want you to do, or else I'm going to bash your brains in with this bat."

The perp looks at him, pretending to be unafraid and slightly amused, but underneath he's nervous because this guy really does look a little crazy. *Maybe he'd do it? But he'd lose his job, he wouldn't really hit me in front of all these people... would he?* So, the perp rallies his most badass, deep, I'm-not-intimidated-by-you voice and says, "The bat couldn't be worse than your breath. Did your wife make you an onion sandwich again? Oh that's right, your wife's dead." (Dang, that's good. I should be writing a blockbuster script instead of this book).

And then wouldn't you know it, the Angry Rager loses it. He starts screaming, yelling, throwing things, kicking over the table, and, yes, hitting the guy with a baseball bat. That is exactly what happens inside of your head. If you aren't deterred by the other cops on the force, and you keep walking towards the fence, the Angry Rager will show up sooner or later to beat you into submission.

"You terrible piece of shit. You worthless worm. He's never going to call you back. You are so ugly. Your legs are so pale and fat and ugly."

"You fucked that project up so bad. You are going to get fired. All your clients are going to leave you and for good cause. Incompetent idiot."

"How could you have said 'no' to her, after all she's done for you? You are a selfish, terrible, asshole jerk. What the hell is wrong with you?"

Beliefs like these are the mental-emotional equivalent of a baseball bat to your nervous system. This kind of heavy abuse can happen all the time inside of our heads. The Angry Rager's influence is the most present before or after we take a big risk. This cop really wants to make sure that:

A. We do not take the risk. And if we somehow manage to sidestep him and do it anyway, then:

B. We never do anything like that again.

So there you have it. Do you see how these guys are showing up in your life right now? How they have been encouraging you, guiding you, and demanding that you remain in your safe zone of no risk, no danger, and no uncertainty (which unfortunately means no real success or love either)?

Do you have other cops on your squad? This is by no means a complete list. There are all kinds of characters we can have in there, generating our self-talk and directing our choices. The most important thing is to identify all the ones that tell you the stories that keep you from facing your fears and taking bold action in the world.

We will be talking a lot more about the Safety Police in the pages to come, as well as how to jailbreak yourself so you are never held back by fear and insecurity again. In the meantime, remember this: everything your Safety Police tells you, every idea or belief, every story, every prediction, is not true. No matter how certain they are. This squad of naysayers is simply designed to say whatever they need to say to carry out their mission: preventing you from taking any action that requires you to leave your comfort zone.

Let's take a look at a few more kinds of stories your Safety Police likes to tell you. This insight will help you peel back the layers of confusion and misdirection that keep you from exploding past your fears and creating a life of extraordinary confidence and joy.

Ability Stories

"Whether you think you can or you think you can't, you're right."
- Henry Ford

Preach it Henry. He's right you know. And right now in this moment you have a list of stuff in your brain that you believe you are capable of doing, and a list of stuff that you believe you are not capable of doing. It's all there in your head. Even if you've never even thought about doing something, when the time came, if you were asked to do it, you'd have an immediate sense of *Sure, I can do that (or learn that),* or *No way I could do that. Not possible for me.*

The Myth Of I Can't

A few weeks back I was speaking with a client who wanted to be more of a leader in her company and in her life. As you may know, being a charismatic, powerful leader is way more than just knowing what technical decisions to make. It also contains a huge social component of being able to speak to people, influence them, and ultimately inspire them to be their best. My client was working on this area.

She had incredible technical knowledge and skill, and was highly qualified to make decisions and lead others. However, she often held back in meetings with people she considered more powerful due to their senior status and years of experience. She compared herself to them and found herself lacking, which lead to self-doubt and staying quiet more than she preferred.

As we discussed the kind of presence she wanted to have in meetings, she described a colleague who seemed very confident in herself. She spoke her mind freely, offered suggestions even if she wasn't directly asked for them, and seemed to be unfazed by someone disagreeing with her opinion.

As my client described her colleague, she said, "I wish I could do what she does, but I can't."

"Really?" I replied. "What is one specific thing she does that you really like?"

"I notice she speaks her mind freely, even if someone might disagree with her. If she has a thought about something, she just says it. She trusts in herself."

"So when she has an opinion or perspective about the subject being discussed, she will speak up and share it? I asked, verifying what I'd heard.

"Yes."

"Great! That's very specific. So which part of that could you physically not do?"

"Well..." She paused for a moment, reflecting on the question. "I mean I *could* physically speak up. But I'd feel so nervous doing it. My voice would sound weak. I don't think I could pull it off."

"Pull it off?" I asked. This was a fancy technique I learned from one of my old school psychologist supervisors. When someone says something vague, you simply repeat the statement as a question and they'll usually get more specific. Take that tip and use it as you will. Bonus.

"Yeah, I imagine they would think I don't know what I'm talking about and judge me for not knowing enough about the subject. If *I* spoke up like my colleague, it would not be met with the same reaction as when *she* does it.

"So you can use your voice and speak up in any way you like. There's no physical limitation there. But you imagine others will respond negatively and so you feel afraid to do those things. Is that an accurate way of saying it?"

"Yeah, I'd say so."

I decided to push it slightly more just to see if she really got the point. "So you *can* do this, but you are afraid to, so you're choosing not to."

"Yes."

This may seem subtle, but it was a huge shift for her. She started to see how much she told herself throughout the week that she couldn't do the things she wanted to do. And she believed it. It was a form of self-hypnosis, or as Napoleon Hill would call it, auto-suggestion. She had repeated it so many times that she just accepted it as the truth until we had that conversation.

How often do you tell yourself you can't do something?

Here's a fun list of things. Notice if your initial reaction to each item is *Yes, I can do that (or could eventually with learning and practice)* or *No, I can't do that (and would never be able to do that).* Read each one and then pause for just a second. Long enough to note your inner response.

- Give an engaging impromptu speech.
- Earn $500,000 in a year.
- Have an outstanding relationship with a person who rocks your world.
- Run a half marathon.
- Start a conversation with a stranger for no reason.
- Become excellent at sales.
- Comfortably dance while being completely sober.

So... what did you notice? Lots of "cans" or "cannots"?

Remember even if you don't feel like you can do something right now, if you feel like you could do that thing if you invested yourself in learning it, then that's just as good. It's a sign of self-efficacy, of believing in your ability to learn something and get good at it with practice. It is a form of belief in yourself and your capability.

Now, why on earth would we tell ourselves we can't do something that we actually *could* do if we invested ourselves in learning how to do it? It's the same reason we tell ourselves any other story... avoidance. To avoid the imagined pain of failure, rejection, and anything else that might happen if we were to take action towards our dreams. We may even be afraid of success, of getting everything we want. Our stories protect us from that too.

So the next time you catch yourself saying "I can't do that", take a deep breath. Break the pattern, snap the hypnosis. You are telling yourself a lie. It's complete bullshit. Yes, you can. If you invested your time, energy, money, and focus into it, you could. Whether you want to or not is a different question, but in terms of capability, the short answer is you can. You can do anything from that list above, and anything else you deeply want to do. Once you remove the obstacles and stories, learn how to deal with fear, and consistently take massive action, there is no end to the level of confidence you can achieve and the list of exciting things you can experience in this life.

Yes, you can.

YOU.

Trying Is Weak

"Do or do not. There is no try."
- Yoda

Yes, trying is weak. In fact, I don't think anyone should try to do anything, ever.

But wait, what about trying something new? you may be asking. *Trying something outside of your comfort zone? Shouldn't your client try to be like that confident guy? I mean you even said he can do all the things that guy does if he just practices and applies himself.*

Nope. He shouldn't try to do anything. Because trying is weak. While "try" technically means "to make an attempt or effort for an outcome" that's not how most people use the word. Most people use "try" as a weird form of verifying they can't do something.

Selma: "Can you get that report to me by Friday?"

Adam: "I'll try."

Guess when Selma's getting that report? I don't know, but probably not by Friday. Because "try" is what people say when they don't want to say "no." Then, when it's not done, Adam can say, "Well, I tried." Then he's off the hook because, hey, he tried.

In the moment, we believe we can't do something. *I can't get that report done. I can't get those sales numbers. I can't meet new people at this networking event.* But instead of saying "I can't" because that sounds bad, we say the more socially accepted version, "I'll try."

When we're trying to do something, we are coming from a weak place of dabbling. I'll put some effort in, but I already believe I can't. So, when I hit an obstacle or experience some discomfort in the process, I will stop. I will tell myself, I knew I couldn't do this, and reinforce my old story. That's what trying is, and that is the level of results we get when we try.

So what do we do instead?

Own up and say what's true. "I have a lot on my plate and that report is too much for me. I can get it done by Tuesday. Will that work? What will happen if I get it to you by 9am Tuesday morning?"

If there's something you're scared to do, don't say, "Well, I'll try." Instead work through the fear (next chapter), learn how to overcome it (also next chapter), or pick something less scary to start with. Then do it. Or don't do it. And say you're not going to do it right now because you don't feel like experiencing that much discomfort. That's totally okay. You can say that. Just be honest with yourself. That's where the trust in yourself comes from, and from that trust comes deep confidence.

Your Stories Live In The Future

So far you're seeing how your stories serve as protection against doing scary things outside your comfort zone that could lead to painful outcomes.

The best place for them to focus on then is the future. Because it hasn't happened yet, so it's the perfect place to fill with terrifying predictions about what will happen. If your mind can make the predictions numerous or bad enough, this is a highly effective way to stop you dead in your tracks. *Everyone would laugh at me? Really? Everyone? Geez, that does sound pretty bad. I certainly wouldn't want to feel that...*

Here are just a few of the top future predictions that come up for people:

- It won't work.
- No one will show up.
- I'll fail and everyone will think less of me.
- They will fire me.
- I'll mess up the presentation (and then they'll fire me).
- She won't want ot talk to me.

- He will eventually leave me for a younger woman.
- They'll reject me.

Do you notice these stories in your mind? Mine spits them out all the time. I learned a long time ago to not believe what it says because they are often so off base. Even though your mind presents these stories with compelling certainty, its prediction abilities are pretty bad. Because your mind is not interested in accurately predicting the future. It is trying to protect you. It is giving you whatever story it needs to in order to stop you from taking action.

That's so important it's worth saying again: Your mind will say whatever it needs to in order to stop you from taking action.

Don't believe the stories. In order to break free, we have to do the exact opposite of what this voice says.

If it says you can't do a presentation, do a presentation.

If it says you'll get rejected if you ask for the sale, ask for the sale.

If it says no one will come to your event, create an event and invite as many people as you can.

Do the opposite of what the story says to do. Doing so puts you on the fast track to liberation and massive success, income, growth, achievement, fulfillment, and love. In order to pull this off, however, you will need something else. You will need to know how to overcome fear.

For audios, videos, and more free resources on how to change your story, go to, http://SocialConfidenceCenter.com and enter your email address to join my newsletter.

WHAT'S UNDERNEATH THE ROCK?

When I was about seven years old, I was best friends with a kid named Jeff. One Spring his parents invited me to spend four days with their family at a cabin out in the woods somewhere. I was super excited and my parents agreed to let me go.

It was as awesome as I imagined it would be: running around unrestricted in a forest that stretched for miles in all directions, staying up late watching bad movies like "Swamp Monster," and spending lots of time with my homie.

One early morning we decided to go out exploring in the woods. One of us figured out that if you lifted a heavy rock, the earth underneath would be wet and soft... and filled with all kinds of things. Sometimes worms, or beetles, or other creepy crawlies. We ran from rock to rock, peering underneath and laughing in delight at all the strange bugs we saw.

Eventually, Jeff came to one extra large rock and flipped it over. He was about eight feet from me and I saw him jump back with a yell and a look of horror on his face.

"What is it??" I asked as I ran over to the hole.

There inside the wet earth lay a small, jet-black scorpion.

Whoa. I'd never seen a scorpion before. They were poisonous. I knew that much. Could a sting kill you? Maybe. My heart pounded. Together we carefully put the rock back on top of the little creature, making sure to dramatically jump back as we did so, just in case he leaped from the bottom of the hole onto one of our faces.

We stared at each other, wide-eyed and panting. Birds chirped all around us. The early morning sun was hitting the tops of the tall fir trees. As we looked at each other, it became clear we were both thinking the same thing at the same time.

"Want to find more?" Jeff asked with an excited smile.

"Yes!" I responded immediately.

So what's underneath your rock? Remember, the first protective layer is made up of excuses. Beneath that are all these limiting stories about your identity and ability. And what's beneath that? When you lift off this heavy rock, this dead weight, what's really underneath it all?

A scorpion.

No, don't take the story above literally! It's a metaphor man! Stick with me. What's underneath your excuses and stories is what we felt when we discovered the scorpion...Fear. That's it. Plain and simple. Good old fashion heart-pounding, stomach-butterflying, hand-sweating, generally-uncomfortable-in-my-chest-and-stomach fear.

And guess what? This is fantastic news. This is the best news you have received all week, all month, all year. Because this news will liberate you. It will set you free. Fear is just an emotion. An energy. It's got nothing on you. By the end of the next chapter you will have completely transformed the way you see fear, feel fear, and think about fear. And by the end of this book, you will smile at fear as you boldly step into the most incredible life you can imagine for yourself.

CHAPTER IV:

FEAR

"All our fears are fears of feelings."
- Christian Mickelsen

AVOIDANCE

Do you like pain? I sure don't. And if you're a living organism on this planet, you probably share my viewpoint. We, as humans, don't like pain. Whether it's the physical pain of hitting your thumb with a hammer, or the emotional pain of someone telling everyone how stupid you are for making a mistake, it matters not. We just plain don't like it.

And so we do what any sensible creature would do. We avoid it. We see the potential for physical or emotional pain and we go the other way. No thank you.

This makes sense and seems reasonable at face value, but there is a problem with this plan. Can you see it? Have you personally experienced the pitfall of this approach to life?

(Un)fortunately, the game of life seems to be set up like this:

1. We are all going to die.
2. Everyone we know and love will die, too. (Sorry, I didn't make the rules).
3. It is impossible to avoid all pain and discomfort.
4. The more we try to avoid short-term discomfort and pain, the more we experience long term discomfort and pain.

That last one is huge. Read it again and ponder it for a moment. Have you seen this in your life or in the lives of those around you?

If we avoid the short-term discomfort of getting our ass out of bed in the morning to work out, we eventually experience the long-term pain of heart disease, diabetes, and a bunch of other unpleasant stuff.

If we avoid the risk of speaking up at work and instead choose to lay low and avoid all assertion and confrontation, we may dodge some short-term pain or discomfort. But we will soon start to experience another, more depressing kind of discomfort. We will feel powerless, ignored, or not respected. As time goes by we start to experience the daily pain of being stuck on the same level of the company while everyone else has been promoted. Or we experience the pain of working in a job that we don't like but are afraid to lose.

Is this making sense? Can you see the truth in this? I'm hammering this one home because our pull to avoid discomfort is so strong that it takes quite a bit of repetition for us to break free of it. To put it more simply:

Avoidance = relief in the short-term, but PAIN in the long term. Or, even more directly:

AVOIDANCE = PAIN

What kind of pain? The pain of not doing what you know on some level you are capable of doing. The ache of watching your life pass you by without you fully participating in it. The shock of look-ing back at the last ten years and seeing how little has changed. The sorrow and anguish of regret. The pain of hundreds or even thou-sands of missed opportunities for connection, excitement, happiness, and joy. The pain of a life not fully lived.

Does this make you uncomfortable? A little shifty in your seat and unsettled? Good. That's exactly the kind of wake up call we all need because all of us are avoiding things on some level. We are all looking for the easier way, the safer route, or the less difficult path. And we're doing it so habitually that much of our avoidance is un-conscious. We're not even aware of it.

That's what all of those excuses and stories are about. Avoidance. Avoiding what we're afraid of. And what we're afraid of is pain. Somewhat physical pain, but mostly emotional pain. Painful feel-ings, such as uncertainty, embarrassment, unworthiness, shame, and vulnerability.

And the more we avoid these painful feelings, the weaker we be-come. The stronger our fear grows and the more anxious and re-stricted we are. We become able to do less and less. The cage grows tighter... Until we decide to break free.

APPROACH

The best, most effective, and only way to overcome fear is to stop avoiding it. To approach it head on. This can take many forms, which we'll talk about below, but ultimately, we must be willing to face our fears to be free of them.

This does not necessarily mean doing the thing you're scared of right away. In fact, the first place to start is inside of your own mind and body. Most people are terrified of physically feeling fear, dread, or other uncomfortable emotions, because they are upsetting, un-pleasant, and agitating. We want them to go away. Or we want to get away from them.

If you want confidence, though, you must change this habit. Many clients come to me because they want confidence, and their definition of confidence is "I never want to feel this stupid fear or anxiety ever again." I tell them I can help them become completely free from their fears, which they love. Then I tell them it will involve being willing to feel your fear more than you ever have, which they love a lot less.

To gain true and lasting confidence, you must commit to turning towards the discomfort, and towards what you fear - both internally and externally. You must be willing to do this again and again, not just once or twice. You must be willing to make this a way of life. That will give you all the confidence you seek. It will bring you an incredible quality of life and amazing experiences. It will bring you everything... If you're willing to walk through the fire.

Below you will find five powerful tools and methods that guide you through exactly how to do this. You'll discover how to face fear, deal with fear, soften fear, smile at fear, and ultimately walk right through fear. Each one of these five habits is in itself a life-changing lesson.

I have spent the last twelve years of my life obsessed with this. I have not stopped studying it. I can't for some reason. Having been so scared of so many things for so long, I created a magnificent obsession with how to be free of fear. I've read hundreds of books, listened to just as many audiobooks, attended dozens of seminars and invested hundreds of thousands of dollars and years of my life learning these secrets. Then I tested the hell out of every single one of them thousands of times, with myself and with every single one of my clients. This is the best of the best. If you apply it, this shit works.

Ready?

FIVE WAYS TO OVERCOME FEAR SO IT NEVER HOLDS YOU BACK AGAIN

1. How To Resolve Fear

Facing fear does not start with doing a bunch of stuff in the world. It doesn't involve being a macho badass, storming into the boardroom, or boldly approaching that group of attractive strangers at the bar. All that stuff is great if you want to do that sort of thing, but it comes later.

The first fear you must face is the fear of your own feelings. Across the board, people are terrified by negative feelings. We don't like them. We feel ashamed of having them. We fear people will judge us if they knew we experienced them. We hate them. We try to make them go away as quickly as possible. We try to escape.

What's on TV? Turn on some music. Listen to a podcast. Check your email. Sign on to the web and say, "Hmm, what is it I need to look up? I need to know something right now." Grab a drink. Roll a joint. Buy a pack of cigarettes. Eat a chocolate bar (or two). Get a Big Mac and a milk shake. Preferably strawberry. Mmm, delicious toxic milk shake. Where was I?

Ah yes, avoidance of our feelings. We all do it. And if you want to have ultra-high levels of internal confidence and outer success, you will need to stop doing it. We must face our feelings in order to resolve them. To let them go. To release them.

How do we do that?

It's actually very, very simple. So simple a six-year-old kid can do it (although your mind wants to make it overly complicated so that it can avoid doing it). Let's learn it by doing it together now. All you do is focus your attention on the sensations in your body. Don't think about them, analyze them, try to figure out where they came from or how to make them go away. Just feel them. That's it.

I told you it was simple. Easy? Not really. We have a lot of momentum pulling us away from our feelings. It takes a commitment to breaking the pattern of fear, a strong desire to be free, and a good deal of courage to consistently turn towards our feelings and allow ourselves to really feel them.

Our patterns of avoidance can be so automatic, or so subtle that we don't even know we're avoiding fear. We might not even be aware of the fear. We just might have a strong urge to go order a heavy, salty, deep-fried lunch, or to flick on our computer and go to our favorite porn site.

We want to become very curious about these decisions and actions. Not harshly judging and condemning ourselves as weak-willed pathetic losers. Just curious. *I wonder what I could be avoiding right now? I wonder what I'm afraid of?*

When we start really looking, we don't have to search very far. Remember, we are most afraid of our feelings, not necessarily the events surrounding them.

Let's use an example to make this concept clearer. Can you think of something you'd like to do, that would really move you forward in your life? Something that would help you double your sales or your income? Something that would help you meet an amazing partner, or make more friends? Something that would bring more to your life, but involves doing things that scare you?

Got it? Good. Think about doing that thing now. Maybe it's giving more sales presentations, or cold calls, or approaching that influential person who has the kinds of connections you'd like to have. Maybe it's asking for a raise or increasing fees for products and services in your own business. Maybe it's walking over to that attractive man and smiling at him as you say hi. Maybe it's telling your wife something you've avoided telling her for months.

Feeling some fear? Some angst? Great! Bring your attention right to it. Focus your awareness on the physical sensations in your body.

Slow way down as you read this. Read these next few paragraphs very…very…slowly.

Breathe.

If you feel discomfort in several places in your body at once, just pick one of them and focus on that area. If it moves, follow it. Go right into the center of it: the place of the most discomfort. See if you can drop your resistance to the feeling. Almost always our default approach towards our uncomfortable feelings is, *Ughh... You again?!* See if you can soften that resistance a little (or a lot). Try saying, "I consent" instead.

This feeling is already here now. *Ok, you can be here. I'm going to allow this.* Can you accept the feeling and just let it be there without trying to change it in any way?

Breathe, relax, and just notice it. Let it move through you. Give it all the time it needs (which is usually not that much time, even though it might feel like forever).

That is how to face fear. And rejection. And failure. And any other negative emotion that comes up as a result of some external experience (or imagined future experience).

This is the most useful, powerful, and effective thing you can do to overcome fear in your life. The more you do this, the less scared you will become. You will stop running from your feelings. And since all of our fears are really just fears of feelings, not events, we stop running from the events we once were avoiding experiencing.

After going through this process enough, fear dissolves. Sometimes it takes five minutes, sometimes it takes fifty. You don't have to do all fifty minutes straight (although that's an incredibly powerful experience). You can just face it for five minutes at a time over the course of a week. Whatever it takes.

As you sit with the fear, simply being with it without trying to analyze it, solve it with your brain, or make it go away, it will often dissolve. It's just energy. You will stop bottling it up and it can pass right through you, leaving you with a sense of peace and a clear head.

Commit to doing this whenever fear comes up for you. Or start with just five minutes per day. It will transform your life.

2. How To Love Fear

As you stop running from your uncomfortable feelings and start meeting them with acceptance, magical things start happening. You will notice more confidence, more strength, and more boldness. However, there is something else we must do, if we want to become completely free from fear holding us back. We must learn how to love fear.

Now I know that might seem like a stretch. We were just talking about acknowledging fear and not judging it. Maybe even accepting it. But loving it? I mean come on! *It's so uncomfortable! And it's weak and pathetic. I shouldn't be feeling this fear anyways. Love the fear? That sounds way too woo-woo and soft.*

I was actually just speaking with a client about this several hours ago. His reaction to this idea was that it feels weak and embarrassing that he would even have the fear in the first place, let alone need to send it love.

If that's how your mind is reacting that's ok. That's just fear too. For men there is often a fear of gentleness, because it is seen as too feminine or not "manly" enough. However, many women I have worked with are also scared of and uncomfortable with treating themselves and their emotions with love and tenderness.

There's so much unquestioned, junko conditioning in our brains that makes us mistrustful and skeptical of just giving ourselves a break. Unfounded stories about how we'll be apathetic, unmotivated, and otherwise ineffective unless we hate the shit out of ourselves for being scared or having some other "unacceptable" emotion.

How has that been working so far as a strategy? What kind of results does it produce? Usually mediocre at best, with lots of unwanted side effects. Want to know a much better, faster, cleaner, and more effective way to move from fear to a life of extraordinary confidence and success? Love the fear.

Fear comes from pain. Pain about feeling pain. Or pain about the idea that in the future we will experience more pain. The fear is like a wound, and your attention and love is like the healing salve that will bring you back to health.

So as you pay attention to the fear and stop resisting it, go one step further and send it love. If your mind says "how?" that's it just throwing up another roadblock to self-love. It's still a little freaked out about the whole idea (*if I don't hate and bully myself, then how am I going to win at life?*). That's fine, you can just send love to that part of the fear too.

Just breath in and out. Take slightly deeper breaths, right into the area in your chest, throat, or stomach that feels tight. Focus right on the sensation, just as you did before, but this time, also silently say in your mind, *I love you.* Keep gently repeating this, telling the sensations *I love you* again and again. Open your heart and hold the uncomfortable sensations with as much patience, forgiveness, and tenderness as you can muster. Like holding a scared child who just woke up from a nightmare. Bathe the sensation in love.

I love you. I know you're scared. It's ok. It's ok for you to be here. You can be scared as long as you like, and I'm not going anywhere, little guy. I love you.

Put your hand on your chest, right over your heart as you do this, and keep it there. Do this for three, four or five minutes straight. Set a timer on your phone for four minutes, and just do this practice fully until the alarm rings. You will be amazed at the effect. It might feel like a long time as you're doing it, but in the big scheme of your life, is four minutes really that much time? Is it worth doing this once or even several times per day if it means living in much less fear and with much greater confidence and joy?

You can also comment on what you are noticing and choose to love and accept whatever arises. That would sound something like this: *Even though I'm feeling scared right now, I love and accept myself.*

Even though I feel tension in my solar plexus, I love and accept myself. Even though I am worried that I will bomb in my presentation tomorrow, I love and accept myself. Even though I'm frustrated with myself, and telling myself I shouldn't be scared, I love and accept myself.

Basically, you are just narrating whatever arises: a thought, a feeling, a sensation, and then saying that even though that's happening, you love and accept yourself. Taking a deep breath and sighing in between each statement makes it even more impactful.

To discover an even more detailed breakdown of this life-changing strategy, I encourage you to go to http://YourConfidenceCode.com.

SUPPORTING THE SCARED PART

The part inside of you that is scared and creating all that inner commotion needs acceptance and love. You can think of it as if it were another person outside of you. If your best friend was really anxious—I mean really terrified of something—how would you respond?

Most likely you would talk with her. You would listen, offer empathy, support, encouragement, and love. You'd be with her in her time of need.

An incredibly powerful and effective technique for loving your fear involves speaking with it directly. As you pay attention to your fear and send it love, focusing on the place of discomfort in your body, notice what that discomfort would be saying if it could speak.

If your chest feels like it's full of pressure and about to explode, focus right on the most intense place in your chest, breathe, and listen. What little (or big) voice is yelling in your head? What does the pressure in your chest say?

It's usually something simple. Such as:

- Ahh, I don't like this!
- I don't want people to die!
- I hate losing friends!
- No one's going to come!
- I'm going to fail!
- I want them to like me!
- They're going to think I'm stupid!
- I hate this!

Whatever it says, you will respond in the same way: with compassion and empathy. Start with "yeah" or "of course."

Yeah, you don't want for no one to come. You're scared of no one showing up and it being embarrassing. That would be difficult.

Of course you don't want to fail in front of all those people. You're worried about your speech. That's ok.

Yes, you're scared that he'll never call back and of getting rejected. Of course! Who wants to get rejected?

This is in direct contrast to how most people deal with their fear. Instead of just allowing it, they brace themselves for battle and try to beat it back. This is usually completely ineffective, makes the fear grow stronger, and increases tension in our bodies because we're squeezing our innards even more by trying to make a feeling go away.

When I guide clients through this exercise in one-on-one or group coaching sessions, the most common way they try to relate to their fears is with something along the lines of, "Oh, it will be ok if no one comes. You'll learn from it and do better the next time!"

This is the old "pep talk" approach, which seems well-meaning on the surface, but actually falls horribly short in effectiveness. It comes from our parents or other loving adults who did this with us when we were kids because they were not that sure of how to handle painful feelings themselves. Seeing their beloved child suffering made their hearts hurt, so they tried to make it go away as quickly as possible. "There, there now. Stop feeling that way. It's time to cheer up and look on the bright side."

This doesn't truly work. It's sub-optimal.

Instead, let's use empathy. That means acknowledging their pain, and describing it to them. It's giving them a reflection so they know that someone else sees them, gets them. This is a profound human need.

When my son falls or gets hurt in some way, and he runs to my wife or me, crying, we pick him up and hold him close. This is somewhat helpful, but he calms down much faster if we also narrate what happened. "You were standing on the step, and then you fell over and hit your head." He'll respond with an emphatic, "yeah!" and will stop crying instantly. We all want this. We all need this. Start by giving it to yourself.

Let's look at a real example:

Scared Part (SP): Ahhhh!!

Me: Hey buddy, you sound pretty scared.

SP: Yeah, I am.

Me: What's going on?

SP: There's so much going on. We're getting this house remodel done, and it seems behind schedule, and the baby is coming in November, but maybe sooner. I don't want him to come early. I'm scared of him coming early and dying or needing all kinds of medical attention and then dying. Ahh!

Me: Whew, yeah man, that's intense. That would be really painful to lose your son. It's such a vulnerable thing to bring a new life into the world.

SP: Yeah, I hate it! I don't want to get hurt.

Me: I bet. That would be a really painful experience that would take a long time to heal from. You'd have to feel a lot of grief along the way. You don't like losing babies, or people you love.

SP: No, I don't. Now I'm scared of someone reading this and judging me. They might think, "This is terrible. I can't believe he's writing this. How is this supposed to help me, he's just blathering on about himself the whole time."

Me: Yeah, you don't want people to judge you. You don't like when people judge or criticize you. You also don't like being exposed to potential judgment. I think it makes you feel really vulnerable.

SP: People might say, "This book is terrible; not as good as his first; pure garbage!"

Me: You're scared of being publicly criticized. I get it! Who would want that? Anyone who puts himself out there is impacted by reviews and prefers good ones to bad ones. That's true for authors, artists, poets, filmmakers, actors, and many more people.

SP: I won't be able to earn enough money to support my family.

Me: You're worried about not having enough money to support the family. Sure, that would be an unpleasant situation. Like you won't have enough money for food and shelter?

SP: No, that we don't have enough to pay all of our bills.

Me: Ok, so not basic survival necessities, but other bills?

SP: Yeah, like a car payment, or life insurance, or business expenses such as hosting all the stuff I do on the web.

Me: Sure, you're scared of not being able to have a car or insurance to protect your family in case you die. That would be difficult to have to cancel that insurance. I love you. You are doing such a great job of seeing the potential dangers and threats to our family. You're doing a great job.

SP: Really?

Me: Yeah, I think so.

SP: But you're always telling me I'm full of shit and that none of these things will ever happen, and that I should stop believing my thoughts, and feeling scared is bad and it's all my fault.

Me: Hmm, I guess I have been pretty hard on you lately. I've definitely been trying to ignore you, or talk you out of being scared, saying everything will be fine and to stop bothering me. I'm sorry. I think you're actually a really important part of the team.

SP: Really? That's a relief.

Me: Yeah man! I mean you are out there all day looking for potential threats and letting us know. You're the one who's got to face the hard things out there. Thank you for what you do.

SP: Thanks.

Me: Hey, I have a question for you. Why do you always predict we're going to fail before we do a new project or endeavor?

SP: Because I don't want you to do it.

Me: But aren't you worried about money? If we never did anything in the business, we wouldn't earn any money.

SP: Yeah, I don't want that either.

Me: So you don't want to do new things *and* you still want to have money coming in.

SP: Yes!

Me: Haha, ok. I was just curious. I like your style. I love you.

SP: I love you too.

As I did this exercise, there were moments when I felt profound relief. This part of me just needed my attention, empathy, love, and understanding.

When he started mentioning not being able to pay certain bills, I really wanted to offer a counter. To tell him that we don't really need any of that stuff, that it's materialistic and doesn't matter anyway, so stop worrying about it. I realized I've been treating him in a cold, dismissive manner. As soon as I uncovered this and thanked him and truly appreciated him, I felt a tremendous wave of relief flood through my entire body.

Can you have this kind of conversation with yourself? Or, perhaps a better question would be, are you willing to have this kind of conversation with yourself?

What if you just dropped the resistance for a moment, and just let that fear be there? Sometimes when I'm struggling with a fear and trying my best to make it go away (yes, I still get stuck in that pattern sometimes too), my wife helps me out. I'm laying there in bed, kind of distant and withdrawn, because I'm trying to use some of my mental CBT, NLP, or other 3-letter acronym mental jujitsu to banish an uncomfortable feeling.

When I eventually confess what's going on and allow my wife to help me, she sometimes says this: "Imagine that scared part of you is a little kid and you're giving him a warm bath. He's shaking and frightened and you draw up a nice, hot, relaxing bath. You put some shampoo in his hair, sing him some songs, and then afterwards wrap him up in a nice cozy towel."

If that's not love, I don't know what is. (She's much better at this "loving the fear" stuff than me). Give that scared part of you a bath. Imagine putting him into a nice warm tub, and offering him as much love as you can muster. Profound relief is just a conversation away…

3. How To Take Fear Less Seriously

"I've lived through some terrible things in my life,
some of which actually happened."
- Mark Twain

A while back when I was growing my coaching business I was plagued with persisting feelings of fear and insecurity. Ironic, given that it was a confidence coaching business. But I always knew it wasn't about me being perfect, it was about me being willing to continually work on myself and to overcome the next obstacle, so that I could turn around and help thousands of other people do the same.

One source of that fear was a doom and gloom story that everything would somehow fall apart. Things had been going well for over a year, I was earning more than I ever had, yet I was terrified that all my clients would leave, none would come back, no more books would sell, no one would buy any new training programs, and the whole thing would evaporate into a cloud of mist. Oh, and then I guess my family and I would die from starvation under a bridge.

At the time I was working with Steve Chandler, an incredible coach who helped me reach the next level of liberation, power, and confidence in myself and in life. He's a sage man with decades of coaching experience, a poof of white hair, and the deepest voice I'd ever heard, save for James Earl Jones of Darth Vader fame.

One time I was listening to an audio interview he did with some-one on our home stereo system. My wife walked into the room and said, "What are you listening to?"

I told her it was Steve interviewing someone.

"His voice is so…deep!" she exclaimed with wonder.

Anywho, in one session I was telling him all about my story of woe and how anxious it made me feel and he asked me this question.

"Aziz, what if you took the fear less seriously?"

"What do you mean?" I asked. "I know what it's saying is not true, but it feels so believable. I emotionally respond before I can do anything."

"Well," he paused for a moment. "You have a son, right?"

"Yes."

"Imagine you were walking down a hallway in your house with your son and just before you opened the door to a closet he said, 'Dad! Don't open the closet door! There's a monster in there that will bite your head!' In that instance, would you be scared to open the door?"

"Haha, no" I laughed, imagining the scene unfold in my mind. "It's cute."

"What would you do?" he asked me.

"Well, I guess I would say, 'Really? Are you sure? Let's open the door and find out.' Then we'd open the door together. I don't know, maybe I'd get a golf club or something so he felt like we could take the monster down if we needed to."

"That's how you want to be with your fear story," he replied. "It's like a kid who's afraid of a monster behind the closet door. It's not real. You don't have to take it so seriously."

That conversation was a huge breakthrough for me. For years I thought I had to not feel afraid or somehow push through the fear until it vanished. I never considered that the fearful voice could keep going and I could just watch it with amusement.

What monsters does your mind imagine are behind doors in your life? What if the next time your mind predicted something awful, instead of getting carried away by it and spooking yourself, you simply smiled at it. Imagine a kid with a spaghetti strainer helmet and a plastic sword, cautiously walking towards the door, waiting for the monster to spring out. It puts a smile on my face every time I think about it.

Note the key point in the metaphor is that you actually open the door and reveal that there is no monster. If you turn around and run the other way, screaming, "Monster! Monster! Honey, our boy told me there's a monster in the closet! Ahh!" then you know you're taking it seriously. In order for this approach to work, you have to smile at the amusing nature of the catastrophe story, and then walk through the door to greet whatever is on the other side of it. Again and again. That is what the next chapter - Action - is all about.

Just remember this: the predictions in your mind about what is behind the closet door—or what will happen if you hired a new person, had that sales conversation, or asked that person out—are not real. They are not even accurate. We are terrible at predicting the future. So the next time your mind tells you something about the future, just smile. Then go find out what happens when you really open the door.

Just FYI, at the time of writing this, I have yet to be bitten by a monster when opening a door (although that doesn't stop my mind from predicting that there certainly will be a horrid monster behind the *next* door).

4. How To Turn Fear Into Power

Fear is just an energy. It's a collection of sensations in your body - tightness, squeezing, pumping, tingling. It can include worried thoughts or images in your mind of bad things happening. But all of that is just an energy moving through your body. It may be unpleasant, but there's definitely a charge to it. It makes you antsy, restless, and uncomfortable. It makes you want to get up, move around, pace, run away, or do something to get rid of it. In this way, it is has great potential to be converted into something else: Power.

How do we do this? Simple. Remember, fear is a response, activated by your nervous system when there is a perceived threat. When the danger arises, our body kicks into high gear and is prepared to flee or fight. Fear is the flee part. We feel scared, powerless, helpless, incapable, small. We want to run away.

But the same energy in our nervous system could be used to fight. To charge the predator, to defend the herd, to respond with power.

That is what you need to activate in order to turn fear into power. No, that doesn't mean hitting your colleagues in the face when you're nervous in a meeting. But it does involve using your voice and body in ways you might not be accustomed to. Perhaps in ways you've never done before in your life.

The simplest way to illustrate it is to use an example that everyone's seen. What do football players do before they get on the field, especially before a big game? Do they sit there, stationary and pensive, waiting for the death clock to reach zero before they have to face their fate? Do they slowly walk out onto the field, limply waving at people?

Absolutely not. Absurd, right? What do they do instead? They get pumped the fuck up. Before the game they have someone give them an inspiring speech about how badass they are and how they are going to crush it. They stand up, start moving around. They wave their arms and hit their chests. They start chanting and yelling things.

I know one football player who would say this at the top of his lungs during a pump-up session: "I am an incredible, unstoppable, sacking machine."

"I AM AN INCREDIBLE, UNSTOPPABLE, SACKING MACHINE!"

He would yell this, bang his right hand against his chest, then belt out an incredibly loud, "Hwahhh!" He would perform this routine dozens and dozens of times before a game, working himself into some kind of frenzy.

Sound crazy? So what? This shit works! That's why every athlete does some version of this. But you don't have to be a professional athlete to have permission to do this. You can just decide to start doing this right now.

Start by being alone where no one can hear you. This way you won't be self-conscious. Well, not too self-conscious to do it at any rate. Then put on a song that gets your blood pumping. Then just start ranting, waving your arms, hitting your chest, and yelling shit. It doesn't matter what you say, it's about tapping into that energy and physical power in your body.

Feel silly or stupid? Good. Keep doing it. Get even more intense. Jump up and down. Shout out the word, "Yes!" My favorite one is a really simple phrase that reminds me how I want to be everyday of my life.

I AM BOLD!

I like to shout this out at the top of my lungs in the car.

At my live weekend events, I create a setting where people get to practice this many times throughout the day. During the first pump-up, some people are a little hesitant, skeptical, or reserved. But once they see others and myself jumping around like primate maniacs, some part of them wants to as well. It's probably their inner kid who loves to jump around like a maniac (remember how fun it was to jump on the bed when you were little?).

The results are noticeable and dramatic. By activating this much power in their bodies, people are able to do things during the weekend that they've never done in their entire lives, such as creating an engaging conversation with a group of strangers, or approaching a beautiful person and asking them out.

As you are building your energy, you can also go on a rant about how badass you are, how you nailed it yesterday, and how you're going to crush it today. One client I worked with became the poster-child for pump-ups. He was in a group I was running and he became this technique's biggest advocate. Each week he would tell the other members how excited he was about it. His routine would start in the shower where he would hit his chest, flex his muscles and say, "Dude, you got this! You're the man! You crushed it yesterday. Today is going to be even better. You are a badass leader. Everyone wants to talk with you. Everyone looks up to you. You're the man!"

He would continue this on his drive to work, and in his head sometimes throughout the day. This allowed him to turn his nervous, fearful energy into power. And it made him take much bolder action in the world. Within one month of starting the group, he blasted through his fear of talking to anyone in his office. Within three months he was giving stellar presentations and getting noticed. The next month he was invited to a small group conversation with the CEO of his company and he said he talked casually, made jokes, and "just chilled with the CEO like it was no big deal." I'm telling you, this guy is the poster child for pump-ups.

Do it. Seriously, just do it. Just give it a shot. Do it several times and see what happens. This shit works.

If you want to get the master's level version of how to do this, how to anchor it into your body so you can access it whenever you need it, and much more, I highly recommend my program Confidence Unleashed! It will help you obliterate fear and transform it into an endless source of power. You can learn more at, http://ConfidenceUnleashedNow.com.

5. How To Use Fear To Guide You

I didn't learn this one until just last year. I was doing quite well before then, but when I discovered this secret, the brakes just exploded off. My personal growth, income, and zest for life skyrocketed. When clients I've worked with have adopted this approach, their confidence, dating lives, businesses, and profits dramatically increased.

Seriously, it's the golden ticket. But here's the catch: you can't do it unless you have mastered the other ways of working with fear. That's why it's number five on this list of steps. So, once you've got a handle of those first four steps, use this one to break through to the next level. Here's how:

Whenever you hear that little voice of the Safety Police in your head that tells you that you can't do something, that you'll fail, that you'll get rejected, that it's too much, that you're not good enough, and so forth…Do the exact thing it is saying you cannot do.

In fact, start listening to that voice, not to guide you *away* from things, but to give you a clue as to exactly the next thing you can do to explode your confidence and success in life.

My good friend and colleague, Ben Allen summarizes this philosophy in a simple and extremely powerful phrase: Fear is an invitation. It's an invitation to take action, to approach, to do the very thing that part of you wants to run and hide from.

So when that voice says, *Don't speak up in this meeting, it won't go well,* that is a direct indication that you need to be speaking up in meetings more. It's showing you the next thing you can do to make your life even more awesome.

Here's how this progression has worked for me.

My Safety Police said, *You can't switch from clinical psychology to coaching. No one will hire you as a coach.* So I switched the work I was doing, created a new website, and started offering coaching.

Then the voice said, *You can coach people in person, but not over Skype. You won't be effective and you'll fail.* So I started coaching people over Skype.

Then the voice said, *You won't be able to coach people over the phone.* So I started doing phone coaching as well.

Then the voice said, *You can't do groups over the phone. No one will come, and it won't work.* Double whammy. So I started a coaching group over the phone with men from all over the country. I was intending my first group to have six people. We ended up beginning with seven. Could these predictions be any more off-base?

But they kept coming. Next it said, *You can't do one-on-one weekend intensives, no one will come to one of those.* I've done dozens by now.

You can't do a larger in-person training. No one will come to that! Guess what I did next?

I think you get the point. You can use your negative, fear-based stories to guide you towards your next step. It's scary, it brings up fear, and it forces you to work on your stuff directly. And it produces confidence and results like nobody's business.

It's like running down a hill where you never quite catch yourself. You keep going faster and faster and your mind says you're going to fall and it will all be over, but you never really fall. Or you do, and you get back up again and keep going and it's no big deal.

You can use this for any aspect you want more confidence in: public speaking, dating and relationships, starting conversations with people, networking, sales, presentations, leadership, marketing, business. Find the thing that scares you, the thing that your mind says you absolutely cannot do, and go do it.

In order to pull this one off, you will need more keys. You will need to know how to take massive action, unlock unstoppable courage, and pursue what you want in life with relentless determination. All of which you will discover In the next chapter...

CHAPTER V:

ACTION

"Fear is the only thing in the world that gets smaller
as you run towards it."
- Tiamo de Vettori

"Take decisive action and your fear won't matter. Take that decisive
action enough times and your fear won't exist any more."
- Dusan Djukich

THE KEY TO CONFIDENCE AND SUCCESS

Action is the ultimate key to ever-increasing confidence and massive success in any area of life. The flipside of this is true as well: inaction is the primary reason for low confidence and a lack of success.

All of the other chapters in this book were designed to help you remove the blocks to action. Excuses, stories, the sensation of fear - all of these tend to block action. And once you bust through them and take action, that's when things really start to accelerate.

Imagine this (only slightly) wacky scenario for a moment. Let's say there's a vast, wide-open field of vibrant, green grass. Way down at the other end of the field is a pot of gold, or career success, or the respect of your peers, or the love and attention of a beautiful partner. Whatever would inspire you the most to get out on the grass and go across that field. Imagine you're not the only one out there. There are hundreds of people out on this field. People of all ages, genders, cultures, ethnicities, classes and economic statuses.

Everyone wants what's at the edge of the field. And yet, you notice something strange. Not everyone is out there running towards that compelling thing that excites them most. Some are walking slowly. Some seem turned around and are actually walking the wrong direction. Others seem stopped entirely, frozen in place. Still others seem to be moving in wide circles, never really moving beyond a certain point. You notice several people sitting on the ground, facing the opposite direction. There's even a guy sprinting the dead opposite direction from what he wants most.

What the hell is going on here?

The people who are stopped in place are most likely paralyzed by some excuse or story. *I can't move forward because* _____(insert story here, such as: something outside of my control that's not my fault, and/or I'm not good enough to get that pot of gold or love)

Those who are moving in the opposite direction of the pot, are most likely retreating due to fear. Much like the brave, bold Sir Robbin from *Monty Python's Quest For The Holy Grail,* when they encountered something scary, they turned and fled, saying, "Run away!"

When they get to what feels like a safer distance, they may turn back around and set out again. Or they may sit down and entrench themselves in a story. *I tried and it didn't work. Therefore it never will work. Sorry, thems the breaks.*

So you have all these people running around in all directions in this field. Excuses, stories, and fear running amuck. It's chaos. Pandemonium.

What about the people moving forward towards the pot of gold, love, and creative fulfillment? They are taking action.

Each step towards that goal comes in the form of action in your daily life. Sometimes it can be big, dramatic action, but usually it's small, simple, basic action. It's making a phone call, asking for the sale, sitting down to write the proposal, blocking off time to complete the project. It's moving towards that beautiful stranger who excites you, it's taking the risk and going in for the kiss, it's saying "I love you" first. It's deciding to go to your friends' dinner party rather than retreating for yet another night of binging on *Game Of Thrones* and Chunky Monkey.

Those are the people moving forward on the field. Action moves you forward. Nothing else. Positive thinking, affirmations, visualization, wishing, hoping, thinking about it, talking about it, and saying you're going to do it: all of these habits do not move you forward. They might help you remove the inner blocks to action but at the end of the day you must *take* action if you want to create the confidence you want in your life.

Some people on the field might be running, some jogging, some walking. It doesn't matter--any forward motion is good. And, it is possible to get into better shape so that you can easily sustain a nice jogging pace towards your ultimate goals. Take that next step. Each step forward is action. Action ultimately leads to confidence, progress, power, and success.

You may be nodding your head as you read this, ready to dive in and tear shit up in your life. You may be slightly shaking your head from side to side, wondering *how do I take action? What action? What if it's too hard or scary? What if I fail?*

Shut up! Stop your whining and get onto that field you sissy! Now run! Go go go! Move!

Oops, sorry. My friend who was a sergeant in the army told me to write that. He says it worked wonders for the "softies" at boot camp.

Where were we? Ah yes, taking action. This chapter is going to help you get into action. Massive, rapid, powerful, fucking unstoppable action. You're going to discover a scientifically proven method to creating huge reservoirs of courage so you can face whatever you need to face and slay whatever dragons and demons you need to slay in order to create the life you want.

You're going to learn how to completely change the way you see action so it's no longer overwhelming, stressful or terrifying. You're also going to learn how to blast through confusion, uncertainty and other delay tactics.

And finally, you're going to break free from any fears of rejection that may be holding you back from taking the actions you know you want to take. You'll discover the real source of pain around rejection, and how to let it go so it's no longer such a big deal. You'll learn how to handle, overcome, and heal any fears about getting rejected so you can float your way across that grassy field, more easily and quickly than you ever imagined.

Read this chapter. Read it twice. Apply what you learn. Do this, and your life will never be the same again.

You'll soon get to experience firsthand the joy of moving gracefully forward towards goals that excite and inspire you. You'll feel the joy of increasing confidence and self-esteem. And you'll see that the ultimate victory is not in getting the pot of gold, or success, or love. It's about the mastery of moving across the field with grace, peace, and joy. Because as soon as you get to that pot of gold, you'll see another one even further down the field, and you get to do it all over again.

THE SCIENCE OF CREATING COURAGE

Courage is what will catapult you into action. As you break through layers of excuses and stories, you'll start to make contact with good old-fashioned raw fear. The kind of fear that induces the fight or flight instinct, minus the fight. Courage is what you need in order to face fear, to challenge your fear, and to become the master of fear.

Before we go any further, there are two things you must know about courage:

1. Courage can be built systematically. The more you practice it, the stronger it gets.

2. You cannot beat yourself into courage.

These are key points and we'll talk about them more in a minute. First, let's define what courage actually is.

Courage Defined

The best definition of courage I've ever come across wasn't in a dictionary, or on Wikipedia, or in a personal development book. It was on a t-shirt. In fact, it was so good I actually asked the guy wearing it to pose for a photo so I could take a picture of it. Here's what it said:

Courage, also known as fortitude, is the ability to confront fear, pain, danger, uncertainty or intimidation. It can be divided into physical courage in the face of physical pain, hardship and the threat of death, and emotional courage in the face of shame, scandal and discouragement. Its vice of deficiency brings cowardice, and its vice of excess brings recklessness.

There you have it. It's a powerful definition. I'd suggest reading it again. Notice how it does not say, "a man or woman who does not experience much fear because they are badass." Yet this is the definition most people unconsciously have for courage. They imagine that courageous people don't feel anywhere near the level of fear that they do. *If I were more courageous, I would feel less fear.*

But the truth is that courage requires fear. We must have the fear in the first place, so we can exercise our ability to confront it. That is the part that is courageous confronting the fear.

In a moment, I'll share with you the formula for creating courage, but before I do, it's worth highlighting the approach virtually everyone takes towards building courage. It's incredibly common, it's recommended and used all over the world, and it doesn't work.

Beating Ourselves Into Courage

The most common approach to courage-building goes something like this:

We notice we are scared of something because we shy away from it, or we get a racing heart, or our minds spin out of control with worrisome thoughts. Then we decide we need to overcome this, take action, and stop being held back by our fears. So far, so good.

But then we attempt to carry this out by saying something like this to ourselves:

Come on! Just speak up for yourself in the meeting! Everyone else can do it. Why are you just sitting there like a passive piece of furniture? You are such a wimp. Everyone there doesn't take you seriously because you can't even open your mouth. And then when you do, it comes out so weak and quiet that people can't even hear you. No wonder you're still in the same position after all these years. Pathetic!

Truly inspirational. Now I feel ready to show up confidently and just crush it in the next meeting. I am ready!

Actually, it has the exact opposite effect. This kind of self-criticism does not increase courage or confidence. It completely demoralizes us and makes us even less likely to take the risk of speaking up in a future situation. It comes from an outdated understanding of human motivation that is based on this principle: If I punish myself relentlessly then it will be incredibly painful. That way, when my mind is given the option to choose between the pain of speaking up or the pain of my self-beating afterwards, I'll speak up to avoid the beating!

Terrible.

Does it really work? Does it work in your experience? Probably not.

Even if it does somehow manage to get you to do something you're scared of, you're not coming from a strong, centered place of powerful confidence. You are tense, scared, pressured, and uncomfortable. You are sheepishly walking up to talk to that person because there's a big dude with a stick behind you saying he'll whack you upside the head if you don't. How is that going to make you relaxed, open, charming, and authentically yourself?

An enormous amount of research has been done on this very topic, which can be found in the dusty archives of clinical psychology journals. One researcher, Dr. Kristin Neff discovered that the more harsh and critical people are with themselves, the less likely they are to take risks. They become tense and terrified of doing so mostly because of the fear of their own brutal self-attack.

We are getting further and further from courage here, aren't we?

So the next time you notice yourself attempting to beat yourself into performing better or being more courageous, stop. Say to yourself, *This is not helpful. I don't do this.*

And then, do the following instead.

THE FORMULA FOR COURAGE

After studying this stuff relentlessly for twelve years and speaking with thousands of people, I've come up with the formula for courage. Do you want to know what it is? Are you ready to uncover the esoteric secret?

Behold! The Formula For Courage:

Do something you are scared to do. Then do it again.

(Pause for dramatic effect, while holding my arms wide out to my sides in a grand gesture. The prestige!)

Yep, that's it. It really is. If we want the secret to be clearer, more complicated, or different somehow, that's just our minds looking for an excuse to not take action. Because at the end of the day, that is what builds our courage—Action. Nothing else.

No affirmations, no cognitive exercises, no praying. Those things can all help prepare you, but then you have to take the action. You have to do the thing that scares you. Of course there are ways to make this process easier and more effective, which I'll share with you now. But they all start with the understanding that action is the key.

What Are You Afraid To Do?

One question I am asked on a semi-regular basis from clients and potential clients is, "What are you going to make me do?" I might be telling them about a coaching program, my Unstoppable Confidence Mastermind group, or a Weekend Intensive and they'll groan and ask that question.

My answer is always "Nothing. I am not going to make you do anything. I can't. I am going to create as many opportunities as I can for you to choose to step up and build courage and confidence, if you want, at the rate that you want."

And then I like to ask, "So tell me, what would you be afraid to do?" And then I laugh maniacally and tap my finger tips together. It's actually a great question, and it shows us the path towards greater courage, which leads to greater confidence, success, and fulfillment. So, what are you afraid to do? Take a few minutes and actually write out a list.

What I'm Afraid To Do, A List
By Aziz Gazipura

Run a marathon or half marathon.
Run paid ads for online traffic.
Initiate sales conversations with prospective customers.
Become a vegan.

Hire a team of full-time employees.

Host and promote weekend events.

Create and fill confidence mastermind groups.

Talk with a friend about a challenge I'm having with our communication.

Tell an employee I am not satisfied with their work and that it needs to be different.

Interrupt my dad when he's talking a lot.

.... And so on.

Notice how it's a list of what you're afraid to *do*. Not just a list of the four million things you could be afraid of in life (for example, a tornado destroying my house and prized stamp collection).

If you are working on your social confidence and ability to meet people, approach strangers, speak up, and communicate with confidence in work or your personal life, the following might be useful for you.

It's part of a Confidence Assessment I give to my new clients. Just read over the list and notice which ones stand out for you.

Initiating a conversation with a stranger.

Carrying on a conversation with someone you just met.

Joining into a small group of people who are already talking.

Being the center of attention in a small group.

Talking with one person while others might be listening in.

Sharing openly about what is going on in your life.

Listening effectively to others so they feel understood.

Initiating a conversation with a stranger you are attracted to.

Complimenting a person you find attractive.

Asking a person you are attracted to out on a date.

Flirting to build attraction and excitement.

Kissing and escalating physical contact towards sex.

Speaking or performing in front of an audience.

Giving an impromptu speech or talk in front of a group.

Speaking in front of a video camera.

Disagreeing with someone.

Telling someone when you are upset with them.

Saying what's on your mind, even if the other person may not like it.

Telling a server at a restaurant that you didn't like the food.

Speaking with your supervisor/boss directly and honestly.

Requesting a raise/asking for a higher fee for your services.

Ok, now it's time for you to make your own list. It can be as long or as short as you like. Give it a few minutes though. If you have three things on your list, take a moment and dig a little deeper. What are you really afraid to do?

To dig up some fears, start thinking about what you would need to do in order to create exciting and deeply fulfilling relationships, grow your business, radically increase your income, find and date an amazing and attractive partner, and so forth. Look at what you really want, and what you would need to do in order to get there. Then watch the fears start tumbling out.

Go ahead and make your list now.

For seriously. Don't just keep reading. The gym doesn't work if you just walk through it. You have to pick up some weights and throw them around!

Fierce

Great! Now you have a list of (some of) the things you are scared to do.

Notice how all fears are not created equal, though. Some of the items on your list might be mild discomforts or annoyances that you can accomplish without much effort. Some might make you pretty darn nervous, and some would make you downright shaky and terrified if you actually tried to complete them.

Go back over your list and next to each item, give it a rank from 0-10, where 10 is the highest level of fear. If you want to get fancy, you can rearrange your list to go from lowest to highest or vice versa. But that's not necessary. Just be sure to give each fear a number between 0 and 10. Now, are you ready to start building courage?

Actually, let's pause for a second and think about this. Wouldn't it be awesome if you could act on the highest ranked fears now? What if you did them and it was no big deal? What if you could be doing them all the time? What would that do for your business, your sales, and your income? What would that do for your dating life and your close relationships?

Yes, the more you do these things, the faster you will grow, expand, and achieve everything you want and more. It's formulaic. It works no matter who you are. Now, are you ready to start building courage?

Pick an item on your list and do it. Pick a low number if you'd like. Or, if you're feeling fierce, pick as high a number as you can handle and go do that. And then do it again tomorrow, or next week. The sooner the better. And setting a reasonable and sustainable pace is important, too. But the rate is less important than just doing it.

So, go do it now. Get fierce. Take action.

FEAR DOES NOT EQUAL DANGER

Have you ever had the misfortune of watching an absolutely terrifying horror movie? I mean something so dark, twisted, freaky, and disturbing that the awful imagery from the movie just stayed in your head for weeks or even months?

The very first time that happened to me was completely unexpectedly. As a child of the 80s I was a fan of Ernest P. Worrell– the comedic character who played in such classics as *Ernest Goes To Camp*, and *Ernest Goes To Jail*. A bumbling, lovable character, Ernest always starts out as the ridiculed and dismissed loser, but he somehow always manages to save the day and earn the respect of all the other characters. Great fun for a little kid.

But then one day they decided to release *Ernest Scared Stupid* on Halloween. A quick Google search reveals it was 1991, which would have made me eight years old at the time.

In this particular Ernest movie, he was roped into battling some ancient evil troll that wanted to eat children or do something else evil that I don't quite remember. What I do remember is a scene where a young girl is terrified that there might be something under her bed. She sits there hugging her legs into her body, repeating to herself,

"There's nothing under the bed; there's nothing under the bed." She slowly looks down to determine if this is in fact true. Eerie music plays. Tension builds.

But, whew! There's nothing under the bed. The little girl, the entire audience, and my little eight-year-old self all relax with a big sigh of relief. It's just her harmless stuffed animal. She rolls back to lie in her bed, and guess who's right there in the bed next to her, waiting. The evil troll. That fucking grotesque, twisted, evil-looking troll. I screamed my face off. That movie scared the shit out of me.

For weeks afterwards, I was prepared to roll over and find myself face to face with a hideous beast in my bed. I really was convinced it would somehow happen. I was absolutely terrified, and pulled all the tricks. Demanding the light be left on, demanding my brother face me from his bed as he fell asleep, demanding that someone guarantee that I wouldn't be murdered by an evil troll in my bed.

Now, let me ask you this. Was I in danger? Was my safety actually threatened in any way? I venture to guess you are saying, "most likely not." And yet, I was afraid. More than afraid, I was really terrified, tense, anxious, and disturbed. Which highlights something extremely important to know about fear.

Fear does not equal danger.

We take our fear to mean that we are in danger. We think, *I'm so scared that a troll might eat me, therefore I am at risk of being eaten by a troll.* But there is no troll (as far as I know) and there is no danger.

As silly as this story is, we do the same thing all the time as adults. Not with trolls, but with dozens of other things.

I'm afraid of failing. Failing must be dangerous.

I'm afraid of being judged negatively by people. They might not like me or approve of me. Being judged or disliked must be dangerous.

I'm afraid of walking up to that beautiful stranger and starting a conversation. That situation must be dangerous.

When we conclude something is dangerous, we think it really is a threat. Then it makes sense for us to avoid it. We want to avoid serious threats to our health. If a house is heavily leaking gas out of the stove, you want to get out of that house. That's dangerous, and it's a threat to your life.

Getting rejected is not dangerous and it's not a threat to your life. It's a movie with images of a troll. It's scary. It's spooky. But it's not dangerous.

So the next time you're afraid of something, remind yourself, fear does not necessarily equal danger. In fact, the vast majority of the time there is absolutely no danger at all, other than the self-beating that occurs after the failure or rejection. And we'll help you let go of that later in this chapter. Before we do though, let's talk about those yellow-bellied cowards.

Cowardice Defined

No one wants to be called a coward. It's a word and insult that's gone out of favor. I don't hear it being used much, although it would be fun to call someone that. "You did what?? You, sir, are a pitiful coward."

While we might not use that word very often, we definitely can criticize ourselves for not being confident enough, bold enough, strong enough, or "man or woman" enough to just go do it. We call ourselves wimps, sissies, and far worse when we fail to take action, fall short of a goal, or otherwise don't perform at the level we want.

Let's take a moment to look at what cowardice actually is. The dictionary will tell you that cowardice is a lack of bravery. That helps. That's why dictionaries are awesome. Bravery is "courageous behavior or character." Remember, courage is the ability to confront fear, pain, danger, uncertainty or intimidation. So cowardice would be a lack of confronting dangerous or unpleasant things.

And this is where a lot of people get confused. If they don't do something out of fear, then they conclude, *I am a coward.* They make it about their identity and who they are, which actually just further entrenches them into choosing avoidance in the future.

I don't think cowardice is a lack of courageous action. I think when you want to speak up in a meeting, and you are preparing to in your mind, and you're feeling tense and nervous and worried beforehand, and you keep telling yourself you're going to do it, and then the moment comes and you're just about to do it, right now, here is your moment...and then you don't... in my book that choice is not cowardice.

Because you were facing your fear. Now sure, you didn't score the goal. You didn't speak up, approach the stranger, ask for the sale, or whatever it is you wanted to do. But you were certainly preparing to. You were confronting all kinds of uncomfortable feelings inside of yourself. And because of that you are close—very close—to taking action next time.

That's pretty good in my book, and I see that as part of the process of developing courage. We don't knock it out of the park every time. Sure, if you had spoken up in that moment, you would have made more progress towards greater confidence more quickly, but it's okay that you didn't. It's not a race.

Here's what I think cowardice really is: it's hiding behind a story or excuse. It's saying, "I can't speak up because I'm a shy person," or "I can't ask someone out because I'm an undesirable loser." That's cowardice, because when you're believing that story or excuse you are nowhere near taking action. You are in helpless, powerless, poor-me victim land. And you are selling yourself a story that allows you to never take the risk you need to take to overcome your fear. A story about how you're somehow not capable or good enough to take action.

I remember drawing a little map with a client one time. He was eager to break free from his fears and develop greater confidence in himself in dating and relationships, as well as in his career. He had just experienced another repeat of his pattern of "almost" approaching a woman he was attracted to, and then aborting mission just before opening his mouth. Another pattern of his was to start talking with her, and "almost" ask for her number, and then exit the conversation politely without doing do so, only to kick himself for hours afterwards.

Then, he would spend days in hopeless, frustrated despair. He was plagued by thoughts like: *I'll never meet a woman. I'm such an awkward loser. What's wrong with me? How come other guys don't have to deal with this. It's not fair. I'm going to be alone for the rest of my life. I should have figured this out by now...*

So I drew him a map:

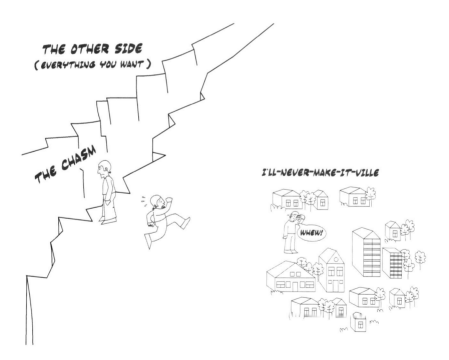

"Here's you," I said as I pointed to the edge of the chasm. "When you get closer to taking the risk to show your interest in a woman, you are getting close to the edge. For you, it's a leap into the unknown. On the other side is everything you want: dates, an amazing relationship with a beautiful girlfriend, advancement in your career, more income, and much more."

He nodded, seeming to agree that everything he wanted was on the other side of this darn chasm.

"Right now, you walk up to the chasm, preparing to leap. This is something you didn't used to do in the past. But now you're stepping right to the edge, and really preparing yourself to jump across. Then some part of you—namely your Safety Police—kicks in and tells you that you won't make it. Then, you retreat to a safe distance, far away from the chasm, far away from actually taking the leap. Over hear, to the safe town of I'll-Never-Make-It-Ville."

In this place, you are safe. No risks, no chance of rejection, no chance of failure, no chance of immediate pain. Of course, this place is full of a different kind of pain – the pain of avoidance, not living up to your potential, not achieving anything, and not being able to give and receive love. It's actually a pretty depressing place to be. But at least it's *safe*, dammit!

ONE CHOICE

You are not a coward. And you are not a courageous person. You are neither of those things, because you are not a noun. You are not a fixed object that can be labeled as always being one way or another. You are a verb. You are constantly changing, evolving, and growing. You are constantly in shift, in flux, in a state of moving and becoming. "I" is fluid, hard to pin down, and its definition depends entirely on what we choose to do in this moment.

In each moment you have a choice. Well, I suppose in each moment you have hundreds of choices, if not thousands. But let's narrow it down to one choice for this discussion on courage and confidence. You, my friend, don't have to worry about if you're courageous or cowardly, worthy or unworthy, good enough or somehow deeply flawed. You don't have to worry about any of that. You only have to decide one thing: will you approach or avoid?

That's it. When it comes to creating extraordinary confidence in yourself, in your love life, in your career, and anywhere else, that is the only choice you must make. The rest follows from that fundamental first decision.

There is an attractive stranger over there. You are powerfully drawn to him or her, as if there is some gravitational force leaning on you to go start a conversation. Do you approach, or avoid? Do you walk right over to that stunning person and say, "Hi there, I couldn't help but notice you from over there. You are absolutely beautiful. What's your name?" Or do you hesitate, wait until the moment has passed, pretend not to notice, act as if you're highly interested in the art scheme on the walls, or just slink away discouraged?

You are in a new division in your company and in charge of moving an aspect of a big project forward. To be completely honest, you are confused and overwhelmed (even though you sold yourself as totally in charge and confident in the interview). You're not sure what to do next or who to talk to. Do you approach or avoid? Do you get out into the hallways and start talking to people? Do you make a list of all the different questions you have, things you would need to do in order to figure out what the hell is going on here? Do you ask questions in meetings, challenge people when they give you vague answers, and dive in head-first? Or do you hide out in your office, waiting for something to happen, waiting for your boss to tell you what to do, and waiting for someone to save you?

In every moment – whether it's when there's conflict with your spouse or children, a limited dating life, unsatisfactory conditions in your career, a dismal social life, or anything else – you have a choice: approach or avoid. It's a choice you've already been making—possibly subconsciously—and most likely the results of your choices are what you are experiencing now. If you've primarily chosen avoidance in an area of your life, then most likely that area is not going supremely well. You probably aren't experiencing much confidence, satisfaction, or success in that area. Because avoidance = pain, remember?

So how do we reverse this tactic, and approach, then? Maybe I'm already preaching to the choir. You're on board. You don't need to be convinced any more. *Yes, Aziz, I get it. I'm ready to approach. But how do I get myself to actually do that?*

I get this question quite regularly with my 1-on-1 and Mastermind coaching clients. It's a valid question, and I'm going to share a number of powerful strategies that will get you into approach-mode, and will help you to take more powerful and rapid action than you possibly have at any other time in your life. But sometimes this question can also be a sneaky delay tactic. I'll talk more about delay tactics in a bit, but I'd like to mention this one before the rest. Because if you're saying to yourself, "Yes, I'm totally ready, I just don't know how to…" you may be sliding back into avoidance territory.

The real question is not "how to", it's "want to." Or, even better yet, "Am I willing to?" We often say, "How do I go over and just start talking to those people?" because we want to make it seem very complex, as if we need a schematic diagram and structural engineering before we can make the first move. *I'd better study this one in the safety of my lab for the next four to six weeks. Then, I'll know exactly how to do it, and then of course doing it will be easy and not scary at all. Right?*

Wrong. It's always going to be scary at first. And maybe for a long time, depending on what it is and how often you go do it. Instead of figuring out how to do it from a safe distance, ask yourself if you really want to do it. *Do I want to walk over to those people and just start talking to them?*

If your fear kicks in here and says, "Hell no! That sounds terrible!" remember that's just your Safety Police talking. Because my guess is that on some level you really want to be able to do the things that scare you. In fact, you desperately want to. You are craving the social confidence and freedom to just freely interact with anyone without self-doubt or judgment. You want the abundance of love and connection that can come from being so bold and open to the world.

So the real question is, "Am I willing to feel some discomfort in order to get what I really want?" Because that's all we're talking about here; just some discomfort. Some fear in your gut, some self-doubt or maybe self-criticism. Some fear of embarrassment or worry about what others think. That's all part of the process. Growth is messy. Breaking through to a higher level of confidence—to a truly extraordinary level of confidence—requires slogging right through the muddy mess of your insecurities to get to the other side. There's no hovering, sterile, future bridge that you can just glide across without any discomfort or challenge. Watch out for that comfort stuff, it will kill you.

NINE WAYS TO TAKE CONSISTENT, BADASS, UNSTOPPABLE ACTION ALL THE TIME

Once you've uprooted your excuses, challenged your self-limiting stories, and learned how to lean into what scares you, you will become truly unstoppable—when you take consistent action.

Using the principles below, I am able to coach individual clients, run life-changing confidence mastermind groups, host multiple live confidence transforming events per year, record a weekly podcast, create weekly blogs and videos, write books, create video training programs, do interviews, and manage as much tech stuff as I can handle. I do all of this while working about forty hours per week, so I can have plenty of time with my wife and two kids, as well as with my friends and loved ones.

I get more done in a week than many people do in a month. I am not saying this to brag or sound superior. I don't think it's because I have some sort of super-power or something. It's just that I've cleared a lot of the excuses and stories, and committed twelve years ago to do what scares me in the service of something greater. Then I applied, and continue to apply the principles below like a madman. I am doing these things all the time.

And I truly believe that you can do this, too. You can spring into rapid, massive, powerful action. You can be moving down that field farther and faster than you ever imagined. This is in you. It's in all of us. Let's step up and activate it now.

1. Get Clarity

*"I was only in there to get directions on how to
get away from there."*
– Principal Skinner, *The Simpsons*

Most of the people I see struggling to get into action are lacking clarity of vision. They don't really know what it is they want to do or accomplish. They are much more aware of what they do *not* want to happen and what they want to avoid.

When someone reaches out to me about Confidence Coaching and we have a conversation, one of the first things I'll ask them to help them get clarity is, "If you had all the confidence you wanted, what would that look like? What would you be doing?"

Quite frequently, I'll get this type of answer: "If I were more confident…Hmm, I'd want to have more confidence with women. Right now I'm completely shy around them, and I'm never able to talk with them."

Or, "I want to be more confident in work. No one there takes me seriously and just last week a colleague who's been there for half the time I have was promoted ahead of me. This always happens. I'm too quiet in meetings and I don't speak up, so people don't think I can handle more. They don't see me as a leader."

This question is asking them about what they want, but notice the hard left turn back into problem-ville. Notice how difficult it is to actually focus on what we really want; notice the discomfort being with our desires causes us. Notice how the problem is just so big and front-row-center that it absorbs all of our attention and it's all we can think and talk about. Notice the lack of clarity about what we *do* want.

From this place, it is very hard to take consistent, effective, badass action. In this place we spin around and around, trying to get away from where we are, but without any clarity as to the direction we want to go. As we spin, we bump into our excuses and stories, and can end up stuck in this place for months, years, or decades.

We need clarity.

What is it you want to do? If you had 800% more confidence in yourself, what would you go do? What would you attempt? Who would you talk to? What would you talk to them about? What would you start or create?

I know you answered some of these questions at the beginning of the book in the first chapter, but we can't ask ourselves this question too often. It brings us back to our goals, our prime direction, our focus. It brings us back to clarity.

So what it is that you want? A more satisfying love life? More dates, more fun dates, more second and third dates? Do you want to freely and easily meet people you are attracted to? Maybe you want to break through to the next level in your career, earn more money, achieve a higher position at work, or step into a higher level of leadership. Maybe you run your own business and you want to grow that sucker – increase sales, expand your team, and earn more while personally working less.

Maybe you want to make more friends, spend more time with those friends, or find new friends who excite, inspire, and encourage you. Maybe you want to play the guitar, paint, sing, take dancing lessons, learn how to program a computer, or create an app for a smart phone.

I don't know. But you do.

Take eight minutes right now and either go back to what you wrote at the beginning of this book, or create a new list. Be as specific and clear as possible. The more detailed you are, the more likely you will be to actually create the things you want.

Ready? Ok, go do that now.

2. Chunk It Down

You may have made lists like this before at other times in your life. Maybe it turned into something, or maybe it became a dusty keepsake that you stored in the bottom of one of your desk drawers, to be pulled out on occasion. "What the hell is this thing? Ahh, those goals. Yeah, those were nice. Anyway, back to real life…"

Here's why most people don't turn this list into action and life-changing results. They fail to chunk it down into digestible, simple, small, daily steps. They don't turn the dream into a project.

Experimental psychologists have found that we can hold about seven pieces of information in our conscious minds at once. As in, a standard seven-digit phone number. Have you ever tried to remember a phone number with the area code as well? Ten things? Holy shit, it's hard. You're reciting that thing endlessly, hastily repeating it lest you drop one of those precious numbers out of the basket of your conscious mind into the abyss.

When we set out to achieve some goal, task, or project, are there usually more than seven things we must do? Of course there are. If it's something like growing your business, it might involve hundreds of things. Even something as simple as "learn how to dance" involves a lot of steps. And when there are too many steps, our mind does something like this: *One, two, three, four, fi…Oh good God! Too many! What's on TV?*

We need to help this out by chunking things down into digestible units that our mind can handle. I like to pick just three or five things. This seems like a manageable amount to me. I also like to tell myself, *Listen, all I gotta do is A, B, and C. That's it.*

For example, when I am feeling overwhelmed with my business and managing all the moving pieces, I will just chunk my list into a few things. *Ok, all I gotta do is profoundly serve my clients, enroll new clients, market the products and services I offer, and create cool stuff that excites and inspires me and others.* Well now, that' just four things. That's not so bad.

Let's look at a few other examples. Let's say you are a single guy and you want to get a girlfriend, but you're uncomfortable initiating conversations with women and you don't feel too confident in this area. Let's chunk your to-do list into just a few big things: *All I gotta do is find women, talk to them, ask for their numbers, and then set up some dates.*

Let's say you want to learn to dance: *All I have do is watch some videos to see what kind of dance I want to learn, then look up classes, then sign up and go to them.*

This sounds exceedingly simple, doesn't it? It often really is. What makes it complex is not what we have to do, it's the stories, fears, and Safety Police that show up when we really consider taking these actions. Fortunately, you know how to do deal with all those suckas.

So, once you have some clarity on what the big picture will look like, you can take the first chunk, and break it down into three to five things. Then start working on the first one. Immediately. As in right now. Not tomorrow, or next week, or in a while. Right now. If that's not possible, then pick a time on your calendar when you will do it and actually schedule it in.

CHUNK UP

An alternative way to chunk things that can be helpful if you're feeling overwhelmed is to chunk up. When we're overwhelmed by all the things we need to do, sometimes it can be difficult to find clarity. Our mind is just churning out all these tasks and items and actions, and it can scramble our circuits. We don't know where to begin and it feels like there's too much to do in too little time.

In this case, we need to vomit all that stuff out of our heads onto paper. Grab a sheet of paper and just let it fly. Write down every thing you think you need to do, big and small, in no particular order. Whatever comes to mind first, just write it all down. This in itself can be a little relieving, because you know you won't lose or forget any-thing. Of course, once you're done it can still remain overwhelming as you look at this list of eighty-four things, thinking, *Oh my God, how am I going to do all this?*

With the power of chunking! (Insert superhero entrance music).

Eighty-four things is too many. Fourteen things is too many. We want to pare that list down to three to five things. Seven at most. So here's what to do. Go back through your list and see what items can be grouped together. What items fall into the same category?

For example, as you scan down your list, let's say you notice many items like this:

- Email Arash
- Email John about tax stuff
- Respond to Mary
- Schedule meeting with Jeremy

All of these can be chunked together into one thing: Respond To People, or Handle Communications. Make a little mark next to each of these items so you know they are each part of that bigger chunk

Then, once you've found three to five categories to put everything into, grab a new sheet of paper. On that one, just write out three to five big things, like:

- Handle Communications
- Dominate Project X
- House Stuff
- Prepare For Presentation

Underneath each one, you can write the specifics of what you'll do, but make sure you write them smaller than these big categories. You want to help your brain out here so it can really see that there are just four things to do. And four is a hell of a lot easier to manage than eighty-four.

3. Fuck It

I have to thank my friend John Parkin for this one. It's simple, humorous and can be profoundly effective. Here's how it works.

By now you know that what stops you from getting the results you want is not a lack of intelligence, natural talent, or good looks. Those are just stories and excuses we tell ourselves to cover the real reason: lack of consistent, powerful, effective action.

And what stops us from taking that action, again and again? Fear. Fear of failing, fear of falling short of our goal, fear of what others will think of us, fear of others disliking what we say or do, fear of others' judgments or our own self-criticisms. A whole big mess of fears, none of which are actually as dangerous to our bodies as we imagine they will be. And that's just the thing. The vast majority (as in all of them entirely) are based in the future. They are all focused on what terrible things *might* happen and how we couldn't handle this because it would be so unbearably uncomfortable.

Enter "Fuck It", or as John calls it, "The Ultimate Spiritual Way."

This is his clever and fun way of letting go. Here's how I use it to great effect. Think of something you'd like to be taking greater action on right now in your life. Something you know will bring greater confidence into your life if you were to do it more frequently, and with that confidence would come the results you want – more dates, more friends, higher income, a more satisfying job, and so forth (remember, confidence is the foundation of all success).

A portion of my clients are single men who are working to overcome their social anxiety so they can meet and successfully date the women they find most attractive. They have spent the majority of their adult lives avoiding doing this, and have either settled for relationships with women they know are not right for them, or have spent huge periods of time alone.

Working together, I help set them on a course towards much

more success in this area. After we blast through the excuses and stories, and guide them out of I'll-Never-Make-It-Ville, we can start making some real progress. That's when the fears kick in and the Safety Police come out guns a-blazin'.

- What if she already has a boyfriend?
- She's not going to want to talk to me.
- She's going to be annoyed and want to get out of the conversation.
- It's intrusive to just start a conversation with a stranger uninvited.
- I'm going to get tense and not know what to say.
- I'm going to freeze up and it's going to be horribly awkward for both of us.

Have you ever been in this situation? Lord knows I have. I spent almost a decade with these fears controlling my dating life, and even more years with these fears running rampant in all other areas of my life. Danger! Warning! Failure and pain imminent!

And yet, if we let this noise overtake us, we will *not* take action. That's the plain truth and the main reason most people are not rapidly moving towards what they most want. In addition to all the powerful strategies and techniques you learned in Chapter IV on fear, you can also use this method right before taking action.

You notice all that noise running through your mind, take a deep breath in through your nose and raise your shoulders towards your ears as you do so. Then let the air out through your mouth with a big sigh, dropping your shoulders as you do so, and say, "Fuck it."

What if she already has a boyfriend? Fuck it.

What if people see me talking to her and getting rejected? Fuck it.

What if I speak up in a meeting and someone overrides me? Fuck it.

What if I call to set up a presentation and they reject me? Fuck it.

Seem simple? It is. And that's where its power lies. Because it's helping you cut right through this storm of excuses. This cloud of anxious thoughts and worrisome future nightmares is not real. This is not a realistic assessment of the pros and cons of taking action. This is a flurry of panicked negative predictions designed for one purpose: To *stop* you from taking action now. To keep you in your comfort zone. To keep you safe.

This way of thinking is not focused on helping you thrive, flourish, break free, and live a life of extraordinary confidence, wealth, happiness and success. That is only achieved by repeatedly stepping out of the safety zone and into that challenge zone. You must do this so often that it becomes the norm rather than the exception. So as we prepare ourselves to dive into the next step, and all those freaky thoughts begin to propel you into hyper-protection mode, we need to take a deep breath in and say, "Fuck it."

I like to add a few other phrases as well, including, "I'm going to die anyways," and "Whatever it is, I'll handle it." These help me keep things in perspective so that I can take that initial leap, again and again.

That's the key piece of this whole puzzle – you have to take the leap. You must. There's absolutely no way around it. No magic pill that triples your confidence, melts belly fat away and creates a life of bright blue skies and green meadows without any effort or discomfort. That myth is twisted (yet highly effective) marketing we've all been ingesting since birth. Fuck that noise.

You must take action. You must step up. You are a warrior and you can blow right through this cloud of fearful thoughts like the vaporous mist it is. In fact, you can just walk right through it. You think you're going to fall down some horribly deep chasm with no bottom, but the most likely worst outcome is a pothole that causes you to fall in the mud and get your fancy armor dirty. Then you get back up and keep pressing forward.

Just say, "Fuck it." Then do it. Now.

In fact, *doing* is so important, it get's it's own section. Let's dive in right now and explore how you can strengthen the most important muscle in your entire body. Your DO muscle.

(If you'd like to listen to my extended interview with author and leader John Parkin, which includes one of the most inspiring and funniest stories I've ever heard, you can listen to these two episodes of my free internet radio show: Shrink For The Shy Guy.

How To Say F*ck It To Needing Approval
http://shrinkfortheshyguy.com/podcast/how-to-say-fck-it-to-needing-approval/

How To Say F*ck It And Do What Scares You
http://shrinkfortheshyguy.com/podcast/say-fck-it-and-do-what-scares-you/

4. The DO Muscle: Think Less and Do More

I'll never forget the moment I met Tim at a Tony Robbins training in Fiji. Tim had decided he wanted to attend this event, but he did not have a ticket or the means to purchase a ticket. So he gathered his items into a suitcase, grabbed a gigantic unassembled bicycle in a cardboard box, and booked himself a flight to Fiji.

The bike was something his company produced. He had invented it himself and they were now selling them around his home town. It had a big space in front of the seat where items, groceries, or even 2 kids could sit. His plan was to show up to the event in Fiji and offer the bicycle in exchange for attending. And guess what? It worked.

We were sitting outside in the warm tropical air one afternoon and he was telling me the story of how he got there.

"Wow, that's bold!" I exclaimed. "What if they had said no?"

"I guess I would have assembled that sucker and biked all around Fiji. Not a bad booby prize," he said with a smile.

I laughed in amazement. This guy is awesome.

"Yeah," he continued. "I've always been a ready, fire, aim kinda guy."

That was the first time I heard that phrase, but I never forgot it. Ready, fire, aim. *Always* ready to fire even before you are certain what you're aiming at. That is the direct opposite of the overly cautious, self-doubting, hesitate-until-the-moment-has-passed kind of way that I had approached much of my life.

That is what the DO muscle is all about. Basically, we have a muscle inside of us that allows us to take action, even when the outcome is uncertain, even when we don't have all of our ducks in a row yet. You just do. Do and see what happens. Do and figure it out.

We can spend so much time planning, waiting, and worrying. What if this happens? What if they say no? What if it doesn't work out? What if I start but can't continue? What if I say yes but then change my mind? What if, what if, what if?

When you hesitate like this and ask yourself all these confusing, disorienting, and terrifying questions, your DO muscle is shrinking. It's getting weaker. And the weaker it gets, the more certainty you need before you take action. And we all know how well that works out, because how certain is anything in life? Almost nothing is, especially not the stuff worth going after.

One of my coaches, Christian Mickelsen, shared this powerful metaphor during one of our group coaching sessions together. Imagine you are in a room with seven doors in it. Each door leads to a lengthy hallway and series of many rooms. At the very end of one of those paths is $50,000 in cash, just sitting there, waiting for you.

Now you could spend hours, or days, pondering which door would be best. *What if I go down door number two and it's the wrong door. What if I go down five doors in a row and I'm wrong every single time? What if I'm too slow? What If I make a mistake? That would be terrible.*

Or, you could analyze the situation for just a moment, trust your intuition and just go down one of those hallways as fast as you can.

Get to the end and see if the money is there. If it isn't, hustle back to the main room and pick another path. The faster you can do this, the faster you will succeed.

Just start. Begin. Do it. Take action. Then solve whatever problem comes up. Address whatever situation needs to be handled. But at least you're in motion now. And the more you just do, the more powerful your muscle gets.

Forget these bullshit lines that keep you out of DO mode and stuck in that procrastinating, fearful, anxious wasteland:

- I need to figure out more.
- I need to know more before I do anything.
- I'm not sure yet.
- I was thinking of doing that, but then I thought maybe I should do this instead.
- I don't know which one is the right one.
- It might go badly, so I'll prepare more and do it when I'm ready.
- I'll do it when I'm less scared.
- I'll do it later.
- I'll do it someday.

These stories you tell yourself are killing your DO muscle and they're killing your confidence. They also happen to be severely limiting your success in all areas of life.

A while back I was part of a high-level mastermind program with one of the leading coaches in the world. To become a part of this group you had to invest a minimum of $47,000, plus travel, accommodations, and other expenses. It was a huge stretch for me, and it freaked the hell out of me to join it, but I did.

What completely blew my mind was that there were a fair number of people in that group who invested that much money in themselves and their business growth who stalled out like crazy. They didn't know what niche they wanted to work with, they didn't know how to create a website, they didn't know how to write materials or marketing. And instead of just doing it hard and fast, they would spend weeks and months exploring "Why don't I do this? What's getting in the way…"

And I was thinking to myself, *What the heck? Are you kidding me? After spending $47,000 I am going to do the shit out of everything I can. Who cares if I'm scared or if I don't know how to do it yet. Let's do this!*

Then I realized I was only able to do this because I'd been building up my DO muscle over the last fifteen years. How do we strengthen this muscle? What would you guess?

That's right, we just DO. We take action. All the time. When you're unsure, take action. When you're scared, take action. When you feel paralyzed by fear, take a breath, then take action. When you don't feel like taking action, take action. When you are uncertain of the outcome, take action. When you don't know how to do something yet, take action and figure it out. When you are certain that you will fail, take action.

When your excuses and stories have been pushed aside and you know how to face your fears and walk through them, then getting into action becomes easier and easier. And the more you do it, the stronger your muscle gets, and then eventually you are doing so much that it boggles other peoples' minds.

So get out there, think less, and DO more.

5. Learn By Doing

You are going to make mistakes. You are going to make errors. You are going to mess up and drop the ball. You are going to fall short of a goal. You are going to fail. And if you aren't doing any of these things, then you are not taking action. Or the action you are taking is so small and safe and inside your comfort zone that it's probably not going to do much for you anyways.

Let's just get that of the way now so we can stop pretending like that's not supposed to happen. We can be so scared to try something because we are afraid of making these mistakes. As if it means something terrible about us as people. This mindset keeps us frozen, rigid, and waiting until we "know enough" to take action.

Instead, I suggest you learn by doing.

A good percentage of my clients had been working on their confidence for many years before they sought me out. They had read books, tried therapy, and done other things to improve their confidence and their lives. And when they approached me, they did so because they wanted to find out what else they could learn that would help them break free.

While we can talk about specific skills or strategies, such as how to start conversations, join into groups, or approach an attractive stranger, this is not where we spend most our time. I know it won't do that much. My main focus is to help them remove whatever is stopping them from taking action. Because I know they will learn the fastest, grow the fastest, and ultimately transform the most only by doing.

We could talk for five months about conversation skills, and they would not learn as much as in five days of having frequent conversations with people. We learn by doing. So if you want to get better at flirting, teasing, and creating exciting romantic connections, then you need to experiment with flirting, teasing, and connecting with the people you are attracted to.

If you want to learn how to speak up in meetings and join into groups confidently, you need to speak up in meetings and join into groups *a lot*. Only by doing this will you learn what works and what doesn't, and *how* to actually do it. This strategy can be very helpful, but only when combined with you putting yourself into a situation where you'll actually learn.

This is in direct contrast to the unconscious and unexamined philosophy that most people have, which is this: I'll learn, then I'll do. I think this comes from traditional education, which is very theoretical, pedantic, and removed from any real world application (think high school math – when am I converting variables in my daily life again?)

I was speaking with a graduate student recently. She was riddled with anxiety and self-doubt because others seemed so outspoken and good at critical thinking. She felt intimidated by them and perceived herself as inferior. This fed into her fear of getting out into the world after her training, being in a job where she didn't know what to do, and not being good enough to handle it.

Her idea was that her two-year graduate program was supposed to teach her everything she would need to know to succeed at any job in her future. I saw it completely differently. Her graduate program was just the beginning of her training. After it's done, she's going to find a job and she's going to continue to learn, she's just going to get paid to do it. As months and years go by she'll learn more and more and get better and better at what she does. She'll develop the experience and knowledge that she desires. But only by doing.

I get paid to learn all the time. The first time I hosted a three-day live event, I was being paid to learn. I'd never done that before. I'd run groups and had been a participant at live events, but I'd never run my own event. So I learned a ton (and freaked out a ton), by doing it.

This is actually the most natural thing in the world. This is what each of us automatically does when we're not being self-conscious or doubting ourselves. This is exactly how each of us learned to walk, to form words and sentences, to draw, jump, run, and use our bodies—everything.

So what do you want to learn by doing?

6. Do Not Delay

If you want to get incredible results in your life—career, financial, relationships, friendships or anything else—do not delay. Delaying, stalling, waiting, and anything else along those lines will slow you down like nobody's business.

So many things can be created and accomplished in a matter of months, if we do not delay. If we do delay, those months can turn into years or even decades. And in those years our negative stories grow in size and strength. *You see, this isn't working. You can't really do this. You aren't cut out for this. It will never work. Look how long it's been. You should be over this by now. If it's taken this long, that means it will never happen.*

All of which is complete bullshit. That's just your Safety Police attempting to keep you small, safe, and deep inside that comfort zone. But it's challenging to see through the murkiness of self-doubt, and it's much easier to get through it if we just don't delay.

Here are some of the primary delay tactics I've used and seen other people use. As soon as you notice yourself applying one, label it as nothing more than a delay strategy and then continue to move toward massive action.

PLANNING

This one is sneaky. Because planning is important, isn't it? Without any planning whatsoever we can get into trouble. We need to have some general idea of what our approach is. But unless we're mapping out the next un-manned space travel jet propulsion circuitry, we usually don't need to plan as much as we think we do.

Underneath the guise of "planning" is often just an incessant busyness in our minds that is actually worrying and preparing for hyper undesirable scenarios that have a 0.2% chance of actually occurring. To prevent this, I suggest making planning a conscious activity that you do as needed. Not something that your brain automatically chews on all day, but rather something you have on your calendar and that you sit down to do for a specific amount of time.

Take sixty minutes to plan whatever it is you need to. The next steps in your project. How to find a better job. Ways you can improve your diet and cook meals that are healthy. How you can start conversations with people and make some new friends. Where you can go to meet potential dates, and what you might say to start conversations in those settings. Some of these wouldn't even take sixty minutes to map out.

Then, once you've had your planning session, conclude it. It's over. Now it's time for action. Put into practice whatever you planned. You don't need to figure more things out. You don't need to know how steps fourteen through seventeen are going to go. Just get started on step one. You'll figure the rest out as you get there.

In fact, many of our best plans must be abandoned after about two steps into the process. Life is not rigid, static, and easily predictable. Life is complex and in constant flux. You might have a great conversation planned out in your mind to woo that attractive stranger, but after your first sentence someone drops a cup of coffee on your pants. You probably wouldn't keep the same conversational thread going, right?

Learning to plunge into situations with gusto and vigor is actually a great way to begin. Learn to improvise in each situation. Learn to make a plan to give yourself a sense of security, and then abandon that plan once you step into the world.

If you notice you are not taking action and are instead feeling a compulsive urge to plan more, identify it as a delay strategy and do whatever it takes to get yourself into massive action. Now.

MINDLESS PROCRASTINATION

Who doesn't know this one? You're all set to begin. You're going to start researching, start making those phone calls, start sending those emails, start setting up those meetings, start going to the gym. For serious, you're really just about to do it. You may have even opened up your mail program and clicked the button to create a new email. All set. And then…

I have to check something real quick. What's happening on my latest social media updates? Did anyone send me an interesting email? Let me check my stats from that last project again. Who played Batman in the movie Batman and Robin? Man that movie was bad. How much was the budget for that thing, and how much did it actually make? I need to check this out now.

And in the blink of an eye, there goes twenty minutes. Or two hours. Or two days. Partially absorbed, compelled to keep engaging in whatever it is we're doing, and mostly mindlessly. Sometimes we have the thought, "I should get back to that project," but it's more of a distant echo than an actual impulse.

Sometimes this procrastination can take a more subtle form, such as "working on" the project at hand. Look, I'm sitting down and writing emails. I'm updating the webpage. I'm creating some posts. And that could be exactly the most effective action you could be doing in that moment. Or it could be avoiding the real action that will get the real result you actually want. Sometimes staying busy with the immediate, attention-seeking tasks is actually a form of delay that is keeping you away from doing the things that really scare you, the things that will actually bring you what you want.

Regardless of which form it takes, it all comes back to fear. We procrastinate when we don't want to face something that is uncomfortable. We're worried about the outcome; it feels confusing or overwhelming; we're not sure we can handle it; it feels like too big of a project; what if I'm not smart enough to do this; what if I fail and everyone sees?

The desire to dodge these fears creates that oh-so-tempting pull to focus on something easier or something mindless. When it happens, just notice. Be neutral and compassionate. You don't need to beat the crap out of yourself. You don't need to tell yourself a big story about how you're a procrastinator and you always do this and what's wrong with you anyways? Just notice it, identify it for what it is (a delay strategy), and redirect to the task at hand.

If you'd like, take a moment and identify what it is you are scared of. Take a few breaths. Use one of the techniques discussed earlier in this book to sit with your fear, face your fear, and ultimately overcome your fear. Then get back into action.

BEING CONFUSED

One time I worked with a client from Italy. When he was about to face something that scared him, he would hesitate and say, "I am in confusion." I like that phrasing. It sounds cool. With his accent pretty much everything he said sounded cool. Unfortunately, he did not think so. He was riddled with insecurity and self-criticism, which lead to this sneaky little way to put off taking a risk.

Confusion is just another delay tactic. I'm confused (aka uncertain), so now I can't do anything. I need to stop and wait until this cloud of confusion passes and I have certainty again. Then I can move forward.

Nope. It doesn't work that way. Because the confusion doesn't mean that you are doing something wrong, or that you're in the wrong place, or even going down the wrong path. It just means your intellectual brain doesn't know exactly what's going on, which happens anytime we are growing, exploring, trying something new, or being fully present in our lives in the moment. Experiencing confusion means you're about to learn something new.

And what's the fastest and best way to learn? That's right, by doing. By getting into action. So when we are confused, we don't want to use that as a reason to stop. It's just a delay tactic and nothing more. Just another way to avoid fear. Another way to stay safe. Keep moving forward even if you're confused. Keep taking action. All will become clear as you continue.

7. Imperfect Action

When I am working with men on dating confidence, sometimes they read me a text message they received from a woman they are beginning to date. The question is always some version of, "What is the exact thing I can say to get her to want to go out with me again?"

When we take action, we want to get the result we are hoping for. If I take the action to ask a woman out, I want her to say yes. If I ask for a sale, I want the person to agree to the sale. If I am reaching out to people for fundraising or investing, I want them to agree to contribute to my organization. If I walk over to a group of people to join into the conversation, I want them to welcome me in and have a great time talking with me. All of this is completely normal and commonplace. Everyone has these desires. The problem arises when we are fixated and heavily attached to our preconceived outcomes. When we feel as if we would just curl up and die if things didn't go entirely our way. If you feel incredibly tense and believe you will be humiliated, embarrassed, mortified, or an utter failure if the outcome you want doesn't occur, then you are in for some trouble.

First, you probably won't take as much action, because the stakes are so damn high. Furthermore, you will probably spend way too long trying to determine the "perfect" action that will ensure the result you want.

My friend and I called this the "grind phase" before talking with a woman. Instead of just moving towards her and striking up a conversation, I would sit there planning exactly what to say in my head. It had a tense, unpleasant, grasping nature to it, as if I were desperately searching for the exact words and phrasing that would guarantee she would want to talk with me and date me.

If you want to stay in massive action and get incredible results in your life, you must be willing to take imperfect action. Let the action be "ok" just as it is. Whatever action you can take, let yourself do that now. Afterwards, assess and take the next action. And the next. Allow each action the right to be imperfect. Let each action guide you towards what you want as best as you can, without needing to know that this very next action will be the final golden key to everything great in the universe.

What if it's not good enough? Who gives a fuck? Do it. Do it now and suck at it. Then learn something from it and do it again. You don't need to be perfect. Every single one of your ideas and creations does not need to be the ultimate image of flawless perfection. Get your hands in the clay and make some weird, misshapen coffee mugs. Then give them to your friends and be really excited so they have to awkwardly accept them and pretend to like them. Then go back and make more mugs. And study someone whose mugs don't look like they are a lopsided pile of melting ice cream. Ask them questions. Copy them. This is the process that anyone who's created anything worthwhile has followed.

When I wrote my first book, I had several people ask me: "Are you worried about negative reviews? What if people don't like it?"

Wow, thanks for vomiting your projected fears all over me. Dick. But I know these were just my own fears coming back at me from the outside world, so I had to come up with good responses to them. And here's what it was: "My first book could suck. But my second one will be better. And then my third one will be awesome." (This book is my second one, by the way. So prepare yourself for ultra-awesome with the next one).

The key is to make a commitment to take imperfect action. This allows you to keep going, to keep making progress. You can course correct along the way and make whatever adjustments you need to once you're in motion. This allows you to build momentum, which is one of the most powerful forces in this world. It allows you to be in a state of flexibility, growth, and continual learning. This is your natural state. This is how all kids are before they've been programmed in junior high to fear making mistakes and "looking bad."

In my Unstoppable Confidence group program, we often start our calls with participants sharing their wins or successes. Sometimes, people have a hard time coming up with any. They are aware of where they are failing, falling short, and not getting what they want. However, when I ask them what actions they took, they usually can recall several. But they don't see those as wins because they didn't get the outcome they wanted.

It's time to change the way you see action. Action is success. When you take action, even if you don't get the exact result you want, you are growing, learning, and moving forward. Imperfect, messy, not-quite-ready-yet action. The more the better.

8. The Long Game

It's kind of a paradox, but one of the fastest ways to speed up our results and get the things we want is to actually expand our timelines. When I was first working on my confidence and beginning to talk with women, I had the expectation that I should get really good at this, really fast. Within a few months I should be able to walk up to any woman, or even a group of women, and confidently charm them by knowing exactly what to say and do in any situation. Sound extreme? It was.

Then, when that didn't happen, I would get frustrated and discouraged. This is the major pitfall with pressured expectations and tight timelines. Our minds tend to conclude that it must not be working if we didn't already get the results.

After many months and years of working on the area of dating and relationships, I became much more confident and successful. I patted myself on the back, recognizing how awesome I'd become. I also thought all the pressure and demand on myself was over at that point. That is, I felt that way until I got into a position where I

wanted to sell things. Uh oh, sales. That means talking with people, offering things, and getting rejected. That means a whole new skillset that I suck at and have to learn. And once again, my timelines were absurdly short and totally unrealistic. *I should know exactly what to say in any situation, and feel completely confident and relaxed no matter what, and not have anything bother me after a sales conversation, ever. Perfectly reasonable. Now, I'll make all that happen in two months.*

When I noticed this thought process happening, I realized I needed to make a few shifts, which would allow for a much more relaxed, self-compassionate, and confident approach to learning something new. First, I decided to focus on the process instead of the outcome. It's not about whether this person wants to date me or not, or if this person wants to buy something from me or not. It's about me showing up, being bold, asking good questions, and getting better at addressing whatever comes up. It's about me learning the subtle aspects of a skill that can only be learned by doing something again and again, hundreds of times.

I also greatly expanded my timelines. I made it okay for me to suck at sales and to learn this for the next three years. I gave myself three years to not know what I was doing, make mistakes, and just fail a bunch. Doing so took the pressure off, which was based on demanding that I be perfect at this as of yesterday.

What about you? What kind of timelines do you set for yourself? What is something you are learning right now? Perhaps it's developing certain social skills, like talking to strangers, networking and making connections for business, or reaching out for dating relationships. Maybe it's public speaking, or learning a new language. Maybe it's being a manager or being responsible for a team. Whatever it is, what would it be like to focus more on the process than any one specific outcome? How would it feel to relax and expand your timelines and give yourself years to learn and grow?

Breathe in and give yourself that gift. Any story you tell yourself that says you don't have that kind of time, that you have to figure this out NOW, or else someone's going to die is just a false sense of urgency created by your mind. And frantic action from that place, where you are entirely fixated on needing to get a specific outcome immediately, will almost certainly push away what you really want. Because it's full of desperate energy, and people (and all of the universe) do not seem to respond well to attached, desperate energy.

So take another deep breath. Relax. Let yourself be as you are right now, learning and growing each day. Focus on the long game, and notice how much more enjoyable it becomes.

9. Post Game: Contraction Spasms

After you've taken action, prepare yourself. Sometimes it's an awesome experience. You feel great. Powerful, liberated, in charge, the creator of your destiny. And sometimes you feel exposed, vulnerable, terrified, and uncertain. Relax. Either experience is good. It really is.

Sure, the first one feels better and we'd all probably choose it if we could. But the second one is actually a very important part of the process. Because, as you take action and do things you've never done before, you will bump right into the face of some of your deeper fears. The more action you take, the more you step into the unknown, and that is where most of our fears tend to lurk.

What are they thinking of me? Did I say too much? Was I too pushy? Did I come on too strong? I didn't say enough. I should have spoken up more. They said yes for now, but I bet they'll back out. They hired me, but what if I can't do the job!

Sometimes it's not even all these fearful thoughts that make you feel uncertain. It's just a super-exposed, vulnerable feeling in your chest and stomach that makes you want to turn and run away while ingesting as much alcohol, marijuana, jelly donuts, and other numbing agents as quickly as you can. It feels different, and different can feel uncomfortable, so our response can be to avoid it at all costs.

And this is all good. Trust me. It's the inevitable contraction spasm that happens after you expand. Don't fight it, run from it, or resist it. Don't spiral into thinking, *What does this mean?? Something must be terribly wrong!* Just be with the feeling of discomfort, witness it, and love it. Expect it, and when it comes, greet it with a smile and a hug.

Your Safety Police and other parts of your brain are continuing to do their very best to keep you from doing all this action stuff. To keep you from going deeper and deeper into the unknown, which happens to be where the life you really want resides. But these guys hate that place, and so they pull out everything they got to make you go back, play nice, play small, and stop right there once and for all.

This reaction is just fear. Breath and find those terrified little pockets in your body and send them acceptance and love. Empathize with them. *Yeah, you don't like doing so many new things at once. You hate all this uncertainty, huh? I don't blame you. It's a lot and it's pretty damn uncomfortable.*

And then reassure them. *It's okay guys. You're safe. You can be here as long as you need to be. I'm not going anywhere. I love you.*

Wait out the spasm, don't try to make it mean anything about whether or not you should keep taking action and growing. Just see it for what it is, send it love, and then get back out there and keep crushing it. When you have these spasms, you know you are on the right track and moving fast toward your goals.

REJECTION-PROOF

Ahh, rejection. Can't live with it and can't live without it... most of us, though, are trying to live without it. We try to avoid it, skirt around the actions that might lead to it, and overall, view it as something that is preferably avoided in life.

And then when rejection (inevitably) happens, we feel terrible. As if something bad or wrong has happened, as if somehow we are bad and wrong. Oh, and then who could forget this delightful cloud of discouraged, pessimistic, hopeless negativity that kicks in?

Why am I even trying? It's so much work. What's the point? It will never work out anyway, I'll never get this. I'll never be able to ____ (make more sales, meet an incredible partner, get a second date, grow my business, build a team, etc.)

Sound familiar? I know it all too well.

But what are we going to do? We can't avoid rejection because it's an essential part of life. Rejection is a "no" and if we want "yeses" in life, then "nos" must exist. It's unfortunate but true, I'm afraid.

The irony is that we try to avoid the nos because they make us feel bad (or so we think). But the more we hold back to avoid rejection, the worse we feel in the long run. Sure, we might feel some short-term relief by not speaking up in that meeting, or avoiding eye contact with that attractive stranger who seems interested in talking with us. But that momentary relief is immediately followed by regret, and then an even worse feeling creeps in. It's the feeling that we can't get what we want in life, that things won't turn out for us (because we're somehow messed up or not good enough). It's a big blob of discouragement and despair. And it's just plain not true.

Dang, so the only way to avoid that terrible mess is to go get rejected? But that feels so bad, too! There's no way out! You are in the right place my friend, because there is a way. But it's not out. It's through...

External vs. Internal Rejection

"I just can't make that decision now. I'll have to think about it and get back to you."

I looked down at the bright green grass, then up at the leafy branches and blue sky above me. It was a gorgeous spring day in Portland and I'd been walking in a park during an extended conversation with a prospective client.

We'd been talking for an hour about his involvement in a group coaching program. I'd tried everything I could think of to help him make the decision to help himself. I was out of ideas.

"Ok," I said.

We agreed on a time for him to get back to me with his decision. I wasn't particularly hopeful; it seemed like a polite "no." (95% of the time, "I'll think about it and get back to you" is a polite "no")

There it was. NO. Rejection. The monster I tried so hard to avoid.

What happens next? A sinking feeling in my chest. An aching, squeezing sensation in my heart. Feelings of sadness, discouragement, heaviness. Negative thoughts about this group, about my potential. It all coagulates into a pessimistic mess.

This pattern can happen so fast that it's easy to assume the "no" is what caused the whole mess. We experience it so often that we just start to think no equals pain. But does it always?

Have you ever been rejected and for some reason it didn't bother you that much? Have you ever been rejected by someone or something you didn't even care that much about, and still experienced it as incredibly discouraging and painful?

One client of mine was working on his confidence for his dating life. He was practicing putting himself out there more, and he had asked a woman for her number. He was not particularly drawn to her and not that invested in dating her. And yet, when she said no, he felt a crushing sense of inferiority and despair.

Have you been there? I know I have. What's going on here?

Internal rejection.

You see, there are actually two kinds of rejection: external rejection and internal rejection. And guess which one's worse?

EXTERNAL REJECTION

External rejection is what the other person actually said and how they said it. In the story above the external rejection is simply the phrase,

"I just can't make that decision now, I'll have to think about it and get back to you."

How bad is that? It's actually quite polite and friendly. External rejection usually is.

No thanks.
I wish I could, but I can't right now.
I'm busy that weekend, thanks anyways.
I'm sorry, it sounds great, but I can't afford it.
I'm sorry but I have a boyfriend.
We regret to inform you that the position has already been filled.
Thanks for asking, but no, I can't.

Those phrases are typically what we will receive as a rejection. In some cases, if the person is really upset, their tone may be harsher or they may leave out the niceties. But this is rare and typically not the kind of rejection we experience in business, sales, negotiation, dating and socializing.

Here's a question for you: What percentage of your pain and discomfort comes from the external rejection? Give it a number now. Out of 100%, what amount would you attribute to the actual words and vocal tone of the person saying no? I think it's usually five percent or less. Maybe if they are really harsh and roll their eyes in contempt or attack your character it can be more towards twenty percent. But usually not higher.

That means ninety five percent of the pain and discomfort and fear around rejection comes from inside of us. Ninety five percent of the damage is self-inflicted... Which is fantastic news. Because what's inside of us is the only thing we can actually do something about.

INTERNAL REJECTION

> *"If there is no enemy within, there is no enemy without."*
> - African Proverb

So how do you do it? How do you turn the mild external "no thanks" into an onslaught of pain? Here's my favorite method:

Step 1: Make the rejection mean something about my own short-comings and inadequacy.

He only said "no" to the group because I'm not good enough. I'm not good enough at sales, at helping him see the value it can bring to his life. I am not good enough as a human. I am a failure.

When I was single and a woman I asked out said no, it was because I'm not charming enough, not suave enough, not attractive or muscular enough, not good enough.

Step 2. Demand that I should be better, and NOW.

I should know what to say. I should be doing better at this. I should be getting this quicker than I am. I am way too slow at this.

Underneath these thoughts lies the demand for a higher success rate at whatever endeavor I'm engaged in. When I inquire into exactly what that success rate should be, I get: *100% success rate, motherfucker.*

Step 3. Conclude that it will never work and I'm doomed to failure.

You'll never find the right people for the group. No one else will want to join (never mind that I've done many groups before and one person is already enrolled for this one). *It's never going to happen. This group will fizzle and fail. And all your future plans, goals, and dreams will also not be realized.*

This one's familiar, isn't it? Insert your favorite dream after "you'll never..." You'll never be able to give a powerful, effective presentation to your company. You'll never be able to speak up for yourself. You'll never find an amazing girlfriend, boyfriend, husband, wife. You'll never sell this much, earn that much, enjoy _____ in your life.

So there you have it. Dr. Aziz's three-step formula for internal rejection. Practice daily for best results.

This rejection is not coming from the person who offered the external rejection. It's coming from within.

Seriously, what are we doing to ourselves? What is all this nonsense? It's Safety Police shenanigans. Remember, that crew jumps into your mind and tries to control your life at any chance it gets. And you just got rejected, so they feel the need to steer you back towards a life of total and complete safety and protection from all potential hurts.

What is your formula? What exactly do you do in your own mind to create the bad feelings after you get a "no"? Study this. The next time you get rejected, slow down. Slow way down. Breathe and pay attention. Ask yourself: *How am I rejecting myself? How am I creating this pain?*

The more you can become aware of the ways this rejection is coming from within, the more power you will have to shift your perspective and let go of the belief that you're being rejected. Speaking of that, let's look at how to let go of this pattern of internal rejection and replace it with something much healthier, much more compassionate, and much more effective for life.

Redefine What "No" Means

"Yes lives in the land of no"
- Steve Chandler

Most people take a "no" as evidence of their personal shortcomings, inadequacy, or failure. The underlying assumption here is that someone else would have gotten a yes. If I were "better" in some way, I'd have gotten a yes. Better looking, better socially, better at sales, better at speaking, etc.

This is so common, we can call it the "default response" to rejection. It happens so fast, so instantaneously. We might not even be aware of the negative thoughts rapidly flashing through our minds in the moments surrounding a rejection. We just notice that heavy feeling, that punch-in-the-gut sensation that leaves us deflated and down. It makes us want to hang our heads, throw in the towel, give up.

But it's all based on a lie. A misunderstanding. An error. The story that a rejection occurred because there is something wrong with you, that you are somehow not enough, flawed, deficient, or inadequate: this is the lie. You need a better story about what "no" actually means. Otherwise, it's all too easy to fall back into the default response, which involves self-hatred, low self-esteem, and an extreme reluctance to put yourself out there again.

What does "no" actually mean? It means, "No, I do not want what you are offering to me right now in this moment." As in, "No, I don't want to talk with you," "No, I don't want to date you," "No, I don't want to buy what you're selling," or "No, I don't want to hire you for this position."

Not right now. Not in this moment. It could actually change in several moments, depending on a number of factors, but for right now it is a no. That's what "no" means. Anything else we add to it is our own story of not being good enough, stalking us and looking for any excuse to pounce on us. In reality, "no" merely gives us information about where the other person is at currently. Then we can proceed accordingly.

Do you want to date me? No? Ok. Now I know. I am going to find someone else then. It really can be that simple. Although our minds want to make it extremely complex and loaded with all sorts of meanings that we generate out of thin air, out of our past, out of reading way too deeply into the situation. *It's because I sent that one text message three weeks ago on a Thursday, wasn't it? I seemed too eager, too desperate. I knew it! It's because I'm too short and don't go to the gym enough, isn't it? I knew it!*

Then, after this onslaught of critical thoughts, we launch into beliefs about the imaginary "someone else" who didn't have these flaws and would never have gotten the no. *If only I were taller, more athletic, and more suave with my texts. If only I knew exactly what to say in response to every objection, then I'd close every single sale. I bet someone else could do it. That person is better than me. I suck.* That kind of internal dialogue is the pain of rejection speaking. It is the internal rejection that makes the whole situation so unpleasant and unbearable. But what if you changed the meaning of no? What if it was just information?

Steve Chandler shared this brilliant analogy with me in one of our sessions. "Aziz," he said in his ultra deep voice, "imagine you were sitting at the ticket booth selling tickets to *My Fair Lady,* and a couple came up and said, 'We want to buy some tickets for the upstairs seating area.'

"You are sold out of the upstairs area and you tell them so. Then you offer some seating in the main area, where there is still plenty of space. They pause and hem and haw and ultimately say, 'No we only wanted to sit up top. No thanks.' And then they walk away.

"Would you spend hours lamenting this situation? 'What did I do to drive them away? I should have said something differently Why am I such a failure?' Or would you just casually say, 'next!'"

This is how we can perceive "nos" in our lives. The more we can see rejection in this light, the less painful the experience becomes. And the more willing and able you are to get out there and receive "nos" the less painful they become.

I have a banner I put up at my live events that says:

CELEBRATE
MISTAKES
REJECTION
FAILURE
NO

And that is exactly what we do at those events. When someone reports that they tried something during one of the real-world activities and they got rejected, we all stand up and cheer.

This is designed to help us completely change our relationship with "no." Instead of it being this terrible, shameful, plagued, vile, wretched villain that we hope to never come across for the rest of our days, we want to see it as a stepping stone to getting everything we've always wanted.

Just recently, I was filling one of my new Unstoppable Confidence Mastermind groups. The group is limited to just ten people, so each person gets lots of air-time, direct support, and coaching to break through to the next level of confidence and success in their lives.

So I created two goals on my whiteboard. Goal number 1: Get thirty nos. Goal number 2: Find ten awesome people for the group. I had no direct control over the second goal. But I had complete control over the first one. I could get as many "nos" as I wanted. I just had to invite enough people.

With each "no" I got, I filled in a little piece of a tall rectangle with some red marker. It looked like one of those thermometer-shaped donation goal graphics that non-profits have. We are this close to getting $50,000 for our new building! Only I wasn't going for the yeses. I was going for the nos. I was seeing how many I could get and trying to reach my quota of thirty.

Because I know that yes lives in the land of no. I know the more nos I get, the more yeses I'm going to get. I know that the more nos I get the more powerful I become. The more rejections I experience, the more fearless I am.

No is good. You want to accumulate nos and you want to do so as fast as possible. When you do this, your dating life, your sales, your business, your income, your social life, and every other thing you can imagine begins to grow and flourish like never before. No is your friend.

Despite the discomfort, fear, and that ball of pain that can get awakened when we hear a no, we want to move towards it. We want to find opportunities to accumulate nos each day. These nos make us stronger, more confident, more powerful, and more free.

"Make no your daily vitamin."
- Les Brown

Failing vs. Being "A Failure"

One of the most painful parts of internal rejection is the sense of failing or being "a failure." Failing, which is just another word for "no" is actually incredibly important and necessary to any sort of growth or achievement. We all spend so much time avoiding failing and not wanting to be failures, that we never even pause to look at what it is we're running away from. Let me ask you a quick question: What is failure?

Think of something right now that you don't want to fail at. It could be in your love life, at work, in a conversation, or a hobby anywhere. What would failing look like in that area of your life? After asking this question hundreds of times, I have discovered it is always the same answer, no matter what person or what situation I'm considering.

Failure = an undesired outcome.

Success, of course, would be getting the desired outcome. So if I want to find a partner and be in an awesome relationship, then anything that does not bring that into my life is a failure. Such as someone I'm romantically interested in saying no to me, not returning my calls, or breaking up with me. These would all be failures.

If I want to get promoted to a certain position, then the promotion is the desired outcome. If I get it, that's a success. If I don't, or someone else is promoted instead of me, then that's a failure. So, failure is nothing more than getting an undesired outcome. Simple, right?

Here's the thing. When you take an action—from asking someone out to putting yourself out there for the promotion—do you know what the outcome is going to be? You may get what you want, or you may not. There is no way to be certain which will occur beforehand. And there is no way to get what you want without at least trying and putting yourself out there.

So sometimes your action is going to lead to the desired result (success), and other times it will lead to the undesired result (failure). There is no other way of going about it; no safer way of going after what you want. The only way to avoid failure, then, is to avoid getting any results, and to avoid taking any action.

That concept is so important, it's worth repeating: The only way to avoid failure is to avoid taking action. And that is just what most people do, most of the time, for most of their lives. They don't try. And because they aren't taking any actions toward getting what they want, they don't feel that fulfilled, excited, or juiced about life, and they just aren't sure why. *Maybe I need a new cologne...*

So there is no such thing as being "a failure." That is a completely made up concept. What would that even mean? Someone who failed eight times? Someone who fails more than they succeed? Every single person who is known for massive confidence and massive success has an endless number of failures under their belt. Every celebrity sports star misses more shots than he or she scores, and strikes out more often than he or she hits home runs. Every business icon has gotten rejected hundreds or even thousands of times, and usually has several completely failed companies under his or her belt. They just don't stop at that outcome, they keep going, until they get different outcomes.

The only way to truly fail is to stop. When you stop taking action, you stop getting results. And then you actually fail. When we stop, we freeze in time and we avoid those pesky thoughts of being a failure. We also end up avoiding our lives, our joy, our true purpose, and what we're really here to do.

I remember in one Mastermind meeting with my coach Christian Mickelsen, I was sharing my fears about hosting bigger live events. "I'm afraid I will rent this big room and almost no one will come. Just two people who will think I'm totally lame." He looked at me and loudly proclaimed. "You are going to fail." He then turned to someone else in the group. "You are going to fail. And so are you, and you, and you. And so am I. We all are."

Before he even finished making his point, I got it. I was spending so much mental and emotional energy fearing failure and trying to avoid it. Instead of just surrendering to the fact that a certain percentage of my endeavors are not going to result in my desired outcome. Some events will have fewer people than I was going for. Some products won't sell much. Some launches will fall flat. And some will succeed. Some will meet my desired outcome. Some will shatter what I expected and succeed beyond what I ever imagined. And I'll never know which ones these will be before I attempt them.

All the fear about failing is not really about making enough money to survive. It's not a life or death matter where you will starve if you don't succeed at your current project, job, or relationship. In reality, the major damage when we don't attain a desired result is to our egos, to our sense of pride. *I'll look bad. People will think less of me.* What we're really afraid of, then, is actually shame. But shame is just a feeling, like all of our other fears. And the best way to deal with shame is by meeting it with unlimited compassion.

Unlimited Compassion

Let's face it: the worst part about a rejection is how we feel afterwards. All of the fear of the rejection, the attempts to avoid it and control our circumstances so that we only get the outcomes we want—all of that comes from wanting to avoid the way we feel after we've been rejected. It makes our hearts and guts hurt whenever we think about it. It causes waves of pain to course through our nervous system.

So in order to truly become rejection-proof, we must be able to handle this feeling. And while the above belief-shifting can greatly reduce the intensity of internal rejection, at some point we must face this feeling.

No amount of mental tricks, reframes, CBT, NLP, or any other "mental technology" will allow us to permanently escape the messy world of our feelings. Trust me, I've tried. And I'm sure you have, too. The only way out is through. Right through the center to the other side. So let's talk about how to do that skillfully.

When you're feeling pain after being rejected, take a few minutes and slow down. Stop checking your email, fiddling with your phone, and watching TV. Turn off those distractions and just slow down. Breathe. Feel.

I know how strong the compulsion to stay in perpetual motion can be. Sometimes I fight slowing down for several days straight. All the while feeling more pain inside, more tension, more dissatisfaction, more irritation. Because I'm staying in motion to avoid my feelings, which takes me further and further from my heart; further from my ability to feel peace, love, and joy.

In fact, just the other day I was spending the morning with my son. It had been a full week, with many rejections in it. I'd been staying busy to avoid those pesky feelings, until Saturday morning came and I could not escape anymore. As I sat there with my son, my wife could tell how miserable I was. In fact, I was making it easy for her to see how miserable I was because I was telling her. But not directly. I was complaining about the messiness of our house, and how I absolutely had to clean things now, instead of playing with my son. "I'm perfectly fine. It's just that there are dishes in the sink. That's why I can't be relaxed right now!!"

Victim-stance anyone?

Anyways, my wife had a workout class planned so she left. A few minutes later, she sent me this text message: "There are endless things to do. The messes don't really matter. Breathe. Feel. Look at our son so happy to be with his dada. I love you."

Sigh. I knew she was right. There was no escape. The only way out is through. So I put some peaceful music on, sat down to play with my son and started to feel my feelings.

How do we do this simple act?

It's really not that complex. Our minds want to make it complex so we can stay in our heads, away from direct contact with those unpleasant sensations. But coming into contact with them is exactly what we have to do to truly liberate ourselves from their affect in our lives. We have to feel the sensations directly.

Start with breathing. Feel your next few breaths going in and going out. Then notice where you feel the uncomfortable emotions in your body. All feelings live in your body, not your head. For me, feelings of rejection cause painful squeezing sensations in my heart and solar plexus (which is in the center of your body, right below your chest and sternum and above your stomach).

For you, the sensation could be similar or it could be something completely different. Tightness in your stomach, waves of writhing energy moving down your hands, sadness behind your eyes, tightness in your neck, shoulders, or back. It doesn't matter what the sensations are. All that matters is feeling them directly.

Stay out of your head and keep your attention right on the sensations. Take deeper breaths, as if you're breathing right into your heart, or stomach, or back - wherever the sensations are in that moment. Notice the pull to go back into your head. To think about the feelings. *Why are they here? I shouldn't be feeling this. What is wrong with that person? What is wrong with me?*

It's endless. Just let your mind do its thing and bring your attention back to your body. Trying to stop your thinking here is like trying to stand in the middle of a river and stop all the water going by with your hands. Instead, simply redirect your attention back into the center of the most uncomfortable sensation in your body.

See if you can drop your resistance to it. Stop fighting it. It's already here now. Can you just allow it to be there? Can you consent? Just accept the feeling as best as you can. If you notice you're resisting and fighting it, just allow and accept the resistance, too. Allow everything. You don't have control over when it stops anyways.

All you need to do is breath and send it love. Your attention is the most basic form of love. You can also gently repeat, "I love you," while focusing on the uncomfortable sensations. You can say loving phrases like, "It's okay. You can be here as long as you need to."

As you send it love, study the sensations. As if someone handed you an ice cube and told you to hold it in your fist as it melted. Notice the shape of the feelings in your body. Is it round like a ball or blocky like a misshapen polygon? How big is it? Is it like a basketball or a tiny stone? How dense is it? Is it thick and dense like a rock or thin and spacious like smoke or vapor? Does it have a clear edge where it stops? Or is the edge diffuse and shifting, like the top of a fire? If it had a color, what color would it be?

These are great ways to keep your mind occupied with the sensations rather than giving in to distractions. It helps you stay directly with the feeling while you breathe and send it love.

Keep doing this. Do it longer than you want to. Usually the first three minutes are the toughest. Our minds grow crazy with resistance, telling us we can't handle it, that it's too much, that we'll die or explode or "lose it" or cry (God forbid!). Don't believe this, it's just resistance.

Your heart is vast and endless. It can handle anything that life throws your way. Anything. All the mind is really saying is: *Ack! These sensations are uncomfortable! I hate feeling uncomfortable!* If you stay with the sensations, they will change. Insights will emerge. You may have a good cry and feel refreshed and soft in your heart again. Give yourself at least ten minutes to do this. Sometimes it takes a little longer.

If that seems like a long time to you, think about how long you've been scared of rejection for. Or how long the painful feelings linger when you try to avoid them. In the big scheme of things, twenty to thirty minutes is not that much time to heal a life-long pattern of pain around rejection.

The really cool thing is, the more you do this, the more you heal and the less future rejections will pierce you. The more you do this, the more you deeply realize you can handle anything that happens. This gives you a newfound sense of power and freedom to go after what you want most in this life.

Self-Compassion is a personal passion of mine and is something I've been studying for over a decade. In fact, I wrote my clinical dissertation in graduate school on the relationship between meditation and self-compassion. To get even more resources on this subject, including in-depth training videos, go to, http://SocialConfidenceCenter.com and register for my free newsletter.

Rejection As Fuel

"Nothin' boosts me more or suits me beautifully, there's nothing you can do to me, stab me, shoot me."

- Eminem

Once you've challenged some of your limiting beliefs about "no" and taken the time to feel your feelings directly, you will begin to see rejection differently. It won't be so terrifying or terrible and it will be something you can face in order to create the life you want. In a sense, you can get through anything.

But that's not fully satisfying to me. If I'm going to face something regularly in life, I don't want to just grit my teeth and get through it. I want to transform my experience into something more powerful. Is it possible to turn rejection into something that actually helps us? That makes us stronger? That provides us with rocket fuel to blast further and faster towards our goals and dreams?

Yes, I believe it is. And here are some ways to do that.

First, let's borrow Nassim Taleb's concept of Anti-Fragile, from his book of the same name. Anti-Fragile, which is a word he created, is the exact opposite of fragile. Fragile things break when they are disturbed, when they are stressed, or when they are pressed. A piece of glass or fine china is fragile. It breaks when you drop it. In this case, a fragile person would break in the face of rejection. They'd quit, give up, or stop.

Many people think the opposite of fragile is resilient. Something that is resilient or strong can withstand being dropped or hurt. It can tolerate disorder, chaos, or rejection. That's a good place to be. But it's not quite the opposite of fragile. Something that is anti-fragile actually becomes stronger with disorder, adverse events, and shocks to the system. Someone who is anti-fragile will actually get stronger with each rejection.

Sound awesome? I thought so too, so I began to make a study of it. How do we actually take this concept and turn it into a real sense of power, confidence, and fearlessness? The first step is to just adopt this belief: *I thrive on uncertainty, disorder, and chaos.*

Tell yourself this regularly. See the truth of it. See how the quest for comfort and everything being predictable and always going your way actually does not bring happiness, satisfaction, energy, and vitality. In fact, it leads to rigidity, fear of loss, and fragility.

Then we can take it one step further to this belief: *I feed off rejection. Rejection fuels me. Each one makes me more powerful.* How do you feel when you say that one to yourself? Believable or BS? Would you want that to be true? What would your life be like if you actually believed this and it were really true for you (not just some affirmation that you tried to convince yourself of)?

Try this out. Remember the last time you got rejected. You asked a friend to hangout and he said he was busy. You asked your crush out on a date and she grimaced. You had a sales conversation and the person said "Absolutely not. And I don't like you."

Imagine that as they said that, a black substance came from them and went into your chest. This sticky, dark, viscous ooze of rejection that went right into your heart. In the past, this black ooze would make you feel pain and lead to discouragement, fear, or resignation. But now, imagine that substance is like oil. It's highly combustible. If you put a match to it, it burns like rocket fuel.

Imagine bringing a flame of powerful anti-fragility directly to that substance. Imagine a 4,000 ton rocket blasting through the stratosphere. What will this rejection propel you towards? What are you even more committed to now because of this? What will you figure out? What you are now even more determined to do with a fire and a passion so strong that nothing will stand in your way?

Feel that fire. Feel the power burn in your core and radiate out to your hands and feet, mobilizing you for powerful, inspired action. There's a setting of the jaw, a breath in through the nose and a deep knowing in your heart that nothing is going to get in your way.

You got this. You are fucking unstoppable.

CHAPTER VI:

MONEY

Let's talk about money. *Finally, we're getting to the good stuff. Enough of this tell myself the truth, face my fears and take action nonsense. I want sex, money, and power, remember?*

Well, my friend, you are in the right place. Because with the skills you've just learned about identifying and removing your excuses and stories, radically overcoming fear, and taking massive action, there is no end to the amount of income you can generate.

And I think you want more than money. We all do. You want a life of extraordinary confidence, which includes a mastery of money. Not just a high number in your bank account (or a big wad of cash under your mattress, whichever you prefer), but a sense of wealth, financial security, relaxation, and enjoyment. The trust of knowing that you can earn enough money to take good care of yourself and your loved ones. Being wealthy in both tangible and intangible ways, which includes being psychologically wealthy.

Because if you haven't had this fascinating (and slightly disturbing) experience yet, you will. Even as your income and material wealth increase, it's possible to feel little to no shift in your psychological well-being. It's possible to not even feel that different at all, and to have the same amount of stress and anxiety in your life as when you were making half as much, or a quarter as much money. As Les Brown says, "We all know money won't solve all of our problems, but we want to find that out for ourselves."

But I'm getting ahead of myself here. First, I want to highlight that you want more than money. You also want love, a sense of personal freedom and power, and a future that feels bright and inspiring. And that is exactly what you are going to create in the second half of this book. These are the results and the rewards of extraordinary confidence. And each one in turn requires more growth and confidence to be able to fully receive what you desire, whether it's money, love, or social power. The more you grow in confidence, and the more you face your fears and take massive action, the more you will expand in each of these areas.

Let's start with money.

MONEY CONFIDENCE

Money and confidence have an interesting relationship. In our heads they are closely linked. Most of us have learned that the more money you can earn, the better you are as a person, which then gives you the right to feel more confident.

In addition, it takes confidence to earn more money. Whether you want to start your own business, double or triple that business, or excel in a professional job, confidence is a requirement.

We also have a certain amount of confidence in regards to money itself. This confidence determines our beliefs about money: whether I can or can't earn money in the world, how much money I can earn, how much my time and skills are worth, and so forth.

This chapter is going to help you maximize your money confidence. It's going to help you shed any negative beliefs that are keeping your money confidence low, which is in turn reducing your earning potential significantly. You will break free from any lingering, demeaning stories about your worth and capability. You will release unhelpful stories about what you are destined for and what you are capable of. Most importantly, you will start to feel more relaxed and confident around this whole topic of money, which creates huge amounts of anxiety and stress in most people. This will not only bring you a greater sense of ease, peace, and confidence in your financial life, it is also the key to dramatically increasing your income.

Before we dive into exactly how to skyrocket your money confidence, it is worth taking a moment to determine what that would actually mean. What would unlimited confidence with money look like for you? What would it feel like?

Would it involve a certain dollar amount in your bank account? A certain income per month or year? A mindset? A sense of being relaxed and carefree while purchasing groceries, because you know you always have enough money to buy exactly what you need in any scenario? We spend so much time worrying about money, what if we took a step back and thought about what it would feel like to just be confident with this stuff?

What did you come up with? Here's what I imagine when I think of complete money confidence:

I have a lot of money.

I can earn whatever I need to support myself and those I love.

I can buy the things I want and enjoy material possessions
   (including unnecessarily fast computers and Apple gadgets).

If something changes (I get laid off, my industry evolves, etc.),
   I'll adapt and figure it out.

I manage money well and I'm a good steward of it.

I can enjoy the money I have.

I give generously to those I love and to causes I believe in, with
   out worry, fear, or guilt

I feel relaxed, knowing I'll always have enough to meet my basic
   needs and take care of myself.

Does this match your idea of money confidence? Are there elements missing for you? Perhaps for you owning a home is part of financial confidence. Or running your own successful business. Or having a nice car. Let's strip away any judgment or ideas of right and wrong in relation to purchasing, and actually investigate together - if I were totally confident about money, what exactly would that look like?

Then take a few minutes and write down a quick list. It doesn't have to be an essay, just a short list will do. Because with money, as with all things, clarity is power.

Your Money Story

Every single one of us has a story about money: a big, complex, mostly unexamined collection of ideas, beliefs, feelings, meanings, and attitudes.

Money is good, and more money is better.
Money is bad and rich people are greedy and exploitative.
Making money means you are intelligent and admirable.
Making money means you're selling out or scamming people.

These are just a few of the dozens of possible stories we can have about money. Do any of these resonate with you? What others pop into your mind when you think about what having money says about you and others.

What do you think of people who are poor and don't make much money? What about people who are wealthy and successful by your standards? Ooh, what about people who you would consider ultra-wealthy and what they're doing with their money? That's usually a good one that pushes a lot of people's buttons.

Notice your beliefs, feelings and attitudes about these different groups of people; all of these come together to make up your money story. Well, part of it anyway, because there is also a piece of your money story that focuses solely on you.

I am good at making money.
I am bad at making money.
I am smart, driven and capable so I'm destined to be rich.
I'm not good enough, don't have a strong enough work ethic, or am otherwise just not capable of earning a good living.
I'm good with money and I invest it wisely.
I'm horrible with money, it just runs right through my fingers.
I'm too stingy.

...and many more. What are your beliefs about yourself when it comes to money? These also contribute to your money story, which creates your confidence in this area.

But wait, there's more! And don't worry, you'll see how this all relates to money confidence (and how to increase it) in a moment. One other set of characters to consider in your money story is... your parents. I know, we'd rather not think that stuff still affects us, but guess what? It does because many of our beliefs and attitudes about money were formed long ago when we were children. You were inevitably affected by not just what your parents said about money, but how they related to it. How they dealt with it, reacted to it, and talked (or didn't talk) about it when you were young.

How did your dad relate to money? Did he have any common phrases he would repeat about it? My dad would often say, "It's only money." How about your mom? How did she see money? What did she say about it?

Even more importantly, what kinds of interactions did your parents have with each other around money? Was it tense? Were they fighting about it often? Many married couples claim that the majority of the stress in their relationship is related to finances. Did you experience this to be true in your parents' relationship when you were a child?

All of these experiences impact us when we are young and shape our perception of money. If dad was stressed about money (as mine was for periods of time when my brother and I were young), then you might feel stressed about money as an adult. If mom was scared to buy things that weren't on sale, you might notice yourself tensing up when your husband grabs that brand name item off the shelf.

Many of our perceptions about money are formed when we are young, and we likely don't talk about them at all. We don't talk about our family's money concerns with kids at school, and most families don't talk about them openly amongst one another. There's so much secrecy around the whole thing. We learn that to ask others about their income or finances is offensive and intrusive and that to share about our own is bragging or airing your family's dirty laundry and should be avoided at all costs. This continues throughout childhood and into adulthood. Most people are only forced to talk openly about money when they are in a significant relationship with a partner with whom sharing finances becomes an option. Then, they unleash the weirdness...

Money fear, scarcity, desire to control the other person's spending, anger, resentment, heated emotional fights that seem way more intense than the money itself, shame, embarrassment, inferiority, inadequacy, confusion, and misery. Bring on the money stories.

When an experience is emotionally charged, then kept secret, it becomes a breeding ground for simplistic beliefs, toxic stories, and shame. Just like masturbation and sex, but talked about even less. And look at all the shame and weirdness we have going on with those topics. This is why taking a few minutes to uncover your money story and the garbage money beliefs that you may be dragging around without knowing why is a very good idea. It's like cutting into a buried wound that has been festering underneath the surface. It's not pretty, and it might not initially feel great, but if you stop ignoring it and actually dig out what's creating the injury and do some work to heal it, you will find yourself on a whole new playing field when it comes to money and to the broader picture of your life.

Let's clear up those garbage money beliefs that keep you feeling bad about yourself, fearful, and inferior. As you release them one by one, your level of confidence and self-esteem will continue to sky-rocket upwards, in your financial life and beyond.

Garbage Money Beliefs

We are all carrying loads of beliefs about money. This includes ideas about what money itself means, how we see ourselves in relation to money, and how we imagine others see us. Most of these are picked up unconsciously, and many actually conflict with each other.

Here is a short list of some of the more limiting and toxic beliefs about money. Notice which ones resonate with you:

Money is bad.
I'm bad for earning lots of money.
I'm bad for wanting more money (greedy, superficial, etc.).
I'm hurting people when I earn lots of money.
If someone pays me, I'm taking from them.
Most people don't have much money.
Making more than X amount of money is bad.
Others will judge me as rich and feel jealous and stop liking me.
Earning more means I'm showing off.
I shouldn't buy nice things.
Wanting and having money is bad when so many people in the world have so little.
No matter what I earn, it never feels like enough.
I'm going to run out of money in the future.

Whew. What a list. Feeling inspired? Lord knows I'm not.

But don't stop here. Remember, we're digging out a festering wound. We just pulled back the top layer of skin and are seeing all the infected tissue underneath. Now is not the time to flee and pretend it's not there. That just makes things worse. Instead, dig deeper. What garbage money beliefs cause you to feel bad about yourself? What do you say to yourself that makes you feel guilty, afraid, insecure, or inadequate?

Make a list right now. It doesn't have to be final or complete. You don't have to get every single negative thought on that list. Just get started and write out the major ones. Some might be from the list above, others might be ones you've noticed in your own life. Go ahead and create that list now, then continue reading.

———◇———

Hopefully your list was equally as inspiring as mine was. Don't you feel all warm and fuzzy inside now? Actually, you might feel a sense of relief for just having gotten those out of your head and onto paper. Now you can see them, work with them, and free yourself from them, instead of leaving them lurking in the shadows of your subconscious, tripping you up whenever you start to experience success.

In a few minutes we're going to discuss the truth about money, which will help you release many of these limiting and toxic ideas that keep you feeling guilty and stuck around money. For now, just look over your list. What do you notice? What is the purpose of these beliefs? What are they encouraging you to do or not do?

Often times this list of money beliefs is dominated by none other than your Safety Police. *Yo, what up S P!* Look who's back on the scene...

Your Safety Police team is highly concerned about this money business. Generally, in order to earn more money, we need to step up and take risks. We need to put ourselves out there, take chances, grow, and do things we've never done before. Your Safety Police hates all that nonsense. Then, to make matter worse, you might not succeed. You might make less money than you wanted, or less than others, and then you are "an embarrassment" or "a failure." And even if you do succeed and make an abundance of money, you still can't be sure how everyone in your life will react. Will they be happy for you? Will they be jealous and secretly critical of you? Will they want something from you, and feel entitled to it? Considering all of these risks, it's much easier to have powerfully strong negative ideas about money that prevent you from reaching your potential in this area. That's how the Safety Police likes it, and that's why most people stay small.

The Truth About Money

Let's clear up some of the most common misconceptions that kill our confidence with money. First and foremost, money is not bad. And you are not bad for wanting it, working for it, or having it. It's a number. It's a game. It's a reflection of how much you've provided the world. It's a sign of service. It's a sign of effort, determination, and continued hard work. It's often a sign of delayed gratification in that what you do today produces the results of tomorrow. Why on earth would it be bad for you to generate this in your life? Are you beating up strangers and taking their lunch money? Are you selling drugs to children?

Below you will find five truths about money that can catapult you toward creating the income and life you want.

1. WANTING MORE IS NOT BAD

So many people feel guilty for wanting more money and for having more money. We see images of people in war-torn countries, starving children, and even our own neighbors struggling to make ends meet and we think to ourselves, *Why should I have so much? I'm bad for having more than others.*

And yet, you still want more, don't you? And then we respond to this desire by judging ourselves for it. At the same time, if we don't have enough money, or as much as we think we should, we judge ourselves as bad for that as well. We feel ashamed and inadequate for not being smart or capable enough to earn more. Or we stay in Excuse Land and continually blame forces outside of our control, like corrupt corporations, politicians, or those illegal immigrants.

So much judging. So much is deemed bad, but why? One of the first ASL signs children can easily learn before they speak is "more." That and the sign for "milk" are the most common ones used by young, preverbal children. What else could you need?

My son Zaim learned the word "more" pretty quickly. Right up there with "mama", "dada", and "nana" (his word for milk). He became obsessed with more. He would point to a jar of raisins and loudly proclaim, "more!" When I gave him a small handful, as he took it, and before he had even put it in his mouth, guess what he'd say? That's right, "more!"

When I saw this, I realized that wanting more is not some diabolical plot of corporate consumer culture. We all come out of the womb wanting more. It seems to be a human imperative. So what if you stopped labeling yourself "wrong" for it and started celebrating it? It's part of your hunger, your drive, your thirst for life. To grow, expand, make more, do more, and become more. What if more was good?

Of course, we can be tormented by a perpetual sense of lack and an insatiable craving for more. This can be a deep hunger for more money, more accomplishments, more success, more recognition, and more pleasure. We've all seen this happen in our world more times than we can count. And we can all be caught in this "realm of the hungry ghosts" as the Buddhists call it. But this, too, is not to be condemned and attacked. This is intense suffering and disconnection. When we notice this in ourselves, we especially need to slow down and meet whatever we are experiencing with love, compassion, and curiosity.

2. MAKING MORE DOES NOT MAKE YOU BAD

Wanting more may not be bad, but what about having more? Many of us have learned that because money in the world is limited, people are separated into the haves and the have-nots. If you have money, then you are automatically putting others in the have-not category. You are bad, selfish, or somehow less caring or compassionate. Worse still, in order to make more money, you must be doing something hurtful to others and taking from them in some way. This is another commonly held belief about money that destroys our confidence.

These challenges are great. If you have struggled with these, then I think it's a reflection of your compassion and desire for equality in the world, which are both good things. You probably have noticed the vast monetary discrepancies in the world, been disturbed by the abject poverty many people experience, and felt saddened by how much some people suffer just because of where they are born. You also might know about how citizens of the United States consume some disgusting proportion of the natural resources allocated to the total world population.

Yes, things are pretty messed up. Societies and civilizations and the global monetary system are insanely complicated. And you are not responsible for fixing everything. So many people feel burdened to change the world and solve all of these problems. Of course, doing so is many lifetimes of work, and even then it is unclear what and how much is solvable. Hell, even what "solved" could be defined as is up for debate. Very few individuals are dedicating their lives to addressing these global challenges. I know I personally am not. That doesn't seem to be my life's work. Most people I know are not either.

And yet, many people carry this burden of guilt around, as if they should be solving all of these problems. And earning more money triggers more guilt, so often people will avoid earning the money in the first place.

Insane. And completely ineffective.

By holding back your talents and abilities, limiting yourself and your career and business success so as to not hurt others by earning money, you become completely ineffective. It's simplistic, unexamined reasoning. By staying disempowered and impoverished yourself, are you somehow bringing about global change? Are you helping someone born into a war-torn country that is plagued by famine? Are you not "buying into the system"? Unless you're living off the grid, growing your own food and roughing it, you're most likely heavily relying on the system. There's no escape. Shit's complex man. And you're not here to figure it all out and make it all "right."

The truth is that you personally earning more or less money has virtually no impact on the greater world. Unless of course, you consciously use the money you earn to do just that.

3.   INCOME IS A NEUTRAL REFLECTION OF OUTPUT

Another limiting belief that stops us from earning more money is the fear that doing so makes us oppressive or manipulative. In order to be making money, we must be hurting others, taking advantage of people, manipulating weak-minded individuals, or doing something otherwise nefarious.

This idea if often propagated by people who feel disempowered and stuck in their economic standing. Increased income and freedom does not feel possible to them because they have given up and allowed themselves to become entrenched in a victim stance. They are upset with those who have more, so they judge or criticize them. Many people hear their parents talking about evil rich people, corrupt CEOs and the like. This creates a subconscious, or sometimes very conscious, resistance to being one of "those people." It also helps write the story that earning money is only possible through exploitation.

Again, there is some truth in these beliefs. People are being exploited in the world and there are some crazy, disturbing schemes that corporations have concocted to maximize profits at the expense of human, animal, and environmental life. But exploitation of the earth and other beings is not a requirement of financial success, and has nothing to do with you.

In reality, money is a neutral reflection of output. The more people you serve, and the more profoundly you impact their lives, the more money you will earn. Service is providing something that people want or need. Something of value to them. The more value you can bring to peoples' lives, the more money you can earn.

You can do this directly through a private enterprise or a small business. Or you can hold a job within a larger company. That larger company is larger because whatever product or service it is providing is impacting a lot of peoples' lives in a significant way.

The money simply flows towards that service. It is neutral. It is like water flowing through a stream. Is that stream good or bad? It doesn't even make sense to ask that question. The money itself is neutral and the direction of the flow is determined by the impact of the service.

If not much is flowing to you, you probably are not serving that many people. This might ruffle some feathers because you might feel like you are already serving profoundly. You might even be doing more than you are capable of and feel overwhelmed. If you are doing so much and so little is coming back, then it's time to get curious. Exactly what are you doing? Is your day filled with the safe, busy activities that don't really produce major results? Are you afraid to have strong fees and prices for your services and products? Are you stuck blaming higher-ups and other aspects of your job that are outside of your control? The answers are for you to discover. Just keep in mind that if you are serving enough people and impacting their lives significantly enough, money is a formulaic result (assuming you're not doing something else to block it).

4.   *Money Does Not Equal Worth*

This one is sometimes a hard sell. I mean, we call the sum total of our assets our "net worth" after all. And yet it has nothing to do with our worth.

Most of us received a heavy dose of this programming: if you earn and have money, you are worthy. If you can't or don't, then you are inferior, incapable, stupid, lazy, or otherwise unworthy of respect, admiration or approval.

This leads to frequent feelings of inadequacy around finances. If there's something you want, but feel unable to afford, you're unworthy. If you are anxious about the weekly grocery bill = unworthy. If your business is just getting by and you are struggling to draw a personal salary = unworthy. You feel shameful and like your lack of money reflects poorly on you.

Of course the money = worth game doesn't stop there. Even as you start to succeed more, you can be just as plagued by it. You are now earning 100,000 USD per year, but he's earning 200,000 for doing similar work. Your business earns a million per year, but those women earn five million. You feel inadequate, inferior, unworthy.

I had a client who sold his company and walked away with forty million dollars. When I met him, he was striving for a billion, feeling inferior and inadequate when compared to the highly successful billionaires he had in mind. This is a game you cannot win.

The only way out is to see through the game itself. Or perhaps to simply see it as a game. You can get better at the money game if you like, just like you can get better at chess, or soccer. But you don't have to. If someone is better than me at chess (which is probably most people who've actually studied that game), that in no way impacts my worth. If you base your self-worth and identity on being the best at any game, you are in for trouble. No matter how good you are, there's someone better out there who will beat you. Even if you're the best right now, it's a short-lived ride of glory.

If you want to learn the money game and master it, then you can do that, too. Study people who are successful, read books, get training, work through all your garbage money beliefs, and do shit that scares you in the world. If you do this, of course you can master the game. Or at least move beyond novice.

Just remember, being good at this game is in no way more significant than being good at any other game. I'm better at the money game, he's better at golf, and she's better at the singing and making art game. Great. We are all enjoying our games and we are all worthy. Which games we choose to play is irrelevant.

5. *Money Gives You Power, Freedom, And The Ability To Make A Bigger Impact*

Money is neutral. What you choose to do with it gives it meaning. More money can give you a greater sense of power and freedom. You can do things, go places, and enjoy activities you wouldn't be able to do without money. You can get access to services and medical care that might be limited.

Depending on how you're earning the money, you might gain more and more personal freedom. You might enjoy being your own boss and working the hours you want to work. Of course, if you're earning the money by being in a meat-grinder corporate executive environment or as a surgical resident, then freedom of time and autonomy don't necessarily come with increased income.

For me, more money means I can work four days per week instead of five. This gives me even more time with my wife and two kids, who I adore more than anything else. It means we can afford to pay someone to help us watch the kids two afternoons a week so my wife and I can spend some quality time together. It means we can get a van (or as my wife calls it, an "adventure mobile") to travel and explore new places as a family.

If this is all sounding way too domestic and in no way desirable to you, that's fine. Because the meaning is yours to give. You can use your money to create a life full of whatever you value. I obviously value autonomy and sharing time with those I love. You might value a fast car, or a big house that can host large dinner parties. Money allows you to experience whatever it is you value most.

Beyond personal comforts and freedoms, money also allows you to create a bigger impact on the world. Through the power of your resources you can help friends and family, support causes you believe in, and actually address some of the challenges you see in the world around you.

This year I chose to give money in support of a little dude in India and to help lions out in Africa. I was able to give a mentor who helped me start my business 10,000 dollars as a sign of my perpetual gratitude to his guidance, support, and love. And so much more. I can't wait to see what I'll give next year. Ultimately, I want to powerfully impact the world. And to me, this kind of giving is small potatoes; I'm just getting started.

Have you heard of Manoj Bhargava? Probably not, but I'm sure you've heard of his product. He created 5-hour Energy, which is like legal, liquid crack in a bottle. It sells like crazy in the US, and all over the world, because people have poor diets, sedentary lifestyles and are addicted to caffeine and other stimulants. Regardless of my thoughts on the product itself, Manoj is amazing. As his company skyrocketed and he earned billions of dollars, he decided he was going to dedicate 99% of it to charitable causes he believed in. He founded a lab that is currently working to solve major problems facing humanity, including global energy and clean water crises.

That is an example of the positive power money can have. We all might not choose to give away 99% of our money, but we certainly can give whatever feels right. The more confidence you have in yourself to continually earn money, and trust that you and your loved ones will be taken care of, the more freely you can give. And the more you give, the better you feel, and the more confident you become.

The Truth About You (And Money)

No matter who you are, no matter where you came from, and regardless of your past history with money, you can become extraordinarily confident in this area of your life. Any story in your mind that tells you that you're no good with money, not smart enough, not capable, or otherwise not good enough to earn and invest money is just that: a story; a fiction that you tell yourself. One that you've told yourself so many times it seems like a fact.

But the real fact is that the biggest problem most people have with money is not based on intelligence or worthiness, but is a lack of education. In school, we are taught virtually nothing about earning, saving, and investing money. Parents often don't teach their children much on the subject either - because they themselves do not feel confidence around money, or the topic is confusing, uncomfortable, and loaded with shame. And so we grow up ignorant. We don't learn how to earn money, other than being advised to "get a good job." We don't learn what actually draws wealth and opportunities into our lives. We don't learn what people will pay for and why they will pay for it. We don't learn anything about sales, marketing, and promotion. We don't learn anything about the stock market, or real estate, or investing.

And each of these subjects can feel like an impossible mountain to climb. The knowledge is shrouded in jargon that we don't understand but think that we should, so we're embarrassed to reveal how little we know. On top of that, you might be spending money to learn these skills, and still be making mistakes along the way. And no one likes to lose money. Ever.

So we remain uneducated, unsure of ourselves, and frustratingly clueless around our money, and how to both earn and spend it. This holds us in a place of frustratingly low confidence. It also leads to endless stories about why we're not capable and somehow not as good as other people who seem to have their relationship with money figured out.

But the truth is you are highly capable. And you are capable of becoming more capable. If you don't know how to do something, you can learn it, apply it in your life, and get the results you want.

I discovered this when I was twenty-one years old and started actively seeking solutions to self-doubt, low self-esteem, and social anxiety that had caged me in for ten years. I began studying a video training program called "Double Your Dating" and reading a book called *Feel The Fear And Do It Anyway*. Between the videos and the book, I discovered things I never would have learned on my own. I received guidance and encouragement and took action. While my journey to extraordinary confidence and social freedom was far from complete, after this first experience I was hooked.

If you come to my house you will see books everywhere. Three on the dining table, four next to my bed, and six on top of the back of the toilet (they tend to accumulate there). The topics range, but they are all about whatever I am needing guidance and training on in that moment. I read books on making money, time liberation, and achieving career success. I have books on being more loving, how to practice positive discipline with small children, and how to be a better father. I cannot count how many times I've experienced a challenge, then read a book, or spoken with someone and found a way to break through.

What really boggles my mind is that many people do not do this. A few days ago a good friend of mine stopped by our house to drop off some food and see our new baby. While I was heating up the food in the kitchen we were catching up, talking about business, life, parenting, and health. He was telling me that he runs several times per week but keeps it very short because he is afraid of injury. I had experienced the same type of injury, and so I did what I always do: I read some books about it. I actually read about a dozen, and worked with a coach, but was eventually able to heal years of chronic injuries that prevented me from running, biking, lifting weights, and playing soccer. Now I can do all of those activities freely and easily. It is an incredible blessing that I am deeply grateful for (although I sometimes forget that gratitude when I'm getting up at 4:30am to go for a run before the kids get up).

And so I said to him, "I know a book that has been profoundly life-changing for me and many others. It helped me overcome years of injury and fear of injury."

And he said what he often says when I suggest a book, "Yeah? How long is it? I don't have much time in my life right now."

Translation: "No, thank you."

During this conversation, I was reminded of a similar one we had about a year earlier. We were standing on a street corner after a delicious meal at one of the many superb Portland breakfast spots. He had just been telling me about his relationship challenges, and I had been listening, asking questions, and offering suggestions. During that conversation I had recommended a life-changing book as well, which he had turned down.

So I asked him, "How many books would you say you've read about business, finances, and real estate?"

"Hmm, maybe a hundred. Two hundred? I'm not sure." He owned two successful businesses in real estate and property management. He was a really sharp guy and I always learned a ton from him.

"I see," I replied. "And how many books have you read on communication in romantic relationships?"

"Umm." He paused, recalling. "Maybe a few pages of one while browsing in a book store." As he said this he laughed because he saw my point.

Guess what? I don't think he's ever read that book. And chances are his romantic life is evidence of that.

So how many books have you read about money? Have you applied what you learned and taken action? Have you studied this topic and decided that you are going to master it like the other areas of life that matter to you?

Most people have not, and will not. They will continue to feel confused and disempowered by money, struggle to earn it, and struggle to feel confident in their abilities. Then they will reside in Excuseville and Storyland. *I couldn't because of this. Those people aren't hiring. I'm not smart enough. I tried once and failed so that means its impossible for me. I don't have the time. I don't have the resources.*

All misguided, all unhelpful, and all untrue. Even if some elements of the stories are accurate, they're not what are really stopping you. What really stops you, and any of us, is one thing: Fear. We use these stories to avoid our fear; we avoid it by not taking action, and we avoid it by staying small and stuck. We will even avoid reading books on the subject we wish to conquer out of fear (although we'll say it's because we're just too busy).

THE WINDING PATH TO MONEY CONFIDENCE

The path to lasting confidence with money, which includes having a deep trust in yourself that you can earn what you need no matter what happens, is right through the valley of our deepest fears. To forge this confidence we have to learn new things, admit we are beginners, challenge family beliefs and programming, and take risks. We have to get outside of our comfort zone, make changes in our jobs and careers, and put more of ourselves on the line. We have to speak up, be seen, be heard, stand behind our ideas, and lead. We have to fail a ton and get rejected even more. We have to hear "no" many more times than we hear "yes."

Once upon a time, I, too, had many dismal stories about money. I was ignorant, should know more than I do, immature, not a real man, and incapable of earning money. How did I know these things? Who told me so? I told me so. I was a self-proclaimed failure. Sure, I was good at school, I could pass tests, but I didn't have what it really took to make it in the real world.

Much of my work life involved earning woefully inadequate amounts of money through menial labor jobs, most of which I quit after several months. I decided to pursue higher education and after the astronomical costs and accumulation of loans from graduate training, I was not only not earning money, I was hemorrhaging it. All the while I was working in clinics and outpatient facilities for free (they call them "practicums" in the clinical psychology world). After two final years of internship and residency, in which I was pulling down big time salaries of $24,000 and $30,000, I was released into the professional world. At that point I had gained four years of undergraduate qualifications and six years of graduate specialized training, and absolutely no business sense whatsoever.

Many of my colleagues found jobs in clinics, treatment centers, hospitals, and the like. That path sounded highly unpleasant to me so I decided to set out on my own in the wide world of private practice psychotherapy. I started by speaking with several psychologists who had successful private practices. What did they do? How could I model after them? Several of them told me it would take three years to create a sustainable, thriving practice.

So I did what I always do in new situations. I read books. I read books on creating a therapy practice and filling it, then I applied what I learned. I hired a business coach. I took every chance I had to do things that scared me in order to put myself out there. And I filled my therapy practice in less than one year. Of course, all the while my Safety Police were loudly proclaiming that I was doomed, that I didn't have what it took, that I would never succeed. But that's just their job, and they might spook me and make me uncomfortable, but they certainly never stop me now.

All the while, I knew a therapy practice as a psychologist was not my final destination. It was actually a stepping-stone to my true life's work, which is helping people radically increase their confidence in all areas of life. This involves writing, teaching, creating audio and video training programs, coaching, running group sessions, and hosting live weekend workshops. For many years I knew I wanted to do this, and my business coach helped me get started on that path earlier and faster than I would have on my own.

So I dove into the wide world of coaching. If clinical psychology was 18th century Victorian England, coaching was the wild mother fucking west. No guidelines, no regulations, no malpractice insurance, no governing body. Do whatever you want man. Do whatever people will pay you for. Oh, and there's no barrier to entry so someone can call themselves a coach with absolutely no training whatsoever. Literally none.

I had my work cut out for me. I needed to distinguish myself from the many other coaches out there, attract people who were looking for help in the areas where I knew I could help them, show people that I could really help them, prove I wasn't some untrained internet huckster, and then offer them coaching or training.

I learned how to post blog articles, shoot videos and record podcasts. I wrote a book and published it through Amazon. I did interviews and wrote for online magazines. Each step in this process was uncomfortable and had my Safety Police up in arms. *This is going to fail! You can't do this! This will never work! No one will hire you!*

I created and wrote and taught for free for a year and a half before anyone hired me for coaching. All the while I was studying Internet marketing and learning how to get my message out there. *If only people could find me,* I thought. *Then I'm all set.*

But then I realized that people don't hire a coach in the same way they go to a therapist. When they seek out a therapist, they are ready for help. There are no sales involved, no resistance from a potential client, no objections. They are generally ready to go after that first phone call inquiring about your services. The fact that insurance is probably covering the majority of their bill helps too. But coaching isn't covered at all. People need to invest a lot of their own money, time, energy, and focus into growing and becoming the most confident and successful version of themselves. It feels like a huge risk. *What if I fail? What if it doesn't work for me? What if I put all this time and money into it and at the end of the day I'm no better off? That would certainly suck.*

I had no knowledge of any of this, of course. All I knew is that people seemed to like what I was teaching, seemed to really need the help I could give them, and then decided not to work with me for some reason.

"Later," they'd say.

"Soon..."

"I'd love to, but…"

After each conversation with a potential coaching client I felt like I was back in the dating world and getting those polite rejections. "Yeah, you're a great guy and all, I just don't see you in that way..."

Then it hit me, I suck at sales.

Sales? Eww. Aren't sales bad? I shouldn't have to sell someone on coaching, or on getting a confidence building video training. That must mean they don't want it and I'm being bad and manipulative, right?

Yes, it does. At least that's what three psychologist colleagues told me one day. They brought it up in a consult group. They said that selling was bad and that what I was trying to do with coaching was also bad. Fortunately, I had enough business sense to know something there was fishy. That, and any time someone tells me I can't do something, I have an incredibly strong urge to go do it. It must be the younger brother in me.

So I began to study sales and marketing like nobody's business. I learned how to ask good questions and address peoples' fears about coaching and investing in themselves. I did all of this because I believed in what I was selling; because I know that coaching is a powerful force for change. I've worked with many coaches over my life and it's like reading life-changing books on steroids. It's the fastest way to get results in the world. So I had to get better at talking about fears, about exploring the concerns about money, and uncovering anything else that was getting in the way for my potential clients.

I had to face my own fears of being seen as pushy, or sales-y, or somehow bad for persisting in a conversation when someone seemed uncomfortable. I had to overcome my fears of talking about money, of having strong fees attached to my services, of charging what my coaching was truly worth. And most of all, I had to learn how to move beyond the torment I experienced when faced with rejection.

I had thought it was all behind me. I'd overcome so much in dating and relationships and now I was married to the love of my life. I'd conquered the rejection mountain and summited the peak. Or so I'd thought. Apparently, there's another, higher peak to climb, and that's the mountain of fear regarding sales rejection. Fortunately, I had some pretty good tools, and I happened to be spending 24-7 with one of the world's leading confidence experts.

I knew the pain of rejection was not contained in the other person's response and delivered to me when they spoke it. It wasn't even about me; it was about them. The real pain was from whatever I did with the rejection in my mind afterwards. So I set out to get 100 rejections and master the inner game of it all. Along the way, my business exploded and I had more clients than I could handle working with. So I expanded to groups and live weekends, which turned out to produce even more powerful and rapid results than I could have imagined.

So what does this all have to do with money confidence?

What do you think? Why am I sharing all of this with you? What are you finding most valuable? What's standing out to you?

No one is born confident with money. No one is just "a natural". Everyone has to stumble through the learning curve. Everyone. We all have to face our fears of not being good enough and take action in spite of these doubts. We all have to fail, fail again, and hopefully fail better. We all have to make messes and be confused, and then learn to find our way out of it.

Money confidence, like any form of confidence, is not bestowed upon you. It's forged. You build it piece by piece. You learn it book by book. You master it mistake by mistake. And the more you do this, the more confident you become, the more secure you feel about money, and the wealthier you are.

What can you do to forge that confidence in yourself? What excuses or stories would you need to let go of? What is the next fear you can face that will take you one step closer to money confidence and your ultimate destiny of definite, major purpose?

Good. Now, when are you going to do it?

I'm not sure about your exact situation, but I have a good guess that "later" or "someday" is not the right answer for you. More on this in the final chapter of this book, but before we conclude this conversation about money confidence, I do want to highlight one thing that can get in your way of creating the financial security and confidence you seek. And those are money traps.

Money Traps

Money traps are the malfunctions in our mental programming that can cause use to get stuck with money. They keep us frozen in fear, doubt, hesitation, and procrastination. They're like the Windows hourglass or the Mac spinning rainbow beach ball. No matter how pretty they try to make it, it still enrages you when it comes on the screen. So let's highlight these traps now so that you can break right out of them when they ensnare you.

Future Loops

Future Loops are like *Kellogg's* Fruit Loops, only much less colorful and fun. In fact, they're downright painful. A Future Loop happens when we time travel from the present moment into an imaginary future scenario in which we are suffering some terrible financial calamity. Although the scenarios may vary, they all usually boil down to, *and then I'll run out of money and terrible bad things will happen, and then I'm going to die!*

This is enough to spike our feelings of fear and shoot adrenaline and cortisol through our nervous systems. If you're an ambitious mofo like me, then it may send you spinning into the next money trap of Double More (which we'll discuss in a moment). Or it may just keep you up at night, leave you chronically tense, and make you freak out about spending the extra dollar for avocado on your rice bowl. *A dollar! Good lord that's a lot of money. If I keep spending like this I'm going to run out of money and die in the gutter!*

For most people, and probably for you, the imagined end-result catastrophes are highly unlikely. There would be many steps to take between where you are now to being completely homeless and without any possessions or money, roaming the streets and looking for hand-outs. You would probably have to actively try to make that happen, consciously resisting opportunities, help, support, and ways to turn things around.

But this fear, like most of our fears, is not a rational one. It's about survival. It's a response to being a vulnerable creature on this planet who can experience pain and who eventually will die, and knows that. Fear's primary goal is to stimulate your body into responding, taking action, burying nuts for the winter, and doing anything else that will ensure survival and avoidance of pain.

People often unconsciously use fear as a motivational strategy. Adrenaline can be a powerful fuel, even though it gunks up the engine over time. A variety of psychological research demonstrates that we humans will do twice as much to avoid pain as to gain pleasure.[7]

---

2 This is pattern is known as loss aversion and has been heavily researched in economics and decision theory, especially by Amos Tversky and Daniel Kahneman.

We hate pain, discomfort, and loss. So what better way to fire up our motors than to imagine future pain and strategize how we can avoid it?

A number of years ago my brother was studying for the BAR exam to become a practicing fancy-pants attorney. This exam is particularly beastly, takes months to prepare for, and is highly stressful. Many people do not pass. As he was studying like a madman he told me his strategy to stay motivated was to imagine he was going to fail. No matter how much he studied, or how well he did on the practice tests, he would tell himself, *I'm going to fail.* Not score lower than he'd like, but straight up fail. Guess what this did? Sent a wave of adrenaline and energy through his nervous system. Who needs coffee?

When I heard that I thought to myself, *psscch, what a fool. That's a terrible strategy.* After all, I do like to feel superior to my older brother. But then I began to realize that in many circumstances I did the same thing all the time in my life. I constantly was telling myself business ventures weren't going to work, projects were going to fail, and products wouldn't sell. Even when there was clear evidence to the contrary, my mind would fabricate a reality in which everything fell apart. This would give me endless juice to rapidly achieve and complete tasks. My superiority was short lived (although I contend that I am still the better looking brother).

Do you get stuck in Future Loops? What do you think the payoff is? Does it give you energy and fuel to take action? What do you get out of it? Every repetitive pattern gives us something, even if it has unpleasant consequences. Sometimes people think that by imagining terrible scenarios and worrying about them they are "preparing" somehow. As if not worrying about that terrible scenario would somehow bring it about, and your worry and anxiety is what keeps it at bay. Absurd.

The way out of these future loops is by staying out of the future in the first place. Some targeted planning or focused problem solving is good. The rest of the time, leaning into your future is a way of avoiding something in the present. So bring yourself back to this moment right now. Feel the book in your hands and the coolness of your breath as you breathe in. Notice whatever's going on in your stomach, your chest, and your jaw. Feel what's actually happening right now. The more you can do this, and the less you resist and flee from it, the more present, confident, and powerful you will become.

Double More Insanity

I am a productive person. I like to accomplish things. Get tasks done. Achieve. Succeed. Excel. I like doing a lot in a short period of time and seeing the results of my efforts. And I am insane. Well, part of me is. I think we all have some insane parts in our heads. Here's what I mean:

I have a part of me that always wants more. He wants more money, more security, more success, more safety. He wants more tasks to be accomplished in a shorter period of time. He tells me there's so much to do, too much in fact. It's too much with too little time to do it. So stop sitting around, stop interacting with your family, stop relaxing. Get the fuck to work. Now!

Do you have this part too? One day I sat down to have a little conversation with him.

"Hey there," I said. "I've been working a lot and accomplishing quite a bit. We seem to have plenty of money to support ourselves and even give some to people and causes we support."

Without missing a beat, his immediate response was, "You need to do more. You need to record more podcasts and videos, create more programs and products, reach more people, help more people, make more money, write more books, spend more time with your kids, and spend more time with your wife. You need to do more."

"Wow," I replied. "That sure sounds like a lot. How much more?"

"Double."

Hence, that part of myself is now called Double More.

Do you have your own version of Double More driving you relentlessly to keep doing? You may be quite familiar with the feeling of not satisfying him. That sense that you aren't doing enough, that you need to get more done faster, that you just don't have enough time to get it all done. Oh, and that you should be earning more money faster and be ahead of where you are now. You also shouldn't be "wasting" your time with entertainment or relaxation and should instead always be doing something productive.

Then when you've accomplished everything, earned all that money, achieved all those goals, only then you can completely relax and enjoy everything you've worked so hard for, right? Actually, that's wrong. This is what Double More tells you will happen. He uses that sweet future land of blissful relaxation, fulfillment, and peace as a carrot dangling from a stick. He holds it out in front of you, which keeps you going hard and fast in the present. Tense, driven, stressed.

What actually will happen is this: as soon as you reach those goals and accomplish all those tasks, it will turn out there's more to do. How much more? Double!

This is insanity. We need to slow way down. Take a step back and let's look at Double More's strategy and approach to life. It might seem necessary at first glance, but as we look deeper we see that his plan doesn't bring happiness or fulfillment. Instead, it kills our confidence because as long as we're in his grips we are never enough and have never quite arrived yet.

What does Double More really want? He says it's more money and achievement, but what's underneath that? From what I've seen in my own experience, and the experiences of thousands of others, it's a sense of security or safety and a sense of finally proving that I'm good enough.

If I just have *enough* money, then I'll be safe and secure. In some delusional way, we unconsciously believe that if we have enough money, we will be protected from pain in life, such as the pain of loss, or the pain of grief. *If I earn enough money I will be protected against the pain of losing my loved ones, or my health, or anything else I feel uncomfortably vulnerable about.*

And if I achieve enough, show I'm the best (or at least better than most), then I'll finally prove that I'm good enough. I'm a winner, I'm impressive, and I'm finally worthy of love and respect.

Insanity. Because it doesn't work. It's a weird trap. You aren't protected. People and pets you love will die. Your children could die before you. Old age, sickness, and death awaits us all. There's no escape.

Additionally, you already *are* enough. There is an abundance of love you can give and receive right now, without improving on any part of your life or achieving one more goal. In fact, seeking to be significant and "the best" at something are actually cheap substitutes for love, which is what you really want. Part of you just tells you that you aren't worthy of that love until you've earned it. We will get into this much more in the next chapter on love.

I think we focus on frantically doing more to avoid the fact that pain is unavoidable in life and we're all going to die. We try to hide from it. Then we convince ourselves it's because we really do need the money, or we really do need to accomplish more. We've got bills to pay and mouths to feed, so we have to focus on this like crazy.

Crazy indeed. And it hemorrhages the confidence we could be building up in ourselves. Because even if we're earning and achieving, we're still running: running from feelings, from death, and running from fully living with an open heart.

As you've seen throughout this book, we cannot gain confidence by running. The only way to strengthen ourselves and skyrocket our confidence to extraordinary levels is by facing things head and on. Facing our fears, facing our feelings, and not running from anything.

So how do we release Double More's grip on our minds and achieve, earn, and succeed with more peace, ease, and love?

Stop dreaming hippie, get back to work!

Sorry, that just slipped out. Here's what seems to be working for me and many clients of mine who are ready to release the insanity:

First, realize there is only so much you can accomplish in one day, and one week. You could conceivably increase that amount if you worked eighty-five hours and didn't take care of your body, sleep, spend time with friends, or see your family and the other people you love. Which to me sounds unsustainable and painful.

For me personally, forty hours of work each week seems pretty reasonable. It's a tried and true number that's been around for quite a while and it gives some balance to the achievement-bot inside of me. So in those forty hours, there is only so much you can physically create, do, complete, or accomplish. And in eight or nine hours in a given day, there is only so much you can do. It's finite.

During those eight hours we want to be focused, clear, effective, and driven. We want to prioritize the most important tasks that will serve others and generate income for our business or employers. We want to be aware of when we get lost in busywork and other menial tasks that are easier, but don't actually generate income or provide true service. We want to breathe throughout the day, eat food that keeps our minds clear and focused, and drink lots of water.

And then, at the end of the day, when we are just about to close our laptops and snap our briefcases shut, we want to pause. Look back on all that you created that day, all the good work you did. All the life energy you invested in your labors. Take a deep breath in, smile, and congratulate yourself for a day of work well done.

Choose to know and remember the sweet pleasure and relief of an end to a good day's work. You did it. You've done just enough—the perfect amount.

When Double More chimes in on your drive home, reminding you of the four thousand tasks you have yet to accomplish, breathe and smile. *Yeah, you want more. Double more! Double faster, double double.*

Thanks for your energy and your input and helping me accom-

plish so much today. Thank you so much for your passion, your drive, and your desire to do and create. It's incredible and amazing.

And now you can relax. I'll drive for awhile and you can just chill out. You've already done more than enough. There's only so much that we can get done in a day. I love you.

It never hurts to throw an "I love you" in there whenever you're talking to a part of yourself. It scrambles their circuits.

As you do this, bring your attention to your breath and to your chest. Breathe in and out from the center of your chest, as if you were breathing directly in and out of your heart. Feel what is there. Run from nothing. You are a warrior.

GRATITUDE

Underneath all the fears and stories and planning, wealth is nothing more than a feeling. It's not a certain number in your bank account, or a certain salary or income. It's a feeling of abundance, of security, safety, and freedom. It's a sense of confidence that you can take care of yourself and the ones you love.

No matter how much we have, nothing determines our money confidence and sense of wealth like our perspective. You can have more money than eighty five percent of the people on this planet do, you can be swimming in comforts and luxuries that only royalty had several hundred years ago, and you can still feel frustrated, upset, and impoverished. You can be focusing on how they messed up installing your fine granite countertop during the remodel and so now you have to wait another two weeks before you can use your kitchen. You feel upset, outraged, or scared. It's a travesty.

It is so easy to forget how rich we already are. If you are in the United States as you read this, you are rich. You have a faucet that spits out clean, drinkable water. Hell, your toilet is filled with drinking water for God's sake! You have a bed and a roof over your head. You have so many things that a large portion of the global population endures life without.

In any given moment, we can focus on the injustices we face, or we can change our perspective to see the blessings underneath. One of my dad's favorite topics to discuss is how broken our health care system is in the U.S. He talks about how insurance premiums keep going up, how some people pay too much, and how there seems to be no solution in sight. I actually agree that there are some major flaws in the whole system. At the same time, I am so grateful that we have access to incredible medical care. The science of medicine and what can be done with it is utterly amazing. If it were one hundred years ago, my wife would have most likely died during the birth of our first son. Or maybe our son would have died. Who knows? I do know that the hospital down the street was amazing and everyone there knew exactly how to perform an emergency C-section.

You could fall from a ladder and shatter the bones in your leg and you will be whisked away to a facility where they will remove your pain, fix your broken leg, and help you get set up to heal and walk again. That's amazing.

We are so rich, so wealthy. We have such an abundance of food that you can drive in your horseless carriage for five minutes and get virtually anything you want. How does my car get me there? I don't even really know. Magic is my best guess. And while I'm driving I could be talking into a device that somehow encodes my voice and shoots it through the ether to a person on the other side of the country.

Each morning the sun rises and warms us. The rains come and water the earth for our food to grow. We have warmth and shelter and people who love us. We have insane amounts of comfort and pleasure available to us. We have access to more information and knowledge than any other time in history. And you can access it all from a device in your pocket.

What are you grateful for in your life? What could you be more grateful for if you wanted to be?

Breathe in and feel that now. Feel the fullness, the richness of what you already have. You are blessed.

EARN IT OR DON'T

Stories, fear, and self-doubt aside, the truth is: you can earn money. You can create whatever you want. If you're dedicated and driven, and you continue to model after successful people, learn new things, and take massive action, then there is no way you won't earn more money. It's inevitable, as long as you don't stop and don't quit.

If you'd like, you can earn a shit ton of money. And it's good to do so. You will stretch and grow like crazy along the way, and the process of transforming who you are will be way more rewarding than any number in your bank account. You will also end up contributing even more to society, to humanity, and to the world as you earn more. If that's what you are inspired and motivated to do, that's great. Go for it.

Alternately, you don't have to do that. You don't have to want to continually increase your income or get more things. You don't have to want a bigger house, a nicer car, or private school education for your kids. There is nothing wrong with you for not wanting to earn more money and for choosing not to.

The key is to make it a choice. Don't let your fear and self-doubt decide for you. Whatever you choose, stand by it. Own it. Give yourself complete permission to go after wealth and abundance with reckless abandon. Or give yourself complete permission to relax, enjoy all of the other riches of life, and not strive so much to earn more.

You are the architect of your life, the captain of your ship. You can create whatever life you want for yourself.

CHAPTER VII:

LOVE

It takes a great deal of confidence to love. It takes confidence to give love freely, to fully let in and receive the love others give us, and to express our love openly and unabashedly. It takes confidence because it's scary. Actually, it can be downright terrifying.

Loving fully is probably the biggest risk we can take in this life. Because it requires opening our hearts and putting ourselves out there, where we most definitely will get hurt at some point. And since our hearts were so open, we'll feel that hurt deeply, and it will be painful. And yet, despite this risk and the inevitable pains that come with it, we all want and need to give and receive love.

Man, what a set up.

Fortunately, there is something we can do to increase our confidence in this area. We can cultivate the personal power, courage, and confidence to boldly put ourselves out there to receive love and face whatever comes back. We can continually expand to feel the deep and profound joy of really, vulnerably loving others, which magnifies our enjoyment of life thousands of times over. And we can learn to face the inevitable moments of pain and loss that are the consequence of loving fully and deeply with willingness and surrender.

As a result, we can love more, which makes life much more enjoyable and fulfilling. You can feel more connected, more supported, more at peace. You can have better sex and more sex, and feel really good about it. You can feel so joyous about being with someone that your heart aches in the most delightful kind of way.

You can also have people there to support you when you're struggling. Those you love can rally behind you to soothe you, encourage you, and sometimes just take you to a bad movie where you sneak pizza slices underneath your jackets.

Let's dive in together and look at what blocks us from having the rock-solid confidence that would allow us to love more boldly and deeply. We will uncover and clear away the core fears that stop us from feeling more love, and then we'll discover new and powerful ways of approaching love that inspires courage and lasting confidence.

Ready? Let's dive in!

THE PRIMARY CURRENCY

We all desperately want and need love.

Now, I know that's not the right thing to say in a self-development book. I'm supposed to say, "All you need is within you now, and you just need to love yourself. You don't need other peoples' love. You are love. It's your core essence because you are moonbeam stardust after all."

While this stuff sounds good and can be somewhat empowering, it's also not really true in my experience. We humans are incredibly social creatures. We depend on connection and being part of a group to survive. Tons of psychology and sociology research concludes that being isolated and lonely is incredibly hard on peoples' moods and physical health. We need others.

We crave relationships with other people. We need them to be around us and we need to be around them. We need to love them and we need to be loved. Without that social experience, we shrivel up and die. Just look at babies and small children. It's profoundly obvious how much they need our ongoing attention, love, engagement, and physical touch. Without it they don't develop properly and can even in some cases get physically ill or die. Love is the primary currency.

Cheap Substitutes

When I was in fifth grade I traveled with my dad, mom, and brother to India. I have a collection of spotty memories, including the Taj Mahal, a guy with no legs begging outside when we got off a train, and an epic rug negotiation showdown between my dad and a rug merchant.

I also remember being fascinated with the idea that you could get a knock-off Rolex watch for thirty bucks. I had no interest in Rolexes back home and never even cared about them. But then, when I found out I could get a phony one for so cheap, I became obsessed. I had to have one. Imagine showing back up to my fifth grade class after my world travels brandishing a shiny new (fake) Rolex watch. I'd clearly be the man.

So I badgered my dad until he finally agreed to get me one. We found some dude brazenly selling knock-off Rolexes out in the open off of his classy blanket-on-the-sidewalk display area. I found a nice one with a fake leather band and a small fake gold face. After haggling hard core, as my dad is wont to do (he is Pakistani after all), we got the guy down to six hundred rupees, which was like twenty dollars. Score.

I promptly strapped on my glorious new watch and proudly strutted through the streets with my dad. I was a baller.

Unfortunately, my glory was short lived because on the plane ride home, even before I was able to show it off to friends and strangers alike, the gold crown emblem - that indicates it totally is a real Rolex

- fell off and slid down the watch face to rest just below the 7. Fail.

While we all desperately want real love more than anything, giving and receiving it is an inherently vulnerable (and thus scary) thing to do. I could get hurt, I could be rejected, I could lose the people and things I care about. That's freaky.

So instead, we often settle for love's cheaper, safer substitutes. The fake Rolexes if you will. These include trying to get approval and attempting to impress others. They may not feel as good, and they may not truly, deeply meet our need for love, but they're less risky and safer dammit.

GETTING APPROVAL

Approval is defined as "accepting something as satisfactory." Pretty uninspiring. But that is what most of us are unconsciously going for when we interact with others, be it a co-worker, boss, potential date, friend, spouse, or stranger. The main way we usually try to be accepted as satisfactory is to avoid doing anything that might be deemed unsatisfactory. That is, we avoid anything the other person might not like.

Here's our unconscious plan: If I avoid stepping on toes, don't disagree too much, and stay away from touchy subjects, then my interactions with others will be smooth. They won't have anything to disapprove of because I'll be so agreeable, pleasing, and nice. Then, with nothing they could possibly dislike being displayed, they will have no other option but to shower me with approval.

I personally ran this strategy for almost fifteen years. It was pretty dismal. How does it work for you?

Usually, not very well, I'm guessing. Because even if you somehow manage to contort yourself into that little box that you think the other person wants you to be in, you don't win much. At best, you get some approval - aka to be "not disliked." How's that for a shitty booby prize?

Does the other person know you, connect with you, feel power-fully drawn to you, or love you? Not if you're running the approval strategy. Because in that game, they don't really get a chance to see you. You're hidden back there behind all the people-pleasing maneu-vers. So they can't really know you or love you, and you aren't able to receive any of the most primary currency that you desper-ately need and want.

It's like being thirsty and instead of drinking a tall glass of pure spring water you swig down a toxic dehydrating glass of soda. It doesn't give you what you really need.

Even worse, it often doesn't even give you the cheap substitute. Instead of walking away with approval, you often walk away feel-ing (or actually being) rejected. You're still thirsty and probably even more dehydrated after drinking that soda. Others aren't as interested in you; attractive people scan around the room for someone better to talk to; and your boss overlooks you and gives the new project man-agement role to someone else. What the fuck?

I was trying to get approval, why didn't this work?!

Because people can sense that pattern of desperate approval-seek-ing. They pick up on it subconsciously and it often repels them. At best they're just not that drawn to you for future interactions. "Oh yeah, that Aziz guy. Yeah, he's alright."

"Do you want to hire him, date him, or be his friend?"

"Mmm, nah. He's alright and all, but I'm just not interested."

At worst, people are actively turned off by this and try to get out of the interaction or relationship with you as soon as possible. I've been there and it's painful and it's confusing and it sucks. Approval is a dismal substitute for the real thing. And the pursuit of trying to get approval from others leaves us hollow, yearning for more, and often lonelier than we want to be.

If approval seeking is an ongoing challenge you have been deal-ing with, you will benefit greatly from the next chapter in this book, which is focused on increasing your sense of personal power. For additional resources on increasing power, eliminating approval seeking, and letting go of caring so much about what others think, visit http://ConfidenceUnleashedNow.com

ARE YOU IMPRESSED?

Another shitty substitute for love that we spend way too much time trying to acquire is admiration. We want to impress others with how smart, successful, or popular we are. How many friends we have, how much we've achieved, or how much we earn.

This desire to impress others can motivate us in hundreds of ways, from what car we buy (or lease because we can't really afford to buy it but want to look like we can), to the level we excel in our career and how much we earn, to how good of a parent we appear to be in the eyes of others.

Behind all of this lies an unexamined chain of logic. If others are impressed, then they'll admire me, which means they'll want to be around me as a friend, employer, customer, or romantic partner. And that is close enough to love for me, especially since I don't have to risk much in order to get it.

It's like that old transitive property from Boring Math 101 in some grade. A=B and B=C. So A=B=C. So therefore A=C.

Impressed = Admired ≈ Love

Therefore:

Impressed ≈ Love

(The squiggly equal sign means it's kind of equal to that. Close enough.)

But it's not. It really isn't. It leads to endless pursuits of things we don't really want or actually need. And it can create the horrible monster known as perfectionism, which I struggled with for many years (and still do sometimes).

This is perfectionism in a nutshell: I have to be perfect and amazing and impress you in order for you to love me. If I show flaws, weakness, uncertainty or insecurity, you will certainly reject me as the unlovable wretch that I am.

Perfectionism comes from trying to impress others as a safe, cheap substitute for love. It's not love. It's not even close. It's pain and loneliness.

Let's drop the grasping quest for these substitutes. Just let them go. People might approve of you, or be impressed by you. Or they might not. It's okay, you don't need either one. What you really need and want is love. And the good news is there's tons of that to go around and you don't even need that much of it to thrive wildly.

The only problem is we have a bunch of subtle clever maneuvers to actually block love from ever reaching our hearts. Insanity! Why on earth would we do that? Because we humans hate pain, remember? We hate even the possibility of pain. So that other natural instinct—to keep ourselves safe—is an effort to protect ourselves from pain. We try to get all the goodies, joy and pleasure without having to take any of the risks. But love doesn't work that way. You have to step up and put yourself out there in order to play. Risk is an inherent part of the game.

Let's look at the main ways we keep love away, and then how we can break through to experience new levels of love, connection, and joy in our lives.

LOVE HURTS: THE FEAR OF PAIN

Why do we push away or block the very thing we want most? Because it comes with a scary price tag. And while we stand to gain all the benefits of love, including joy, connection, peace, and purpose, we also know on some level that we might have to pay for it in several painful ways.

Let's uncover the main fears around love right now, so we can see what we're dealing with. This will help you feel more at ease and confident, because uncovering and facing our fears is always better than ignoring and hiding from them. When we examine our fears in the light of day, we often see how strange and exaggerated they really are. This diminishes their power so we are free to let in all the love we truly want.

Fear Of Disapproval And Rejection

"None shall pass."
- The Black Night, Monty Python
And The Quest For The Holy Grail

One of the first fears that shows up when we are considering love is the deep fear of experiencing criticism, disapproval or rejection.

This one can be summed up as this: *I'll open up my heart and put myself out there and the other person will say, "Eww, no thank you. You are unattractive and unworthy of my love. I don't like you."*

We can be afraid of this scenario at any point along the process of connecting with others, from the first meeting, to the first date, to the fifth year of our relationship. In fact, we can become more afraid of this as time goes on because we become more and more connected to the other person. Now if they reject us, it hurts even more. It matters more.

I like to think of this one as the Gatekeeper Fear. It often comes up first and prevents us from even entering the playing field of love. I have worked for many years with people struggling with social anxiety. The fear of strangers and of new people rejecting us is rampant in this scenario. Time and again, I would hear a client say, "I desperately want to meet someone, feel a connection, go on dates, fall in love, and have a great relationship." And it was true. Part of them did want this.

But the Gatekeeper would get the best of them. Before they could even walk over to the person to open their mouth and start a conversation, the fear of rejection would overtake them. They would feel a sense of absolute certainty that this person, who was so beautiful and confident, couldn't possibly want to talk with them, let alone date, sleep with, or spend years of their life with them. And so they would never even try. Safety Police, anyone?

This is a way of dodging the potential pain of disapproval and rejection. But it also obviously dodges the potential pleasure of love and connection. Why would we choose to go without love, to starve ourselves of the primary currency, in order to avoid rejection?

Because rejection hurts.

There are things we do to make it hurt way more than it has to, and we talked about some of the most powerful tools in the world to handle rejection so it never holds you back again in the Action chapter.

But, you'll notice I never said something like this, which is the favorite dogma of the self-help world. "Rejection does not have to hurt at all. In fact, the only reason you feel pain is because you're making it so by giving it a negative meaning. Just change the meaning and it won't hurt at all."

Bullshit.

What are we, robots? Ultra logical Vulcans?

The truth is even without negative meanings being attached to it, rejection can and does hurt. Not all rejections have to be painful, and not all rejections hurt equally, but pain is often part of it. When I muster up the courage to start a friendly conversation with someone I am drawn to, and she gives me a look of utter contempt and dismisses me, that hurts.

When I spend ninety minutes talking with someone, giving them my full attention and trying my best to serve them, and then they say, "No, I don't want to work with you." That can hurt. When

I go down into the kitchen, walk up to my wife, and wrap my arms around her as she prepares some food, and she tightens in her body and moves away slightly, that hurts.

I know rationally and intellectually that the rejecting woman could be in a bad mood, that the potential client may have some block to trusting me, and that my wife may be struggling with something that has nothing to do with me. And yet it can still hurt in my heart.

Simple, and often dismissive, statements like, "just don't take it personally" usually don't help. The truth is this: rejection hurts. And another truth is that we can handle this hurt.

We just have to be willing to feel. To go into that painful sensation right in the center of our hearts, directly and fully, breathing deeply all the while. Wow, what a sensation! It can hurt so much. Not always, and not equally for each rejection, but wow. Ouch.

In order to become extraordinarily confident, you'll want to become way more familiar with this sensation. We think it's horrible, and that it means something is terribly wrong with us, the other person, or the world. But the secret to extraordinary confidence in love, and many other areas of life, lies in the center of that feeling of pain. We will discuss this more in just a bit when we get to the section on loving fully and boldly. For now, let's move to the next fear that stops us from loving fully.

Fear Of Being Left

A primal fear every human has is the fear of being abandoned. I think it's deeply hardwired into our nervous systems from birth, since at that time abandonment would have equaled death.

Now, as fully capable adults, we may not consciously fear that we will be abandoned and be unable to take care of ourselves or survive. But deep in our hearts, we still fear being left, which can bring about a great deal of pain and tap into this old primal fear of abandonment.

This showed up for me pretty early in life with nightmares and separation anxiety. I remember sleeping in the same room as my brother when we were young kids. As we each lay there on our individual twin beds, I would repeatedly request, "Tariq, face me." I wanted him to be facing me as I fell asleep. If he were to turn over I would feel a growing sense of anxiety and dread. I was afraid of being left.

As an adult this manifested as me starting relationships with women and then leaving them fairly quickly, thus preventing me from ever being the person who was left. *I'll do the leaving here, thank you very much.* Later still, I noticed this fear showing up in client relationships. I would sometimes experience a nagging and persistent fear that all of my clients would leave me. In my experience over the years, this is not something I have much control over. The brave and willing stay through the process to profoundly heal and grow, and a certain percentage of others choose to pull back to the safe and familiar life that they lived before. Nonetheless, a fear of being left persists.

This often shows up in people's romantic relationships as well. It could be a chronic fear of their partner leaving them, no longer finding them attractive, or cheating on them. It can also show up as a perpetual fear of being fired for no major reason. All of these are forms of the fear of being left.

And we hate that feeling. Being left tends to dredge up all kinds of negative self-worth stuff. Or, to be more exact, all kinds of "clearly I'm not worthy of love" stuff. We hate the feeling that we are not enough in some way. Part of that feeling is this chain of reasoning: *If I was only better looking, smarter, funnier, or more of something or other, then I would never be left. But I was left so therefore I'm inadequate and inferior.*

What a mess. No thank you. I'll just steer clear of that love nonsense and then I won't have to worry about being rejected or left or abandoned or any of this other unpleasant stuff. I can just stay in my apartment, get take out, watch TV, play video games, maybe spend a little time with a friend or two who I know won't leave me, and call it a life. Sounds comfortable, predictable, and safe.

Sound familiar? It's a choice we all might make on any given day, or month, or year.

Fear Of Hurting Others

Another major obstacle to love is the fear of hurting others. This is especially common if you fancy yourself a "nice" person. You don't like conflict, you try to be polite to everybody, and you just can't stand it if someone doesn't like you or something you did.

If this sounds like you, don't worry. I can relate. I spent a decade of my life as the nicest guy you could ever imagine (on the outside), even though inside I was anxious, uncomfortable, suffering from chronic low self-esteem and deep down quite angry – I just didn't allow myself to feel it.

As part of this approach to life, you tend to worry a lot about what others think and feel. The last thing you want to be seen as is a selfish jerk who hurts other people. So you lean toward the opposite extreme and do whatever you can to make sure everyone feels great all the time. If someone is upset, you take it upon yourself to remedy the situation, even if it involves saying and doing things you don't actually believe. Whatever it takes to make everything smooth again.

This pattern gets especially challenging when it comes to love. Because love is the biggest risk of all and people are going to get hurt. Before dating someone, you can't know if it's a perfect fit. You have to spend time together and figure out if there's enough connection and chemistry. You might not feel it. He or she might not feel it. Someone's going to be disappointed, sad, or rejected.

Even if you two hit it off extremely well, and you are a match made in heaven. Even if you love the hell out of each other, and the sex is great, and you treat each other as gentle as you please. Guess what? Someone's still, inevitably going to get hurt.

There is no way that two humans can agree on everything. They can't have the same feelings about the same things all the time. They can't always want the same things. So there are going to be some unavoidable moments of frustration, some conflicting desires or preferences, and definitely some disappointments. If you are both being authentic, expressive, and honest, it cannot be any other way.

This is where the nice guy in me freaked out. *I can't disappoint a woman. I can't say no to her if she really wants something. I can't tell her I'd rather spend the weekend "doing my own thing." That would crush her! I would be such a selfish monster.*

To make matters even more confusing, when you are living as the "nice guy" or "nice girl" you tend to attract partners who may unconsciously use this to their advantage. They may be highly skilled at running the "guilt trip," for example. "You don't want to spend the weekend with me? How could you do this to me? Why do you never want to spend any time with me? What am I supposed to do all weekend??"

Even worse, what if you decide you don't actually want to date this person anymore? What if you want to break up? Well shit, that's just about as much pain as you can cause in another person, right? Especially one you supposedly love. No, that's too cruel. You'd better just adapt yourself and do some internal gymnastics so you can make it work between the two of you.

Many people I've worked with had stayed in relationships for months or years longer than they wanted to, simply because they did not want to hurt the other person. It's tortuous. No one said being "nice" was easy.

So in order to avoid that whole ball of complex feelings and asking themselves the confusing questions, such as, "Am I a good person if I cause pain in others?" many people just give love a wide berth. They stay a safe distance away, residing in social anxiety, fear of meeting and dating others, or keeping relationships very short and uncommitted.

Of course, what you're really scared of is not only hurting the other person. It's the feeling of guilt that you feel afterwards. And the relentless self-attack that ensues, wherein you tell yourself that you're a bad person, and often believe it. That is what you're really afraid of. And that is something you can be completely free from, which makes life, love, and relationships approximately 4,000% better.

Before we move on to see how we deal with these fears, and how to free ourselves from them, there's just one more fear we have to look at. Even when we accept that to love means opening ourselves up to getting rejected and being abandoned, we're still not in the clear yet. Because there's one more fear that is the granddaddy of them all. The thing we want to avoid most. Loss.

Fear Of Loss

After studying psychology for several decades and working with thousands of people, I believe that loss is one of the experiences we dislike most as humans. We hate to lose anything. Objects, possessions, opportunities, experiences, and of course people and places we love.

The grief we feel as a result of losing something or someone we love is hands-down one of the most difficult and intolerable things we experience as people. In fact, it's so uncomfortable that most people will do absolutely anything to not feel the loss or the grief associated with loss. If at all possible, we will avoid connecting fully and vulnerably so that we will not be as exposed to loss. If we do experience it, we have countless strategies to escape from this feeling, including staying busy, working non-stop, not slowing down, being constantly engaged with entertainment or some digital device, pushing others away, lashing out at people, getting drunk, or spiraling into addiction.

And yet, despite our dislike of this feeling, it's an inherent part of love. It's built into love. Damn.

Everything we love we will lose. In the short term we could lose someone because they might break up with us, or choose to move on. Even if we have the most amazing, loving, lifelong relationship in the world, we will still lose the other person. Old age, sickness, and ultimately death, awaits us all.

On top of that, we have no idea when that loss might occur. There are absolutely no guarantees whatsoever. My children could get sick and die long before I do. My dear friend might get into a car accident when he's just about to have his first child with his now pregnant wife. So much potential loss. Such unpredictability.

It freaks us out. That much uncertainty and that much vulnerability can be hard to live with. So we squeeze the pipe and reduce the flow of love to a trickle. Less gets in, but we unconsciously think: *if I don't feel so much love now, maybe it will hurt less if I lose it later. After all, if I love completely, I'm setting myself up for a world of hurt.*

Yep. You are. That just seems to be how it is. I know some spiritual teachers say they no longer identify with the physical form and that all things are one, so there is no loss. And that therefore, when their husband or wife of thirty years dies, they won't feel grief because they are completely aligned with the way of Spirit or God.

I don't know about all that. I think it's going to hurt a shit ton when I lose my wife, and my parents, and my friends, and my children (hopefully I won't have to experience that last one). But I'm all in. I'm going to keep opening my heart more and more to squeeze every last ounce of juice out of this amazing opportunity.

If you are with me, and are sick and tired of living a guarded life, of trying to minimize the pain of rejection and loss, but at the same time find yourself minimizing your joy, power, and sense of vitality, then good! We are going to explore exactly how to live and love with more boldness and courage. How to be all in and reap the tremendous rewards of taking that risk.

The best way to do that is to uncover the main ways you try to get away from the fears listed above. The specific strategies you regularly use to avoid these fears that are causing you to enjoy less love than you want and need in your life. As you identify and remove these strategies, you will approach life in a less guarded manner, and your heart will thank you for it.

How We Defend Our Hearts

The Emotional Breastplate

Our hearts are one of the most vulnerable parts of our bodies. Any damage inflicted on this area will cause major bodily disruption or death. Knowing this, men who went into combat used to wear extra armor in front of their hearts, known as a breastplate. It was often a thick sheet of metal that would deflect anything that attempted to make contact with the man's heart.

Unknowingly, almost everyone is wearing some sort of mental-emotional breastplate in front of their hearts. It is designed to protect us from the emotional wounds that our vulnerable hearts can experience. Rejection, hurt, ridicule, being unwanted or disliked, or losing people and places we love. These can all be painful experiences, and we don't like pain. So after experiencing a few of these painful moments, we decide to don an emotional breastplate. We pick up patterns of thinking, feeling, and acting that serve to protect us from feeling so much pain in our hearts.

Of course, this armor protects us from feeling anything. While we may sort of numb that ache of loss or vulnerability, we also numb the expansive pleasure of love, or the bright joy of breathing in the fresh, cool air that smells of fall and is heavy with moisture. Instead we just feel stressed, tense, worried, irritable, or impatient. We spend the majority of our time in our heads, thinking about the world and ourselves. It feels a little safer up in there, doesn't it? I know I try to think my way out of feelings all the time. And if that doesn't work, distraction is always good, too. Music, audiobooks, games on your phone, social media, reading the "news", watching endless TV shows, or just going to the Internet and furrowing your brow, asking yourself "Wasn't there something I needed to look up?"

This breastplate may have served you in the past. It may have protected you from pain you didn't know how to manage at the time, like your parents divorcing or losing your first love. Or you may have unconsciously needed to put it on to provide a sense of certainty and safety that you'd never have to hurt that much again. Whatever happened that caused you to initially put on this breastplate, it's okay. We're just tender, vulnerable creatures doing the best we can in an incredibly complex world. Give yourself a break.

In this moment, as in all moments, you have a choice. You can choose to maintain your defended stance towards others and life, marching forward with a breastplate (and maybe even a thick shield in front of that). Or you can choose to live in a less defended way. You can choose to draw more awareness and energy into your heart, rather than less. You can feel your heart and your feelings much more throughout the day. You can acknowledge the vulnerability of life, of those you love, and of yourself. You can accept that you will feel pain and loss as part of living and loving, but that you are powerful and expansive enough to feel all of those things. And this will open you up to so much more joy, happiness, love and life. It's scary, but it sure beats the alternative.

In order to actually do this, you have to become aware of how you construct the armor around your heart. This awareness will help you dismantle the breastplate so that you can love others more freely and fully.

Heart Defense Squad

Let's take a look at your team: your collection of patterns that are designed to help you feel a little less pain around love. I call these patterns your Heart Defense Squad, because that's exactly what they're trying to do. That, and because it's a badass name.

Notice which of the following you do to try and feel less. Less fear, less vulnerability, and less pain of rejection, loss, or being left. If you're like most of us, you'll probably recognize more than one of these patterns in your squad.

Stop Feeling That!

This is a straightforward, simple, and highly effective way to try and get away from feelings. In any given moment, however you're feeling, your mind simply tells you, *stop feeling that!*

Sad? *Stop feeling that!*

Anxious, confused, hurt, rejected, insecure? *Stop feeling that!*

Your mind will provide you with tons of reasons for why you should not be feeling what you're feeling. It will make a compelling case for why you're wrong for feeling the way you do, and should knock it off right now.

Just yesterday I was getting my haircut at a barbershop down the street from my house. Sitting in the chair next to me was a little boy who was getting his hair cut while his brother and mom sat on the big black couch in the waiting area. Towards the end of his haircut, the barber called mom over to discuss a few tweaks. As they talked, the little boy sat there quietly, looking off into the distance. I didn't get a long look at him, but I would guess he was feeling a little tense, anxious, sad or uncomfortable.

His mom picked up on this as well and said, "Jerry, what's wrong? Why are you like this? Smile. This is not like you." Translation: *Stop feeling that Jerry. What the hell is wrong with you anyways?*

Most of us got a hefty dose of this as children, from parents, siblings, teachers, and other installers of programming. It may have been subtle or obvious. More harsh, or more kind. Regardless, the end result is a hyperactive pattern of telling ourselves not to feel something.

Does this actually work? What is your experience?

For me, I've noticed it can kinda sorta keeps a feeling at bay for a little while, but it doesn't actually make it go away entirely. It's there waiting for me in the shadows, building in intensity. Meanwhile, I'm just feeling something unpleasant. Usually this is some combination of tension, irritability, impatience, and general resistance to other people and to life.

One of my favorite feelings to run this strategy on is loss. Whether it's in dealing with a miscarriage or my beloved deceased cat Pimple, my heart defense squad was ready to reduce the pain onslaught (no that's not a typo, his name was Pimple, and yes, I am an adult).

After some arbitrary amount of time, say three weeks for the dead cat, and three months for the lost baby, my mind says: *Ok, that's enough! Grieving time is now officially closed.* After this proclamation, any feeling of sadness in my heart was met with confusion and impatience. *What is this grief nonsense? What is wrong with you? Others don't feel this much or hurt this long. You should be over this by now. It's always something with you, grieving this, feeling sad over that. You're just making stuff up to feel sad about because you're messed up and weak. And bad. Yeah.*

Now as this delightful experience is happening in my head, to be honest I'm not feeling the grief. I don't know what the hell I'm feeling, but probably some mixture of shame, a sense of being defective or inferior, and maybe anxiety. What I do know is that it's definitely painful.

You know the crazy thing though? It actually feels better than straight up grief and feeling the loss. It's somehow more manageable and under control. It doesn't remind me how vulnerable love makes me. It's safer. It's also painful, miserable, self-esteem-destroying and ultimately unhealthy, but it's safer.

The core message of this member of the Heart Defense Squad

(heretofore referred to in shorthand as HDS) is *you don't have a good enough reason to feel that, so don't feel it at all.*

Whenever you notice this pattern running in your mind, label it as an HDS maneuver. Then apply one of the new strategies you'll learn below in the section on loving fully and boldly.

Super Distracto

Ahh, the old Super D. This strategy is king in our modern life. It basically involves continually focusing externally on whatever is in front of us, so we can avoid going inward and feeling the hard feelings.

Super D takes the form of television, video games, our laptops, our smart phones with games and apps and the ability to compulsively check our email eighty-three times per day. He disguises himself as sports, the latest news, what so and so said about such and such, shopping, Internet porn, endlessly reading responses to a Reddit post, researching the list of updates to the latest piece of tech gear. These are just a few of the ways we can focus externally rather than allowing our focus to be on our feelings.

None of these activities is inherently wrong or to be avoided entirely. They are simply some of the many things we can choose to focus on when we need a distraction. But if we frantically focus on the external, moving from one thing to the next without even pausing to slow down and feel, then we're most likely running an HDS strategy.

Sometimes we have done this for so long that is just feels normal. *Of course I'm doing a bunch of stuff. What else am I supposed to do, just sit there and do nothing?*

But if you slow down and become more willing to notice what you are feeling and actually feel it, without running away, something interesting will happen. You'll start to notice the compulsive drive forward and feel the discomfort and tension around it. You may even pause for a moment, or drive somewhere without music and podcasts and talking voices blaring at you. At first, you might feel antsy, bored, or impatient. But what if you didn't impulsively try to get rid of that feeling by ingesting the next piece of stimulus? What if you just took a few breaths, felt your body, and became more aware of what was going on inside of your mind, your body, and your heart?

Super Distracto doesn't want any of this nonsense, so he'll be running overtime to prevent that. With more doing, more activity, and more pleasure comes less feeling, thank you very much.

HEAD GAMES

This strategy is so common and so consistent that it actually becomes a way of life. It makes up how you see yourself and who you think you are. Basically, it involves seeing yourself as residing entirely between your ears, and your body is like an inert sack of potatoes hanging from your head, which is where all the action really happens anyway.

I remember one session with a client named Nick. He had been struggling with self-doubt and social anxiety for most of his life, despite having a family and running a relatively successful business. He was in constant fear of being judged, worried about how people were thinking of him, and whether he was better or worse than others.

He was telling me about a moment when he had felt so nervous about two colleagues who were talking nearby. As usual, he had a hard time being present in the moment because he was analyzing how they might view him, and how he could impress them when he spoke.

In our session, I asked him to pause for a moment, take a breath, and notice where he felt that nervousness, fear, and pressure to impress them.

"Where do you notice that tension or angst in your body?" I asked.

"Uhhh. Hmm. I don't notice anything in my body," he replied.

"Really, nothing? What about in your stomach, your solar plexus, your chest, your neck, your jaw? Can you feel anything in any of those places?"

He paused for a moment, apparently checking. "Mmmm, no. Maybe I feel a little hungry in my stomach. I can't notice anything else."

This man had lived in his head for so long, he could no longer feel his body. My best guess is he retreated to his head to avoid the painful feelings in his body. And after having done that for several decades, he had forgotten how to get back. That, and part of him was really terrified to go back there.

Avoiding the feelings in our bodies is yet another way we can protect feeling so much in our hearts. We retreat to our heads and try to live completely cerebrally. I'll solve the problems, figure out what to do, handle all social situations, even interact with people I love, all through my head. That's the plan anyway. Of course it turns out it doesn't work so well for, you know, life.

As much as we might try to be, we are not completely logical Vulcan-like creatures. We are strongly influenced and impacted by our feelings. We can't think uncomfortable emotions away or banish them by completely focusing on our thoughts. Feelings need attention, presence, and acceptance. This is how they move through us, clearing us out to feel alive, present, and self-confident.

WET BLANKET

This one is a tried and true strategy that people have been using for hundreds, if not thousands of years. It goes something like this: *Don't get too excited. Don't get your hopes up. It won't work out anyway.*

This relationship, this job, this project, your future, anything that matters to you in life—just don't get too excited about it. If you do, you're just setting yourself up for a big fall, which will feel absolutely terrible. Because at the end of the day, people will leave you, things won't work out the way you had hoped, and you'll not only feel that pain, but also the pain of having hoped everything could have work out the way you wanted it to.

No thank you. It's better to just guide your focus away from excitement, optimism, and joy and towards a dismal, bleak future. It's unpleasant and kind of demoralizing, but it's safe.

This is the traditional pessimist's stance. The position of the classic cynic, who may seem tough or like he's made of steel, but underneath he's terrified. He's so scared to open his heart and feel the vulnerable feelings of excitement, joy, and anticipation. He's even more scared to feel loss, sadness, discouragement, or the pain of failure and things not working out exactly as he'd hoped they would. It makes him want to cry.

But he's tough, dammit. So he doesn't cry. And no, he's not scared. He's just skeptical. And he thinks all this positive thinking and self-help stuff is stupid and for mindless people who can't think for themselves. Not him, he's a tough realist. The only one who's not afraid to tell it like it really is.

In reality, he's living with walls around his heart that are so high and so thick that very little love can get in or out. He has chosen safety and certainty over love or anything else for that matter. And his heart is dying as each day passes.

SOCIAL ANXIETY AS A DEFENSE

One of my main specialties is working with clients who experience social anxiety. I've worked with thousands of people over the years, and after I wrote the best-selling book, *The Solution To Social Anxiety,* I came in contact with even more people who wanted my help to break through the fear and shyness that was holding them back.

As I worked with more and more clients, I began to see a fascinating pattern. Everyone was of course dealing with the main challenges of social anxiety—fear of being judged, predicting others would not like them, reluctance to take risks and put themselves out there, and the deep-seated feeling that something was wrong with them and they were somehow unlovable.

The fascinating pattern I discovered was that many of my clients had experiences in their lives when they did, at one point, feel very open, very free, and very loved. It may have been when they were kids, or when they first fell in love as a young adult. And then something happened—their family moved and they had to leave all their friends, they entered middle school and started comparing and criticizing themselves, or their beloved moved away or ended the relationship.

For example, one of my clients moved every two years when he was a kid. Sometimes he made friends at each new school, and sometimes he endured two years of being heavily teased.

Another fell deeply in love when he was twenty years old. He was a lover of life, passionate, and excited about his future. After six months his beloved's parents said she could not date him, because they held traditional Indian values and did not feel he was a good fit for her. To his surprise and dismay, she obeyed her parents and didn't even fight for him.

In response to this pain, they both began to experience social anxiety. They began to fear meeting people, asking potential dating partners out, speaking up in meetings, and connecting with people in general.

It seems that one of their common responses to experiencing pain and loss was to make an unconscious decision that goes something like this: *Wow, opening myself up so wide led me to get hurt really badly. It was so painful to lose my friends, lose my girlfriend or boyfriend, to lose that connection. Opening up and deeply connecting with others is extremely dangerous. I am destined to get hurt if I do. So, from now on, I will avoid doing that.*

Enter social anxiety. It's the perfect Heart Defense Squad maneuver. It casts a deep spell on you, telling you that others won't like you, it won't work out anyway, no one wants to talk with you, no one wants you as a friend, no one wants to date you, no one wants to hear your opinion, and on and on.

And all the while, it's guiding you towards holding more and more of yourself back. Hiding in a shell of protection, away from the chance of getting hurt as a result of connecting with others and the world.

And then, in a final stroke of genius, the social anxiety gives you one major problem about yourself to focus on. *I have this social anxiety problem. It makes me really different and messed up. I can't talk to people or connect with them because I have this social anxiety problem.* And then your mind and energy can be focused on your problem and how different you are. All the while, keeping you safely removed from all real contact with other people.

Pay no attention to the man behind the curtain...

BRING IT ON: LOVING FULLY AND BOLDLY

Despite all the fears, and all the ways we try to avoid pain and emotional discomfort, guess what? You want love. You need it. And so do I. We all do.

So let's talk about how you can have the confidence to face those fears and take that risk. To remove the armor from around your heart, and be willing to open up and fully let love in. Because, as with all things in life, when you face your fear and get to the other side, the rewards are tremendous. And no reward is more valuable, more fulfilling, and more deeply satisfying than love. It's the jackpot.

What Is Love?

"What is love? Baby don't hurt me. Don't hurt me, no more."
- Haddaway

It's a cheesy song, and yes, it's from *A Night At The Roxbury*, which some people consider a classic. And by some people, I mean no one. But it asks a great question: "What is love?" I know, it's a big question and there are a million answers out there - from poets to musicians to hardcore scientists measuring peptide counts. I am just going to provide a simple, clear, relatively unscientific definition here.

Love is something that is felt and expressed. It's something you do, not just something you feel. Feeling is a big part of it. It can feel like a warmth in your chest, excitement in your body, energy, joy, uplifting. It's a sense of "yes" to someone or something. More please.

It can also be felt as an ache in the absence of the person, animal, or place that we love. Longing, pining, or yearning for our beloved. This is part of the feeling of love, too.

Another component of love that is equal to that feeling is the doing, the expressing. In order to fully feel love, we must express it. We must say it, share it, show it. If we don't, it withers and dies inside of us.

Have you ever had the joy of saying "I love you" to someone, and then hearing them respond with "I love you, too"? Not the automatic rote version that you might say with your husband or wife as you leave to go to the cleaners. I'm talking about the moment when you are really feeling it. Really present and aware of what you are saying, and of the depth of the feelings in your heart. In that moment, when your love is received and their love is shared back with you, what happens? The feelings in your heart intensify, don't they? They magnify and become even more powerful.

We can express our love in countless ways. You can tell someone directly that you love them, you can touch them, hug them, hold their hand. You can buy them a gift, surprise them, or write them a heartfelt note. You can listen to them when they're hurting and reassure them when they're scared. You can treat them with kindness and acceptance, even when they make a mistake. You can praise them for their qualities and accomplishments (ladies, we men especially like this last one). This list could go on for twenty pages. The number of ways to express love is endless. The more you do it, the more love you feel. The better your relationships, the better your life.

All the fears we talked about above can get in the way and prevent us from experiencing the feelings of love. Our fear and self-doubt can also significantly block us from expressing love as freely and openly as we truly want to. Let's see how we can free you up to more boldly and openly feel and express love whenever you want.

Expressing Love

How freely can you express love? How boldly do you put it out there? How willing are you to do it again if the first response was not exactly what you wanted?

In my experience, most of us are hesitant and a little scared to express our love. It feels vulnerable, and we could get hurt. So instead we play this game. I call it the Certain Love Game, and it goes something like this: *I'll hang back and wait for you to express love first. Then, when I know it's safe, I'll share too.* Of course, this gets a little problematic if both people are playing the same game.

This hesitation to express love can show up at every level of connection and in all relationships. Because expressing love is not just saying "I love you." It is the expression of any positive energy towards someone. Being attentive, interested, curious and open with someone is expressing love. Giving someone a compliment is a form of expressing love. It might be a less intense dose of love than writing a passionate love letter is, but it is the same kind of energy on a much smaller scale.

So where do you hesitate to express love?

Some people are reluctant to approach people and warmly engage with them. Others hold back and don't give someone a compliment or ask them out when they really want to. You might hesitate to openly share that you are enjoying talking to someone and that you'd love to hang out again, or be friends. You also might avoid sharing what's really going on in your life when someone asks, and instead keep it superficial and change the subject.

All of these examples are actually forms of holding back and not expressing love, because love is nothing more than an exchange of positive energy. And the more we express love, the more we feel love. But often we don't want to do all this because we're afraid we are going to get rejected and that our love won't be received well. Now we're holding back and playing the Certain Love Game. Which might feel safer, but it actually massively restricts the amount of love we can feel. We're determining whether or not we express love based on what we think other people will approve of. We are basing our actions, our expression, and ultimately ourselves on other people, and this never leads to good things.

What if you didn't wait for others' permission or approval? What if you stopped playing the Certain Love Game and just played the I Say And Do Whatever I Want Game? In my experience that one is a hell of a lot more fun. You feel way better about yourself, you enjoy much more love in your life, and people become magnetically drawn to you because you're emitting love, which is what everyone in the world wants deep down to experience more than anything else.

What would this look like? When there is someone you are drawn to, walk over and talk to them. Immediately. Instead of asking yourself these kinds of questions:

Do they want to talk with me?
How will they respond to me?
Will they like me back? (aka is love certain?)

Try asking yourself these kinds of questions:
What do I like about this person?
How can I tell them this?
I wonder who that person is and what they're like?

When I was struggling with social anxiety, if I saw a woman I was attracted to, I would feel more dread and fear than anything else. As I developed the courage and boldness to express love and stopped waiting until I knew it was going to be returned, my internal response changed. It went from *Oh shit!* to *Oooh, who's that?* There was an excitement and a desire to be closer to her.

Then, instead of playing it super cool and never telling anyone what you think and feel about them, why not just say it?

"I noticed you from over there and I had to come talk with you. You are absolutely beautiful. What is your name?"

I would say this kind of thing, with all sincerity, and it was powerful. I wasn't doing it as a pickup line or a tactic to get her into bed. I was expressing love. And here's why it was so powerful—because I was not doing it to get her to like me, I was simply saying what I wanted to say. So, if she responded positively, great! We could now have an even more open and fun conversation. But if she seemed a little tense or nervous, that was okay too. I would even sometimes comment on that and ask her about it.

"Hi Tiffany, my name is Aziz… You seem a little tense. Did my absolutely beautiful comment freak you out a little bit?" I might say with a disarming smile. I was actually curious to find out how she would respond.

Because there was nothing wrong with what I did. Nothing wrong with expressing my love. So often we recoil and shrink back if our love is not met with an immediate, highly positive response. We instantly conclude that our love is bad, and that we are bad and undesirable. Inside we recoil, thinking *my love and attention is unwanted and I am unlovable.*

But this is completely false. It is a horrible misinterpretation of what's actually happening. And when you stop beating yourself up so much and start being on your own side no matter what, you can get more and more curious about what is actually going on. What is really happening here?

Is she scared? Is she afraid I might want something from her? Is she uncomfortable receiving compliments, especially about her appearance? Is she excited about me talking with her and feeling nervous and not wanting to mess it up?

Stop concluding that you know what is happening inside of the minds of others. Start expressing your love more freely and let them have whatever responses and reactions they will. When you are having a great conversation with someone you just met, tell them you're having a great time talking with them!

"This is awesome. I love talking with you Ben, you are hilarious."

Or, "Dude! I really enjoy talking with you. We need to do more of this. I want to be friends."

People can spend their entire lives avoiding saying anything like this. They fear that it sounds desperate, is putting the other person on the spot, or is somehow "too much."

Nope.

That's just the work of stories, fear, and your Safety Police trying to protect you from consistently putting yourself out there and maybe getting rejected. In reality, that kind of honesty is bold, it's courageous, it's loving, it's powerful, and it's awesome.

And when you can do this sort of thing regularly, people will become powerfully drawn to you. They will feel the ease you have with yourself, your comfort with vulnerability, your courage to be real and honest, and they will connect with you instantly. No, not every single person, but many people will. And you don't need every single person in the world to like you - that's an impossible quest anyways.

Bring It On

Have you ever been to the ocean and gone into the water where the waves are crashing? As you walk out into the surf, you have several choices. You can turn your back each time a wave comes, hunker down and protect your chest and stomach. You might get a little less cold, a little less wet. You could actually slowly back your way out into the water, keeping your back to the waves the entire time. Slowly, carefully, safely moving backward, toward the waves.

Or you could turn and face the ocean, face the water, face the waves. You could stand up tall and as a wave comes, let it hit you square in the chest. Thump. Here I am. It might even knock you back a step or two. But there you are, upright, tall, and strong. Looking out into the water, seeing the vast expanse of the ocean as it meets the bright sky. It's magical.

Which one sounds better to you? Which one would you prefer?

We have the same choice when it comes to feeling and expressing love in this life. Do I want to walk facing forward with my chest and stomach open to the world? Able to feel, able to be felt, able to connect, and able to be hit? Or do I want to back my way through life, hunkered down, protecting myself from any sort of discomfort or pain in my heart?

The irony of course is that if you were facing backwards, even if the wave doesn't hit your chest directly, you aren't seeing where you are going. You can't even choose the destination you want to head towards. And, funnier still, you are actually more likely to get knocked over because you can't see the waves coming toward you, so are less able to protect yourself from their influence.

So which will you choose?

I personally prefer to say, "Bring it on." Yes, I can get hurt. Shit, I will get hurt. I will love the hell out of my cat and then he's going to die. I will love my wife and sons so fully and so fiercely that should anything happen to them I will feel such heart-smashing pain that I will barely be able to stand. I will openly express my love to friends, family, clients, and even people I just met, even though it may not be fully received. I will say what I'm really thinking and feeling and reveal who I really am, even if that shows flaws, challenges, weaknesses, or vulnerability. Especially because it shows those things. And sometimes people will judge me. I am going to share what I can with as many people as I can reach and some people will actively dislike me for it. I will get hurt. Yes, all of this is true and inevitable. And, bring it on.

Because what else am I going to do? Eek my way through life, hiding from all pain, suffocating my love, energy and passion so no one dislikes me? I did that for ten years and it was the most painful decade of my life. No thank you, no more. Bring all of it on—the excitement, the unknown, the profound feelings of joy and love, and the pain, heartache, and grief.

Because there is no separating one from the other. You feel love in the same place in your body as you feel grief. If you try not to feel pain or grief in your heart, you will also not feel love. They reside in the exact same location. And I want a life of love, of excitement, of passion, of joy, and of purpose. So bring it the fuck on.

On Vulnerability

We all learned somewhere growing up that we had to be a certain way to be loved. Starting with our moms and dads, we soon discovered there was a right way to act, and a wrong way. As we grow up, we learn that there's actually a right way to be: a right person to be. And if we are that person (or at least appear to be), then we'll receive love and approval.

This person usually possesses qualities like confidence, outspokenness, and experiences no emotional problems that they can't handle completely on their own. They are tough, have it all together, are funny, charming, upbeat, intelligent, kind, generous, and successful. Oh, and they're totally desirable and have lots of sex.

Part of us drives us to be this way and look this way to everyone, believing it's the only way to get and keep love. *No one's going to love you if you are nervous, or dealing with hard feelings, or stingy. So don't be that way, ever. And certainly don't ever show or tell anyone that you are that way. Good God! That would be a mess.*

And so we go through life maintaining our images, wearing our masks. We beat ourselves heavily for not living up to that ideal, with the belief that criticizing, punishing, and berating ourselves will drive us to improve and finally obtain this image and become this perfect person (it doesn't, by the way). And we expend a lot of energy and lose countless hours of worry on whether we appear good enough to others. Whether we pulled off the image and they love us, or whether they saw through the facade and are secretly judging us as the relationship approaches its inevitable end. Because, after they see my weakness and flaws, why on earth would they still want to talk with me?

Have you ever seen the doors that they used to have in old saloons in the Wild West? The two wooden doors that would swing open in the middle as you pushed through, only to swing back to a shut position once you're inside? Each of us has a pair of these doors in front of our hearts (no not anatomically, it's a metaphor, man). And we are choosing throughout the day whether to open those doors or keep them shut.

When they are shut, this is like keeping the mask of perfection on. We don't let anyone in. We don't reveal what's really going on. How was my weekend? Great. How am I doing? Fine. No problems, everything's under control. I'm perfect, remember?

The upside of this approach is that it feels safer. I don't have to reveal anything messy or vulnerable that the other person might judge me for. I don't have to risk them changing their opinion of me or judging me. It's easier and more familiar.

And the downside? Well, what do you think? What have you noticed is the cost of keeping those doors closed?

In my experience the cost was real connection. Deep relationships. Powerful feelings of love and joy. All of those goodies are blocked outside of the saloon doors as well. It also feels profoundly lonely in the saloon now because we don't let anyone fully in. Even if people like us or love us, and even if they tell us so, we still feel lonely.

The saloon doors are closed so that positive energy can't get in. On some level we doubt their love - *They didn't see the real me, they only know my mask.* And if they love the mask, this doesn't do much for us other than offer a few minutes of satisfaction from looking good and being admired.

What if you took the mask off occasionally and started sharing more openly, more honestly? How would your relationships, and your life, be different? Would you have more relationships? Or would you be in a loving romantic relationship?

Many years ago I discovered the link between extraordinary confidence and vulnerability. I saw that the more risks I took to share myself, to face the deep fear of not being enough, of shame, of being exposed and not accepted, the more powerful I would become. Because all fear is the same. When you approach fear and face it, you gain power and it loses its power to hold you back or stop you in any way. My life philosophy was (and still is), "Do what scares you in the service of something greater." And nothing scares me more than being authentic, honest, vulnerable, and real.

After doing this for years, I have some bad news. It always feels uncomfortable. Even though I've done it thousands of times, in friendships, and relationships, and in front of groups of people. It's always a little (or a lot) grindy inside. Part of me resists and freaks out. *Don't share this! Don't say that in front of those people! It makes you look bad! They'll think you're greedy, weak, pathetic, a fraud, a loser, or bad in some way.*

At first, these fears would be enough to get me to keep it all hidden. But not any more. Because I've seen the power of vulnerability. I've seen my friendships, my family life, my relationship with my wife, and my business all transform and flourish through being more and more boldly myself. More importantly, I've felt the profound relief that happens when we share ourselves vulnerably, right in the face of that voice that tells us we're doomed if we do it. And then what happens afterwards is magical. There's a sweaty, tense, awkward few minutes. Sometimes difficult feelings or a challenging discussion might arise. And then comes relief. The deepest relief and relaxation I've ever felt. All my organs that were subtly holding tight without me knowing it, let go. My nervous system realizes it's okay to be me and seems to say, *Whew! Thank God!* as it relaxes and lets go.

And then you can feel a sense of joy and connection that is unparalleled. Because there are no saloon doors blocking your heart anymore, keeping all the good stuff on the outside. You are fully seen and known and loved for it. Not just for your perfection, your image, or your mask. But for who you really are.

Deep down that is what you really want. That's what we all want. And the only way to get there is to be vulnerable. To take the risk of being more real with others. You don't necessarily have to do this with everyone all the time, but strive to be more vulnerable with some people, some of the time. And the more you do this, the more you will see that you are profoundly lovable just as you are. Taking the risks yourself will show you this is true in a way that no words or statements ever could.

Actually, "profoundly lovable" isn't quite accurate. In truth you are neither lovable nor unlovable. You just are. You exist. Is an oak tree lovable or unlovable? The question doesn't really even make sense. It just is. Some people will like the oak tree and others won't but either way it makes no difference to the oak tree's essential being. The oak tree just lives there, doing its thing, regardless of anyone's feelings for it. And the same is true for you.

So you can relax. You can let go. What you were taught is not true. You don't need to be perfect in order to be loved. In fact, it's quite the opposite. If you project perfection, people might be intrigued by or drawn to you at first, but they will soon get frustrated because you don't seem humanly flawed like they know they are. But when they see your struggles, your challenges, and your weak points, others will instantly relate to you. They will feel the same as you, a sense of "we are in this together." And from that sense of togetherness and familiarity comes deep love, connection, and respect.

You are loved. Deeply loved. You just have to let it in.

THE MOST IMPORTANT PERSON TO LOVE

I considered ending this chapter with an impassioned section on bringing it on. I mean, I thought it was really good. I got all fired up. I felt like a deep southern preacher belting it out in the name of the Lord. But as I was dabbing my forehead with a handkerchief afterwards, I realized there was one more thing to share about love. And it might actually be the most important thing of all: loving yourself.

I became obsessed with this topic many years ago when I realized that I lived ninety percent of my life in a state of self-loathing. It was so normal and familiar to me that I actually didn't even realize that's what I was doing. It was just how things were. Until I began reading some books on self-improvement and I realized just how horrible I was to myself in my own head.

That began a serious quest to find out how to actually love myself. Books and programs seemed helpful as I read or listened to them, but I soon found that my inner critic seemed more powerful than I was. And when I went toe-to-toe with him, he always won.

But I continued on my journey, and through the help of countless books, therapy, coaching, a men's group and the most loving wife in the world, I was able to completely transform how I felt about myself.

Now I reside in self-acceptance and self-love about ninety percent of the time. And I'm always curious about how my inner critic devises more clever and sneaky ways to attack me. When I am in one of those states, I notice it immediately and am able to quickly work my way back to being on my own side.

And this, above anything else, is what makes life fun, exciting, and joyful. Because when you are criticizing yourself, attacking yourself, hating yourself, and not loving yourself, life sucks. It doesn't matter what you have, how much money you earn, or even if someone else loves you deeply. If you are not right with yourself, life is not right.

So let's help you get on your own side, once and for all.

Self-Rejection

How Big Is Your Straw?

Each of us has incredible access to the most valuable resource in the world. This is incredible news. It's not money, or oil, or precious jewels. It's love. Love is the primary currency, remember? It's the thing that all humans want beneath everything else, even if they are going after all kinds of crazy things that aren't actually going to bring love into their lives.

But what if I accumulated enough money and oil and wore those precious jewels? Wouldn't that do it?

I'm afraid not. Love is what we want. Love is what we really need. And it is everywhere. In fact, pause for a moment and reflect on this question. Who loves me?

Who are the people in your life who really love you? Friends, a boyfriend or girlfriend, a husband or wife? How about your parents, your children, your grandparents, your aunts, uncles, and cousins? And the people you work with, and those in your community? What about your dog or your cat? Those little guys love people like nobody's business.

There are a lot of people who love you. In this very moment you are deeply loved. You are swimming in an abundance of love. The real question is, how much of that love do you let in?

Each of us has a straw that determines exactly how much love we let in. Imagine an enormous cup filled with your most favorite beverage of all time. It could be filled with anything - deliciously creamy, sweetened iced coffee, Kombucha, or Mountain Dew Code

Red. Whatever it is you crave.

Now imagine you are incredibly thirsty as well, and I mean parched. You've been out working in the yard all morning in the sun, or you've been playing an hour of pickup basketball and you forgot your water bottle at home. And now, here you are, right in front of this unlimited supply of your favorite drink.

Then, instead of drinking directly from the cup, you decide to use a straw. Not just any straw, but one of those super thin coffee stirring straws. You know the ones I'm talking about? So tiny and thin you can barely get anything through them. And no, you can't double them up to be using two at once. Just that one, single, thin, barely-get-any-of-the-drink-I-really-want straw.

Frustrating, huh? It could also be painful, disappointing, and discouraging when we're talking about drinking up love instead of Mountain Dew. And it's all because we chose that shitty little straw. In fact, we thought we had to. We thought, *that's just how things are, how I am, and how it is.* But it's not. And you're not.

You can choose to let in way more love than you can imagine. And yes, it feels better than you can imagine. And the only thing you have to do is get rid of that tiny, limiting straw and just start picking up that cup and drinking big, full, satisfying sips. Mmmm, diet Mountain Dew soda...

What is the straw? Self-Rejection.

Why I Suck, A List

Right now you are limiting the amount of love you let in by how much you reject yourself on a daily basis. You are determining how worthy of love you are and how much love you deserve to receive.

These guidelines are based on nonsense rules you picked up somewhere along the way. *If I perform well and win, then I'm worthy of love and praise. But not too much love and praise though. And if I lose, I'm shit. And I'm not worthy of any love or belonging. I'm a failure and a bad person.*

If you do satisfy the rules and you are able to receive love, you have ways of capping it when it feels like too much. If someone comes up to you after the win and says, "That was amazing. You did an incredible job and I'm so impressed." You might let that praise in and you might enjoy it. If it's above the arbitrary pre-approved limit for love, however, you will deflect it.

Internally you might start to feel incredibly squirrelly and un-comfortable, itching to get away. You may dismiss what they are say-ing in your head. *Oh, it wasn't that great, they are just saying that to be nice.* This one's a doozy because it magically transforms this person's expression of appreciation and love into some weird conde-scending pity, which actually makes you feel less loved. Crazy, huh? Crazy like a fox.

This is all on purpose. It's all by design. You might not have been fully aware of this pattern until this very moment, but it has been serving its function for quite some time, to keep you safe. And to keep those love levels down because too much love equals too much potential pain.

That's why we go around rejecting ourselves all the time. Have you ever stopped to think about why you--and everyone else--do this? We spend huge portions of the day being dissatisfied with and critical of ourselves. *That wasn't good enough, I'll mess that up, I'm too awkward, I'm ugly, look at that gross fat, these clothes don't fit well, they thought I sounded phony, I'm so bad with money, I'm...*

And on and on it goes. All day everyday, like the terrible whirr of a broken fan in an A.C. unit. Absorbing your focus with a shitty list of why you're not good enough, why you suck. All under the guise of self-improvement, of course. *I have to notice my flaws and be hard on myself. It's the only way I'll get better.* (It's not, and it will never work by the way).

Or maybe you're not even using the weak pretense of, "I'm doing this to make myself better." You might just be doing it. You might not even have a good reason or know why you're doing it. It might just be a bad habit that you don't know how to control or stop.

This is how it was for me for years. Virtually every single time I would look in a mirror, I would notice something I didn't like about myself. I'd criticize my face, my eyes, the blemishes on my skin. If I was shirtless I'd criticize my body shape, lack of muscles, or body fat. Every single day, multiple times per day. And that was just my appearance, not to mention my clothes, the way I spoke, how people responded to me, my dating life, and my life in general. These were all fair game, too, in the endless smack down on Aziz. It was terrible. And I thought I was terrible. And it was all horse shit.

STOP THE MADNESS AND START ACCEPTING YOURSELF NOW

How much time do you spend rejecting yourself right now? Do you regularly criticize yourself for falling short, for not being how you "should" be, or somehow not being enough?

Do you criticize yourself for not being successful enough, confident enough, popular enough, talented enough, funny enough, thin enough, muscular enough, or any other "enough?"

And how many times per day would you guess you criticize yourself?

When I was training at Stanford University with David Burns, one of the leading Cognitive Therapists in the world, he suggested I keep track for a few days of exactly how many times I criticized myself.

So I carried a simple 3x5 notecard in my back pocket. Each time I criticized myself, I would pull it out and make a little hatch mark next to the date. It was a little confusing at first. What should I write down if I criticize myself eight times in a row about the same thing? I just decided to make a mark for each critical thing I said to myself. So that would get eight.

At the end of the first day I tallied my numbers up. Whoa. It was high. In the high sixties or low seventies. In one day. And mind you this wasn't some epic day filled with life or death decisions and challenging moments. This was an ordinary, random Tuesday. And guess what? I didn't even catch them all on that note card.

The next day I recorded again and the number was even higher. This is because I started to become more aware and realized I was criticizing myself without even knowing it. Just a shitty habit firing off in the background all day long.

It's a powerful experiment and I highly suggest trying it for a week. It will rapidly boost your self-awareness and help you start to interrupt the pattern of self-attack. It is a great first step in helping you stop the madness and start accepting yourself now.

The next step is to decide here and now that you are done with this nonsense. You are done with this toxic, unhelpful, life destroying habit. Like the smoker who looks down at her last cigarettes in disgust and decides, there and then, never to smoke again. And she does whatever it takes to break the bonds of that nicotine monster's hold on her and from that day forward is a new woman.

You can do that. Right now. You can decide as you are reading this sentence that you will no longer attack, criticize, or reject yourself. Never again. No matter what. I made that decision many years ago, and my life completely transformed as a result.

Does this mean you will never have another self-critical thought again in your life? Absolutely not, that's absurd. We can't possibly control all the thoughts that go through our wacky brains. Have you ever tried? It's crazy-making. In fact, as soon as you make the decision to be on your own side, your critic might beef up his attacks to scare you back into that place of fear and self-doubt. Do not listen to him.

This is about making a claim. Putting your stake in the ground and deciding who you are and what kind of person you want to be. From this place, when you do notice self-attack happening, you will respond to it very differently. You will listen to it, examine it, get curious about what's going on and question it. You'll address it, heal it, calm it, solve it. You are no longer its helpless victim, subject to unending periods of self-hate that you simply allow and tolerate because you think you deserve it. Fuck that. You don't deserve it. No matter what you did or did not do. It's attack. It's verbal abuse. And it's not helpful.

So take a stand. Decide right now to change how you treat yourself. Instead of constantly improving and not having any flaws and only then being okay with yourself, what if you just decided to accept yourself right now, just as you are. Still slightly overweight. Still single. Still in a job you don't love. Still not earning the money you want to —and know you can—earn. Still whatever. Try accepting yourself right now, along with all of those things. Stop saying no to them and fighting them. It's draining the hell out of your energy supply and limiting your resources to go after what you want.

When I notice that I'm attacking myself, I will call myself out. Usually it starts with feeling frustrated, irritated, or impatient. Maybe there's a restlessness or a sinking feeling in my chest. Maybe a fear--*I gotta get more done now or else!*

So I slow down, breathe, and I feel my feelings. *What's really going on? I'm hurting right now, this is a moment of suffering. What am I saying to myself?* Sure enough, when I slow down and pay attention, I can start to hear the cries of the critic in my mind.

You're a bad dad. You should be with your kids more. You're too obsessed with your work.

Client X is not getting the results he wants quickly enough. You suck as a coach. You should be able to make him take action. If you were better you'd know exactly what to say.

That group call wasn't good enough. Everyone in the group doesn't like you. You suck.

Yep. My critic still throws this stuff my way, despite being an amazing, loving and super present father. Despite helping thousands of people improve their lives and getting overwhelming amounts of appreciating and positive feedback for my coaching, groups, programs, etc.

Because it's not about the content of the insults. It's not about what the critic is actually saying. Beware of getting hooked into that and trying to justify or explain yourself to your critic, because it will never be enough. You will never be able to convince or satisfy him.

So instead, when I notice this criticism happening I pause, and take a deep breath in. Then, as I let it out, I say out loud: "This is self-attack and is not helpful. I do not criticize myself."

Then, I work with it. I use one of the dozens of techniques you've learned in this book. I work with the subconscious fears that the self-criticism is trying to protect me from confronting. And believe me, there are always fears underneath. I look at the things that I'm scared to do that my critic is trying to distract me from, or tell me that are not possible. Then I go do those things.

In this way, you end the madness. You stop the rampant, endless, self-hatred. Without taking this stand and working through it, you will never be free. Self-attack does not go away when you reach a certain income or find a spouse. It will never go away until you learn to address it, face it, and dismantle it.

If you would like a wealth of tools, strategies, and exercises to completely neutralize your inner critic once and for all, I highly recommend you get a copy of *The Solution To Social Anxiety*.

When you commit to being on your own side no matter what, when you focus on finding the fear in your body and loving the hell out of it, when you truly want to accept yourself now as you are, then you will be free. Then you will be able to receive and feel all of the love that is already there.

You are deeply loved. You just have to let it in.

Fiercely Loving Yourself

One night we were having a delicious pizza dinner with several close friends and my parents. We had just eaten copious amounts of cheese, our brain's opioid receptors were satisfied and everyone was feeling relaxed.

My wife had just had her birthday earlier that week, and our friends were asking her, "How old are you again?"

She paused for just a moment. I knew she didn't like to say her age, especially with my parents there. She pulled a quick maneuver to buy some time.

"What would you guess?" She said, pausing for just a moment. Then she continued, "What would be the perfect age to keep turning each year? Thirty seven?"

"Whatever age you are." I said, in all seriousness.

Because I believe we all have a responsibility. A responsibility to see through whatever toxic bullshit that we learned from whatever culture we grew up in. I don't care where you are from, your culture has some great qualities that bring out the best in you and some toxic nonsense that makes you hate yourself for being human.

And this was one of the ones that was coming up for my wife: Aging is bad. Especially if you're a woman. You shouldn't age. As you get older you get ugly and undesirable. And it's bad. And love is now unsafe because you're not good enough to keep it anymore because you have wrinkles, or your hair is turning gray.

So what's the underlying message? Don't age.

What the fuck is that all about?

But my wife is courageous and honest like nobody's business, so she told them. "I just turned 43."

And then, they asked me, because I had a birthday coming up in a few weeks. "Aziz, how old will you be turning?" I had to pause for a moment to remember because I generally don't even think about how old I am. It seemed to matter a lot less once I turned 21.

"I'll be turning 33." I replied.

And I knew that one was a doozy for my wife, too. Not only is she aging (which is completely unacceptable, remember?), now she's with a man who's ten years younger. Oh heavens that's even worse!

Later that night we were lying in bed, with our little dude asleep next to us. She was freaking out. So much anxiety, discomfort, and fear. Having supercoach skills helps in situations like this and I helped her get in touch with her body and breath so she could calm down. As she did, we explored what was going on.

Sure enough, there was tons of fear about aging - specifically a fear that she would start looking "too old" and I would want a younger woman. In other words, she would lose my love.

Then there was the fear of what other people might think. They must think it's weird for a man like me to be with a woman ten years older, she thought. He's handsome and successful, he should pick a younger woman. They will think she must have tricked him into being with her. He must have felt sorry for her.

I assured her these fears were crazy-balls nonsense. Who is this "they", and who gives a fuck what anyone thinks about us?

This is where we all have a responsibility. It is our responsibility to see through the toxic cultural demands and resist them. To heal whatever needs to be healed so we can be at peace with aging, with going bald, with whatever is natural, inevitable, and part of being a real human.

Many people hate themselves for aging. They perpetually feel disappointed in their appearance when they look in a mirror. They spend their entire lives resisting this inevitable evolution of their body. They hide it, dye it, treat it, surgery it, whatever it takes to pretend like they aren't getting older. All because they have unconsciously bought into the cultural demand to never age.

If you don't question these demands, you will suffer. Life will be more painful and difficult. And you will feel less joy and love. Your straw will get narrower and narrower. Because these demands result in shame - in you thinking that you're not good enough and not worthy of love. And that's bullshit.

Here are some of the most common false beliefs from American culture, many of which are shared around the globe:

Aging is bad and makes you gross and unattractive.

Money determines your worth. If you earn a lot, you're awesome. If you don't, then you're not man (or woman) enough. You are a loser.

You must be thin if you are a woman.

You must be muscular if you are a man.

You must have a certain shape to your face or body, you must have certain facial features (and not others). You must have blemish free skin and all of your hair.

You must appear confident, strong, and assertive and never anxious or nervous, especially in front of a group. If you are anxious it means you are weak and there is something wrong with you.

Extroverted, outgoing people are better than more quiet, introverted people. You should be more loud and talkative.

If you're a man, you should not cry, especially if others are around. Maybe if someone you loved died you could cry, but only once or twice, and only within a few weeks of the loss.

Do you recognize these? Which ones impact you the most? Are there other ones that are more specific to you that aren't on this list? An essential part of deeply loving yourself and others is letting go of these toxic demands. They are completely unrealistic, and completely inhuman. As in no human can adhere to them.

Notice when you criticize yourself based on one of these beliefs. Notice how commonplace it is for people to disparage themselves or others for not following one of these guidelines. And when you notice yourself using one of these guidelines to criticize yourself, don't buy into it. When someone is joking about how getting older makes you gross, don't play along. Speak up and break free.

I was at a party a while back and someone was talking about their experience at a hot spring. He was saying how there had been a lot of naked people there, but "not the kind of bodies you'd want to see." After he said that, others laughed knowingly. Haha, yeah, ugly and old. Those are the bodies we don't want to see. Real human bodies? No thank you. I only want to look at ultra rare, super fit bodies, so I can continue to hate myself for not looking like that.

I saw a moment to carry out my mission of mass liberation, so I took it. "What do you mean?" I asked in a casual and curious tone. "What kind of bodies?" He paused for a moment and looked at me, hesitating. Perhaps he was unsure of how to answer.

"Just not the kind of bodies you want to look at, you know?" He said with a smile.

"You mean like old bodies, or fat people?" I asked.

"Yeah," he said with a laugh. At this point he seemed a little uncomfortable. Perhaps he didn't want to look like a judgmental jerk. But I didn't see him that way. I was just wanting to call attention to how often we collectively buy into this stuff without even pausing to think about how it's affecting us.

"I don't know," I said, taking an inferior stance so as to not make him feel judged. "I actually like seeing all kinds of different bodies. It reminds me that we all look so different and that there is not one standard way to look." This, then actually lead to a fascinating discussion with him and several others about body image, society, and how we see ourselves.

Seeing With The Eyes Of Love

Several times per year I host live weekend intensives. These are a chance for people to come from all over the world to rapidly break through any self-doubt, social anxiety, or fear that stops them from being the most powerful, successful, and confident versions of themselves they know they can be.

Part of the weekends is always to go out into the real world and practice getting outside of our comfort zones. Because you know me, and you know how I feel about action. During these action periods, people can go out and experiment with talking to others, approaching attractive strangers, and being more authentic and expressive with anyone they wish.

During one of these weekends, I was out with several of the participants, helping guide them to being more expressive, confident and free. One of them became extremely anxious about the idea of starting a conversation with a woman who was sitting and eating lunch in a Whole Foods cafeteria.

So, as any good coach would do, I began to loudly and publicly shame him. "What on earth is wrong with you? What kind of pathetic excuse for a man do you think you are??" Everyone in the entire store stopped and stared, with their eyes popping out and jaws hitting the floor.

I'm kidding. Actually, I encouraged him to have a seat at one of the tables in the dining area. I guided him to his breath and his body. I did the exact same techniques I described above when we discussed how to deal with fear. As he began to calm down, I spontaneously came up with an exercise that I now call, Seeing With The Eyes Of Love.

We were sitting near the checkout area of the store and we could see many of the employees who were checking and bagging groceries. I asked him to look over at a young man who was a cashier in one of the lanes.

"As you sit here and breathe, just let yourself look at him. Notice what he's wearing, how he's moving, how he acts. See if you can see beyond the surface and actually feel what's going on inside him. What do you notice about him? What do you sense?"

My client spent several minutes looking at him, and then said, "I'm not really sure. I notice he has curly hair and that he smiles a lot at the customers."

"Good," I said, encouraging him as he got out of his own head and into the world around him. "Let me share a little more about what I mean. When I look at him, he strikes me as a guy who's really sincere. He wants the customers to feel good, and probably wants them to like him. He seems like he has a really big heart and is really good at loving people."

"Yeah," my client agreed. "I actually see what you're saying. I can see some of those things too. Ok, I get it now."

"What about that woman over there?" I asked as I pointed to a young woman with her middle-aged mother. The young woman was probably about twenty-five years old and significantly overweight.

My client paused and looked at her for several moments. "She seems kind of shy and reserved. Maybe she's been judged a lot in her life for her weight. I bet she criticizes herself a lot for that too."

I thought he was done, but after a quick pause he continued, "She also seems like she has a great sense of humor. Like she could be really playful, too."

"Great," I said. "What do you love about her?"

Without hesitation he replied, "She is strong. She is determined. She doesn't give up."

We sat in silence for a few moments, just breathing and noticing the people around us. Then I asked, "How are you feeling now?"

"Much calmer. I feel way more comfortable and relaxed. I actually feel love for these people."

As I write this, I am actually tearing up. This man had not felt love for strangers in public his entire life. He had only felt fear, criticism, and perceived judgment. Pain. Now something powerful was happening. He was shifting his perspective so he could actually see people around him for what they really were: complex, multi-faceted, deep, beautiful creations with hopes, challenges, desires, pains, and dreams. They all just want to feel loved, to feel happy, and to find a sense of purpose and joy in this life. They are all just doing the best they can with what they've got.

What would your life be like if you approached others with this awareness? What would happen if you could see that attractive stranger, or your intimidating boss in this way? How would you approach the world if you were seeing through the eyes of love?

CHAPTER VIII:

ASKING

"I've never found anybody who didn't want to help me when I asked them for help. Most people never ask, and that's what separates the people who do things from the people who just dream about them. You gotta act. And you gotta be willing to fail. To crash a burn."
- Steve Jobs

I swallowed hard. My throat was a little dry and the sun was beating down on my forehead. I had my thumb out as cars drove by. This was the first time I'd ever hitchhiked.

It wasn't too far of a journey. I just needed to get from one side of the Columbia River to the other. It was a vehicle-only bridge and I was on foot in Hood River, Oregon. *No problem!* I'd thought earlier. *I'll just hitchhike across the river. Who wouldn't want to give me a ride? It's like a three-minute drive.*

After about the 40th car that drove by, I started to question that assumption. *Really? No one wants to pick me up? I'm a clean-cut, responsible looking guy. Are they scared? Indifferent?*

I was surprised by the discomfort that arose as I stood there, getting ignored by car after car. I had no idea that hitchhiking could feel like getting rejected dozens of times. I noticed my mind starting to react as if I were being judged by the drivers of each of the cars that passed.

"Hey, look at that guy standing there with no car, wanting a ride. Yeah, him. What a loser. I don't like him."

As I saw these stories forming in my mind, I smiled. What a great opportunity to bust through a fear I didn't even know I had! I kept at it, and eventually someone did stop to grab me. It took probably sixty cars driving by before one finally stopped.

Later that day I had to get back across the bridge. I wasn't looking forward to the process given my low success rate before. I knew there had to be a better way to do this. And then it hit me - just ask.

Hitchhiking is not asking. Well, it kind of is, in the most passive, easily ignorable kind of way. It's like asking for a raise via email. It's weak and often unsuccessful.

In all areas of life, boldness is rewarded, and cowardice is punished, or at best, ignored. So I decided to ask. This time, I stood on the sidewalk across from where cars were lining up to make a left turn onto the bridge. The drivers were sitting there in their cars and couldn't go anywhere. Most of them had their windows down because it was a hot day.

"Excuse me!" I said in a loud voice to the first car in the line. There was an empty lane in between me and the cars waiting to turn, so I had to make sure they could clearly hear me. The driver was a slightly overweight woman in her thirties. "Can I have a ride across the bridge?"

"No, sorry," she replied apologetically.

"Really? I'm safe, I promise!" I said with my biggest, most charming smile.

"No, sorry," she repeated, looking moderately uncomfortable.

Well, no need to push the issue. I went to the next car and asked them.

"Sorry man, we have two car seats in the back. Otherwise

we would."

"No worries, I totally understand." I replied. Which is true. We currently have two car seats in the back of my wife's car. I wouldn't want some dude back there either.

0 for 2.

I got to the third car. They've seen me ask the last two cars. They know it's coming.

I ask.

The guy nods and in I go.

Three tries. That's it. Versus sixty tries earlier that day. This, my friend, is the power of asking for what you want. Asking boldly, directly, repeatedly. Do this, and you will get everything you want out of life and more.

Ask For What You Want

It might seem obvious, but it's worth saying: when you ask for what you want, you're more likely to get it than if you don't ask.

Let's say you wanted to go on a date with a lovely lady who works down the hall from you. You see her exactly twice per day. Once in the coffee shop on the bottom floor when you're both getting your morning fix (totally coincidentally of course, it's not like you time it that way). And once in the evening on the elevator ride down to the bottom floor. Also a completely random, chance occurrence.

She's a real beauty. Gorgeous long brown hair and bright skin. You know she's intelligent because of the work she does. And her smile and eyes tell you she has a big, kind, loving heart. She would be a fantastic woman to ask out.

Now, imagine it's one month from now, and you still have not asked her out. What is the likelihood that you've been on one (or several) dates?

Zero percent.

Ok, maybe three percent. Maybe you are such a tall, dark and handsome stud that she actually walks up to you one day and asks you out. Or maybe she just happens to be a friend of a friend and they set you up on a blind date. You never know, so we'll give it an outside chance.

If you're reading this and thinking, *geez, I have a three percent chance and I don't have to take any risks or face getting rejected. Those are pretty good odds!* then you may need to revisit the whole first half of this book.

Risk is good, remember? Boldness in life is rewarded. Either in the immediate short term, or in the long term by making you a stronger, more confident, more powerful person.

And three percent is a generous estimate, by the way. I spent years of my life not asking for what I wanted out of fear and the odds of getting dates (or anything else) were much worse.

But let's look at the flip side... If you did take the risk to strike up a conversation with her, and asked her out this month, what is the likelihood you would have one or more dates with her?

42.5%

Actually, I have no idea. How could I? Who knows if she's single or not? Are you her type? How skillful are you at initiating conversations and confidently being yourself around people you find attractive?

All these factors, and many more, will determine your outcome. But I can tell you this with absolute certainty: If you ask her, your odds of getting what you want are astronomically higher than if you don't ask her.

In any area of life, the more you ask, the more you receive. Even if this nice lady said no, if you asked seven other women that month, what do you think the odds of having a date would be?

That's right, much higher. So what do you want to ask for? Who do you want to ask?

Sometimes (but only always), we can have some sticking points or discomfort around asking for what we really want. We'll help you clear those out of the way in just a moment, but first let's actually explore for a moment the places where you could be asking for more, more effectively in your life.

Do you relate to the dating example above? Do you want to ask more people out on dates? Are you in a relationship already? If so, what would you like to ask your partner for? It could be something small, or something big. It could be for more of something, or less of something.

What do you really want to ask him or her? The thing that would be amazing to receive but makes you a little squirmy or vulnerable when you imagine actually asking for it. What about in your social life? If you wanted more friends, more time with those friends, or more things to do, who could you ask and what could you ask them for? Who could you email, call, or text right now?

How about in business and your career? This is a big one. To accelerate your growth in your career, become more of a leader in your field, and double your income, what would you need to ask for? Who would you need to ask it of? If you're in sales, would you need to ask more prospects for the sale? Would you need to ask each person for the sale more times during the conversation? Would you need to ask for bigger sales, bigger accounts, bigger proposals, and ultimately bigger numbers?

Where are these people? How can you find them? Better yet, who could you ask to help you find them?

What could you ask of your co-workers, team members, employees, managers, or bosses?

How are you doing right now? Getting excited? Nervous?

Some people at this point start to actually feel a little tense or uncomfortable. If that's happening, you're in the right place. Even as I'm writing this, I'm thinking about these questions in my own life and I can feel a hot burning sensation in my chest and a slight squeeze in my stomach. Asking for want we want can be scary!

And yet, we can blast right through that fear and reach the other side, feeling powerful, effective, supremely confident, and grateful. We just have to hack down the obstacles obscuring the path to total boldness and confidence.

BLOCKS TO ASKING FOR WHAT YOU WANT

What stops you from asking for what you want? Now that you created that list above, why not simply pick up the phone, or walk down to someone's office, or turn to your sweetie and just ask? Using your newfound powers of self-awareness, what have you discovered? What's getting in the way?

In my experience, it's the same stuff that gets in the way of doing anything - excuses, stories, and fear. Most people, when they imagine asking for what they really want - what they truly want deep down - feel some form of fear. This fear comes out of stories, beliefs, and other things we were taught about asking. Such as, whether asking itself is good or bad, which ways of asking are acceptable and which are unacceptable, bad, and wrong, or what it means about you as a person if you ask. And of course, how others will see you for asking.

Fortunately, these are all just stories and fear. And you know how to uncover the truth, face your fear, and elevate your level of confidence, power, and overall badassery. You've done it before, and healing up our shit about asking for stuff is just another step in the process.

So let's look at the beliefs and stories that get in your way of asking. Think of one thing you came up with above that you would love to receive. If you received it, your life would instantly be so much better. Maybe it was getting more dates with people you're really attracted to, closing more sales, or getting a promotion.

Just pick the one that excites you the most right now in this moment. Good. Now, imagine asking for it. Imagine asking those people out, or asking those people to buy your product or service, or asking your board or managers for more money. Good. As you imagine this, how do you feel? Do you notice some tension, discomfort, or angst somewhere in your body?

Take a moment and just breath and notice those sensations. Feel the center of the discomfort and send it acceptance. Meet it with curiosity. You might even feel some positive anticipation, knowing that you are about to uncover and heal something that will greatly liberate you in your life.

As you notice the fear, worry, or discomfort, ask yourself these questions: *What fears do I have about asking? What am I worried will happen?* Take five minutes and write a list down. Anything you can think of that might be contributing to that discomfort in your body, or that worry in your mind. Go ahead and do that now and I'll see you in five minutes.

So what did you come up with? What are the main fears you have about boldly asking for what you want? What is your top fear? The one that stops you the most frequently? For most people, the number one fear of asking is that they will receive a "no." It's rejection.

Then there's a flurry of other fears that orbit around that major one. Fears about how the other person will respond:

I'm bothering them.
They'll be upset or offended.
They won't like me for asking.
They'll think I'm greedy.
They'll think I'm pushy.
They'll think I'm desperate and needy.

Underneath those specific fears are more general fears about the act of asking itself. These fears involve what kind of person you are for asking, and what is right and wrong. Some of these include:

Asking is bad.

It's wrong to ask.

Asking is demanding.

Asking is being a jerk.

Many of these are subconscious. You might not walk around literally saying these phrases to yourself, but you know they are there when you just feel rotten after asking for something, or about even the idea of asking. This can bring up tremendous amounts of embarrassment or shame. It can also lead us to try to get what we want in much less skillful ways because we think that asking directly is off limits.

For example, I like to receive attention from my wife. I like it when she's interested in what I'm saying and asking me questions about it. She's smart and funny and curious and sweet and gorgeous, so it's pretty much awesome. I used to get as much attention as I wanted, all the time.

Now we have two small children who are both under three years old. It's a mad house. Chaos. They need mom's attention like nobody's business. And sometimes the well is dry. She's sleep deprived and tapped out. So I start sharing something, which is no doubt fascinating, and I'm met with silence and a blank stare. Ugh.

My adult brain knows what's going on. She's giving a ton right now and doesn't have the capacity to pay as much attention to me. It makes sense. My child brain is outraged. *What?? Don't respond to me in the way that I like? Do you know who I am?*

It turns out asking for attention directly is one of the most difficult things I've come across in our relationship. Actually, what I really want sometimes is attention and then acknowledgement or praise. Asking for that is even more cringe-worthy. My mind tells me it makes me sound immature, needy, and pathetic.

For a while this was all happening beneath my conscious awareness, so all I felt was irritated and upset. *God, Candace is so annoying right now. Her responses suck. She's annoying. She doesn't put her dishes away either and I have to do everything around here.*

One day, when I was throwing an inner tantrum, I sat down and had a conversation with this part of myself. After we cleared the first layer of superficial complaints, my inner self kept repeating, *she pays too much attention to the house remodel. It's all she talks about.*

Ahh, there we go. I asked him, *"What should she be paying attention to?"*

"Me!" Obviously.

Before I knew all this, I couldn't ask for it directly. I just felt hurt, ignored, and full of blame. So my highly effective strategy was to just act irritable and pouty, sometimes making comments about having to clean up the dishes. Nice. When we can't ask for what we want, we carry out shitty strategies to try to get what we want instead. As if my being pouty is going to cause Candace to say, "You know what? I've decided to talk about the house less and just pay attention to you my love."

Remember the odds for getting what you want without asking? Three percent at best.

So once I discovered all this, I knew what I had to do - ask! Now there are two ways to ask for what you want. Actually there are probably two thousand ways, but for now I'm going to mention two. You can ask skillfully or unskillfully. We'll discuss this more later in this chapter, but for now all you need to know is this: vulnerable and authentic is skillful; demanding and accusing is less so (but it's a hell of a lot easier and safer).

As I looked back over the last months I realized I had occasionally asked my wife for what I wanted. Well, sort of. I would say, "I feel unappreciated." How's that for vague? Translation: You aren't appreciating me enough. You should appreciate me more. That's pretty indirect, and a little on the demanding/accusing side. Of course, she would feel hurt and want to point out the half dozen ways she had appreciated me that week. It's easy to tell if you asked skillfully or not. If shit breaks down into an argument or completely missing the mark, then you probably asked in a less than optimal way.

So, I decided to try a different approach. I was just honest and vulnerable. I told her how much I loved receiving her attention and that I really missed getting all of it. I also told her how much I love it when she acknowledges and praises me. I even told her about how I feel really uncomfortable about asking directly because part of me judges it as weak and needy.

That was much more skillful. Uncomfortable as shit, and super vulnerable, but highly effective. How do you think she responded? By telling me to "man up and grow pair." No, I'm kidding. She was extremely sweet and loving. She didn't feel accused at all (because I was no longer accusing her). She spontaneously wanted to share things she appreciated about me (because I was no longer demanding it).

Our beliefs about asking for what we want can be submerged in shame. I think this shame accumulates from all the times we said what we wanted as kids and were met with disapproval, frustration, anger, and the message, "Shut up, you're bad." Somewhere in our nervous systems, we've stored all the pain of these responses. And we try to avoid that pain by avoiding admitting what we really want and asking for it directly. Instead, we stay locked in stories about our spouses, our jobs, our bosses, and every other aspect of life. We focus on what they won't give us, and what is wrong with him or her. Blaming feels so much safer.

So many people live with this philosophy: *I shouldn't need to ask for what I want. If my partner really loved me, he'd do the thing I want him to do. If he hasn't done it yet (without me asking), it means he doesn't want to. And besides, if I ask him and he does it, it won't mean as much because I had to ask him.*

Sound familiar?

As Walter from *The Big Lebowski* would say, "You're entering a world of pain." As righteous and seemingly airtight as this philosophy is, it brings nothing but pain to your life. It is also a tough exterior hiding cowardice: utter fear of the vulnerability of asking. If you are living this right now, it's time to break free.

It's okay to ask for what you want. There's nothing wrong for wanting things that someone else hasn't given you yet. You're not bad, and neither are they. All you need to do is ask. And if you can ask boldly, even better.

Bold Requests

Your life is shaped by the decisions you make on a daily basis. Sometimes the small decisions steer the way, like choosing what to eat for dinner or where to go on vacation. Sometimes the entire course of your life changes in a moment when you make a big decision - to move, to get married, to break up, to go all in on a business venture.

Requests have a similar impact on your life. What you ask for each day determines the quality of your life. And the big requests, the bold requests, create opportunities and successes that may have always seemed impossible. Almost every highly successful person has at least one story of making that bold request. And usually they have many more than one.

Apple co-founder Steve Jobs tells a story about how he wanted to build a frequency counter when he was twelve years old. As an eighth grader with no equipment he needed some help. So he picked up the Palo Alto phone book and found the number for Bill Hewlett, the CEO of Hewlett-Packard.

Steve chatted on the phone with Mr. Hewlett for twenty minutes, who decided to give Steve the parts and offered him a summer job at HP. When asked about this experience, Steve Jobs said, "Most people don't get those experiences because they never ask. Sometimes that's what separates the people who do things from the people who just dream about them."

Anthony Robbins, the self-help stud, and founder of the church of the entrepreneur, was known for similar wacky levels of boldness as a kid. He loved playing baseball and had a vision of being a professional athlete. But by the ninth grade it was clear that this was not his path. So he decided to be a sports journalist instead. Instead of writing about his high school teams, though, he sought out sports celebrities who were in town. He called them and asked for interviews, landing one with Howard Cosell, a famous sports journalist at the time. Tony recorded the interview and was able to get a job writing for the sports section of his local city newspaper as a result. At fifteen years old he did this. Wow.

When I heard stories like these years ago, my first reaction was, *What the fuck? Who thinks to do this stuff when they're twelve or fourteen years old?* I wish I'd been that badass as a kid. Instead I was hunched over a table playing *Magic, The Gathering,* and praying I would draw a red manna before I died in two turns.

My next question was, *Am I doing that now? Am I asking for big things?* What would that look like if I did? What would my bold, outlandish requests be? What would your outlandish requests be?

We are so usually heavily self-policed, so polite, and so fearful of being inappropriate, that we just assume that everything we want is out of line and out of reach. But the people who don't buy into that assumption are the ones who profoundly impact the world. Thank you Steve and Tony for being ballsy mofos. I know my life is better as a result. And so are millions of others.

Of course, not all requests are equal. Some are small and easy, while others are big, scary, and bold. Let's look at the different levels of requests we can make, and how to use these to open doors, break through limitations, and create amazing lives.

BOLDNESS-O-METER

There are four levels of boldness in our requests. The lowest level is when we just don't make any requests. We're scared to ask for anything and we live under the thumb of our fear, so we just remain static. We take what life gives us, and then we complain about it. We don't even think to ask because it's wrong, they'll say no, it won't work out anyway, and so on. This kind of life is safe, stagnant, repetitive, gray.

The second level of boldness involves making some requests, but only when you are entirely certain things are going to go your way. You ask that person out after their friend told you that they think you're cute. You apply for the new position only when you are one hundred percent positive that you'll get it. This level of boldness gets better results than Level 1, but not by much. Besides, how often are things in life totally certain? Can you really wait for that perfect confluence of circumstances to do what you want?

The third level of boldness is when you start to come alive. It's when your power, energy, and vitality get activated. It's where you discover your purpose and sense of meaning in this world. It's where you make requests even when you have no idea what the outcome will be. There is risk in this, and that's how you know it is the right choice. You have no idea if someone will say yes or no or storm away in a huff. They might not like the request, resent you, or even find it offensive. Or they may not care one way or the other. At this level of boldness you are exposed to a lot more rejection and a lot more "nos." You also get what you want at an incredibly accelerated rate, more than the vast majority of people. Why? Because you're in the top ten percent; you're asking when others won't.

The fourth level is the icing on the cake. If you spend most of your time regularly making Level 3 bold requests, your life will be awesome. But when you make the Level 4 requests, your life gains a quality of magic and wonder to it. This is when we make our boldest requests even though every part of our being is telling us they won't work out. This is the long shot, the stretch, the dream. The thing we just have to go for, even though it probably won't happen anyways. The vast majority of the time your predictions are accurate, and you don't get what you want. But sometimes... Sometimes they hit...

When I first met Candace, she was married and owned a gorgeous home in the forest outside of downtown Portland. She had a successful career, a thriving social life, and what looked to be a great marriage. After my first extended conversation with her, which lasted two hours, I was in love. I remember coming home to tell my housemate, "I met the most incredible woman! She's everything I could want. I'm in love!"

My housemate, who'd seen me bumble my way through several failed relationships, was ecstatic. "Yay!" she exclaimed, throwing her arms above her head.

"But she's married," I said, slumping my shoulders.

"No!" she said with equal enthusiasm, slowly lowering her arms.

Since it was a Level 4 long shot, and I wasn't too eager to break up a marriage, I decided to let it go. Fortunately, I saw her regularly because she taught personal development workshops that I attended. I kept some distance, but my love for her continued to grow. She was kind, sweet, and funny. She was extremely skilled at communication and highly self-aware. And my lord was she sexy. Torture.

It got so uncomfortable, I decided to take a break from being near her. I took about two months off, during which time I didn't show up to any workshops or evening events she led. I buried myself in studying for my board exams. I tried to forget about her. But as soon as I finished the exams, I couldn't help but think of her again. And again, and again. I decided to take action.

At the next workshop she facilitated, a workshop about being fully authentic and honest, ironically enough, I was encouraged by several participants to reveal how I felt. How utterly terrifying. What terrible advice. I was convinced that if I revealed my web of infatuated feelings that Candace would be repulsed, and her husband would find me and punch me in the stomach. From there things wouldn't go well. After all, I'd only been in one fight in my life. It was in the fourth grade against a kid named Marius, and I resorted to scratching at his eyes.

But, fuck it, I thought, *I'm going to die anyways, so I might as well go after what I want.* So I told her. I told her everything. Well, mostly everything. I told her I felt uncomfortable around her because I wanted her so much. I told her I thought she was the most caring, loving, kind person I'd ever met. I told her she was hilarious and I'd never met a woman who could make me laugh so much. I told her she had a hot ass. (Yes, I went there.)

And then I sat back, bracing myself for the inevitable rejection and subsequent gut punch from the husband.

But that never happened. Funny how our minds can predict something with such certainty, and still be completely wrong. She seemed genuinely moved by my passionate expression. She seemed intrigued. She seemed drawn towards me. Behind the scenes in her relationship, she had been struggling for quite some time to make things better with her husband and she was fed up. She was ready for a big change.

Who knows what will happen when you go after that long shot? This is a success story, and I never would have the amazing relationship I have now without my Level 4 boldness. Sure most of the time, you won't get what you request, but you'll be no worse off for trying. In fact, the act of trying and failing actually strengthens you. It builds your resilience, your courage, and your power. It transforms your identity from the person who plays it safe on the sidelines to someone who's in the arena, fully alive in the adventure of life. So, in truth this type of boldness is always a win, even if we don't immediately get what we want.

Now let's take a moment to look at your life. What are some Level 3 boldness requests you could make in your life? When you think of your work, what would it be? What bold request could you make to advance your career, expand your opportunities, and accelerate your growth (and possibly your income)? What about in your personal life? Your romantic life? Who would you approach? How would you interact with others? What kinds of requests could you make?

And what about the Level 4 requests? What could those be for you? Think big, think outlandish, think unreasonable. What is the most absolutely amazing thing that could happen? The one that would blow your mind and have you shake your head in wonder each time you thought about it. That one. That's the one to go for.

When your center of gravity is at Level 3, your life will flourish. Your confidence will continue to grow because making those requests builds that confidence. You will stand out to others because of your boldness and willingness to go after what you want. And you will receive more than you could ever imagine from the world around you.

How To Ask For What You Want

I taught a few courses at a university when I was fresh out of my graduate school training. It was a great place for me to get teaching experience and overcome my fears about being in front of a group for extended periods of time.

One exercise I would have the students do was around interdependence. I would write "dependent" on one side of the board and draw a circle around it. Then I'd ask them to shout out whatever they associated with that word. Common responses were these: weak, needy, children, incapable, lazy, slacker, helpless, sick, old, and a host of other mostly negative associations.

After that, I'd walk to the other side of the big white board and write out the word "independent" and circle it. As they shouted out their associations to this word, it often included things like: strong, capable, attractive, leader, free, intelligent, likable, and many other generally positive terms.

Most of us, especially if we were raised in Western culture and in the United States, perceive independence as desirable. Being dependent is seen as weak and unattractive and so we strive to not be that way in the least.

However, we are all extremely dependent on so many things to survive. We are dependent on farmers to grow our food, truckers to deliver that food daily, and our local stores to house it and sell it to us. We are dependent on water coming in through our faucet and all the people that make that possible. We are dependent on our garbage and sewage services.

This last week the furnace broke in the house we live in. It was below freezing outside and the house got cold pretty quickly. We are dependent on people who make furnaces and people who can repair them. We are highly connected, highly supported, and highly dependent upon so many other people. To pretend we are "completely independent,"–a rugged individual who needs no one–is completely absurd. We all need stuff and we all need each other.

In addition to all of the survival necessities such as food and shelter, we also need things from our connections with others. Here is a brief list of the things we need, but would rather not admit to:

Love

It's the primary human need. Underneath most of our actions is a drive to gain love or prevent the loss of love. Romantic love, familial love, and friendship are all forms of love we crave, need, and want. When we're missing love in one of those areas, life feels diminished in some way.

Attention

When my brother and I were kids and we stayed at a hotel with a pool, it was a big deal. In addition to swimming races, Marco Polo, and the "who can hold their breath underwater longest" game, there was always lots of "Mom! Watch me jump into the pool. Mom! Watch this."

We all want this kind of attention. Watch me, notice me, see me doing what I'm doing. This doesn't go away once we grow up, it just goes underground and becomes more subtle. Even those who hate being the center of attention secretly want positive attention, they just have so many self-judgments that the experience of being noticed becomes highly unpleasant.

Acknowledgement

We don't just want attention, we also want to be acknowledged. We want people to see what we're doing and appreciate all we go through. We want to be acknowledged for our efforts, our attempts, and our service. We want to be acknowledged for how hard we work, how difficult something in our lives is, and how good of a person we are.

Praise

We want to be approved of and admired. We want people to tell us what we're doing well, and how awesome we are. We want our strengths and our gifts to be noticed and commented on. We want our actions to be praised, as well as our character.

Autonomy

We want a sense of freedom and choice. Especially in intimate relationships, we want to be able to sometimes do our own thing, say no to what we don't want, and be the one to make the choice. We also want this autonomy in our work life. We want to be given free reign to do it our way, to guide our own choices.

Touch

We all need touch, and lots of it. Probably a lot more than you're getting now. Primates spend hours per day grooming each other. Most humans are starved for touch, and many people have hang-ups and old wounds that make them uncomfortable giving or receiving touch. Underneath any learned discomfort, there is a deep desire to touch and be touched. This includes sexual touch, but also cuddling, physical play, holding hands, hugging, and a good old fashioned pat on the back.

Help

This one often gets a bad rap because it can easily be viewed as that wretched dependence that we're all trying so hard to avoid. But we all need it, more often than we admit. We need help learning tasks at a new job, we need help figuring out how to open that file on our computer, we need help getting into better physical shape, we need help taking care of our two young kids. We need tons of help, all the time.

Many people have a terrible aversion to asking for help, and receiving it. They fear it makes them look weak, needy, and somehow inadequate. They might also feel angry and bolster their injured pride by responding with, "How dare you take pity on me! I don't need your charity." This perception of help is extremely limiting and often leads to problems in professional and intimate relationships.

So we have all of these things we need, but perceive as unacceptable, shameful, or otherwise not ideal to reveal. Best to keep them hidden and just figure it out for myself. But "figuring it out" really means, "How can I get what I want without asking for it?" This approach, which is what many people do, is a mess. It leads to poor results and all kinds of relationship drama. In order to thrive in life, to live with extraordinary confidence, you must get over your fears about asking for what you want. You must learn how to be what Dan Wile calls "skillfully dependent."

7 Ways To Skillfully Ask For What You Want

Not asking for what you want and assuming others will read your mind and give it to you doesn't work. Withdrawing, giving them the silent treatment, or angrily demanding it also doesn't work. In fact, most ways people ask for things doesn't work out so well because they have so much shame about asking in the first place that they have to take all these wacky indirect routes.

The first step in skillfully asking for what you want is to simply decide, right now, that you give yourself permission to ask for want you want. That it is ok. In fact, it's better than ok: it's absolutely essential. And that the more you do it, the more people will respect you, and the more you will regularly get what you need from your relationships.

Here are seven ways to become more skillful in asking for what you want. Each is contrasted with its opposite - the unskillful way of asking. This will help you identify what you are doing that is effective and what could use improvement to get better results.

Bold Versus Timid

Regardless of the words you use, your attitude, energy, and vocal tone convey the majority of your message. With asking, as in all things in life, boldness is rewarded.

Think about a situation where you are naturally bold. Perhaps it's around a certain friend; when the two of you get together you're quick to make jokes and laugh, and there's a lightness in your step. Maybe it's when you power up your computer and sit down to play your favorite game; you know you're going to crush your opponents because you're awesome. When you are feeling bold, what are you like?

Most likely you speak louder, stand taller, make longer eye contact, smile and laugh more, speak your mind, and don't worry so much about what responses you'll receive. This is the exact energy you want to bring to your requests. Just put it out there boldly. Don't overthink it, question your wording 50,000 times, or hesitate so long that the moment passes and you miss your opportunity. Just fucking say it. Blurt it out so that you can't go back and you have to work with whatever happens next.

This is very different from the timid approach in which your voice hushes to a whisper, your shoulders hunch, and your eyes dart back and forth like an anxious rabbit on amphetamines. You approach the situation like you're doing something wrong, bracing for your audience to dislike you and maybe even lash out at you. This creates a confusing and uncomfortable energy that people often respond to by wanting to get away from you. And if they want to get away, they're probably less likely to hear your request and say yes, right?

So chuck the timid approach and be bold. The only one who sees what you're doing as bad is you. Step up and ask for what you want. The bolder, the better.

DIRECT VERSUS INDIRECT

When you ask for what you want, it is most skillful and effective to make your request simple, clear, and direct. In an attempt to minimize our fear and our chance of rejection, we can sometimes use way too many words when asking. Explaining why you're asking, sharing why it's okay for them to say no, and giving way too long of a backstory are all ways we water down our requests. We do this because we still feel on some level that asking for what we want is bad or wrong and is going to create upset. So we feel the need to justify why we're doing it. Stop it. You don't need to.

You just need to ask. Take a second before the interaction to reflect on exactly what you want. If you could wave a magic wand and get your exact wish granted, what would it be? How could you ask for this in the least amount of words possible? Is any backstory necessary? Sometimes it is important to explain, and that's okay- just make sure this is one of those times. Be sure it's consciously chosen and designed to be more effective, instead of fear-based.

Let's look at a few examples to make this distinction very clear. Let's say you're at a new job and you are figuring out all your tasks. You've been there for a few weeks now, and part of your mind is telling you, "You should know this by now." But instead of being timid and hiding in your office, you decide to be bold and ask someone for the help you need to excel in your new position.

So you go find Larry down the hall, who is a whiz with the computer system. Here's what you might say if you were taking the indirect approach.

"Hey Larry, when you have a minute I have a question for you about the computer system."

So far so good. He says yes and you're ready to go.

"I was on a call with one of the New York accounts I was assigned. They need to update their priority status and receive their items sooner. They seemed pretty urgent about it. I tried to enter the new shipment date and expedite their order, but the system gave me an error that said I wasn't authorized to do that. I know you showed me how to change things in the system before, but I can't remember where the priority section is. How do I do it?"

This is a very common style of indirect asking. It's so wordy and long, and full of unnecessary information. Why does he need to know all that? So he sees that you have a legitimate reason to ask for help, that you already tried yourself so you're not lazy, and that you almost remembered so you're pretty smart? Stop all the impression management! Just ask the dude the question.

"I want to update the priority status for an account's order so they can get their shipment sooner. Can you show me how to do that?"

Bam. Simple. Clean. Fast and effective. And Larry is much less bogged down with confusing and irrelevant information. The more direct you can be, the more powerful your request, and the more likely you are to get what you want.

Requesting Versus Demanding

Most people struggling with confidence and social anxiety tend to veer toward the more passive and "nice guy" (or "nice girl") end of the spectrum. This means many years and many relationships of not asking for what you want. This leads to a slush fund of pent up frustration and anger. That's why many nice people who tend to want to be really good and polite and perfect tend to have lots of physical pain and health problems. Rage stuffed down in the body.

So when we do finally ask for what we want, sometimes we can have an edge to our tone. We can unconsciously think, *I've compromised so many times already, this time you will give me what I want!* We also have the assumption that if we work up the courage to finally ask, then we should be rewarded just for asking. None of this is true or how it really works, though.

The reality is, when we demand something and have a tone of expectation and our request is tainted with "You owe this to me," people often respond by not wanting to give us the thing we want. It just seems to be how humans work.

Instead, we want to realize that when we ask for something we are making a request. The other person has the right to say no. In fact, it's better they do if that's what they want to do. Because then we can say no when we want to, and your relationship is based on choice rather than fear and obligation.

Keep in mind that just because you ask, doesn't mean you'll receive. And if you get a no, you can ask again or make your case. If the answer is still no, keep in mind you can always find other ways to meet your needs, and that a no might not be permanent.

GIVING VERSUS GETTING

With a chapter focused on asking for what you want, it seems like the focus is on getting. And that's where many of us are focused: on what we can get from others. But the more focused on getting we are, the less we typically receive.

In any relationship, whether it's a friendship, a sales relationship, or a romantic connection, the more we can give, the more we will receive in return. This doesn't mean we have to be the martyr and selflessly give without ever expressing our own desires and asking for them to be met. It just means that if we are focused on meeting the needs of those close to us, they will be more likely to do the same with us.

This is especially true and essential to realize in an intimate relationship. If you are keeping track and waiting around to give only once your partner has given enough to you first, then you are probably going to suffer (or are already) in your relationship. When we are able to regularly meet the needs of our partner, and become skilled at doing so, we will receive so much more in return. And, when you ask in those circumstances, your partner often gives more freely, because their tank is so full.

In any area of your life, two extremely powerful questions you can ask yourself regularly are these:

"What does this person need right now?" and "How can I add value?"

These are so powerful because they guide your mind to focus on what you can give, rather than on what you can get. As you do this more, you will find that you receive more than you might imagine.

Assume Yes Versus Assume No

While demanding and focusing solely on what we can get aren't very skillful and don't usually lead to what you want, there are better alternatives. In fact, here are two ways we can ask that make our requests harder to refuse.

The first one is assuming we are going to get a yes. An attitude of, "Of course you'll say yes. This is a completely reasonable request." With a cheerful, upbeat attitude of collaboration, you ask for what you want.

This is powerful and effective for several reasons. First, your certainty and comfort impacts the other person on a subconscious level.

It makes them more comfortable with the whole process. Additionally, many people are not sure where they stand on many things. They are frequently looking outside of themselves for guidance, certainty, and assurance of what the "right thing" to do is. When you provide that relaxed assurance, it makes it easy for them to say yes.

Furthermore, when you assume a yes, you are not bracing yourself for rejection. When we assume the response will be no, our body and face tighten up, our voice becomes more constricted, and what we might say and do is limited. This fear and bracing make us less dynamic, charismatic and magnetic to others. When we let that fear go and just assume most people will say yes, and that if they say no it's okay, our energy is much more relaxed and open. This allows our light to shine, and many more people will happily extend a hand to help you on your path.

ENTITLED VERSUS APOLOGETIC

The second subtle attitude shift that increases your likelihood of getting a yes when you ask for what you want is to be slightly entitled.

Now I know I said earlier that demanding often backfires, but this is a different kind of entitled. This isn't, "I'm entitled to get what I want and you better say yes to me." This is more about being entitled to make a request in the first place.

This attitude is designed to remove any hesitation or discomfort about making the request. It's the stance of, "Of course I can ask for what I want. There's nothing wrong with asking. The worst someone can do is say no." As you become more comfortable and entitled to asking, you won't have so much fear and angst about it. This will reduce mixed messages and make your requests significantly more powerful.

The opposite attitude is one of apology. In the example above about the new job, many people would start their request with, "Hey

Larry. I'm so sorry to bother you, but..." So apologetic. Why are you so sorry? Why are you assuming you're bothering him? Hell, by saying it now you are implanting the suggestion in his mind that you are a bother. Why assume that in the first place? Maybe you're fun to interact with. Maybe you're a refreshing break from his tasks and he gets to feel a sense of contribution and accomplishment after helping you. He gets to feel smart.

Just leave the apology part out. You are not doing anything bad by asking. We have so much bad programming about asking to let go of. Just start doing it. You are entitled to ask for what you want, in all your relationships, with all people. Even if they get upset at first. Don't stop. Keep asking, and you will gain more comfort, more confidence, and your relationships will transform.

VULNERABLE VERSUS ARMORED

This one is big. It might be the most important distinction of all when it comes to asking skillfully, because the skill of vulnerability is often the hardest and most uncomfortable skill to learn. It's the one that most people avoid because it's messy, unclear, and feels so damn, well, vulnerable.

But if you want to have a thriving, life-long, passionate relationship with your wife or husband, this skill is essential. If you want to have deep friendships and close connections with family, you must face the discomfort. It's even essential if you want to excel in business and become a leader in your career. In any area of life, vulnerability is going to be what gives us the edge.

To ask for the thing we really need or want, that is usually a very vulnerable place to be. The underlying needs are generally tender, make you seem less strong, and sometimes can be deemed unacceptable. These are needs like all the stuff we talked about earlier: attention, love, praise, touch, acknowledgement. This kind of asking requires that we reveal the vulnerable fear or desire underneath, instead of just showing the hard, upset or tough exterior.

Most people make requests in an armored fashion. They reveal little of their underlying need or discomfort. Or if they do reveal their challenges, they're hidden behind layers of sounding angry or tough.

Armored Request: "You talk about the house too much."
Vulnerable Translation: "I miss your attention. I want you to pay attention to me."

Armored: "You work too much."
Translation: "I miss you so much. I feel rejected when you focus on work, and eventually I want to withdraw and reject you, but I'm secretly hoping it will make you come around and dote affection on me."

Armored: "We don't need stuff like that."
Translation: "I'm worried about money, and I also feel like I should be able to provide and not have to worry about money at all. When I fall short of this I feel like a failure."

Armored: "You just go on and on at parties."
Translation: "I feel shy at parties and you are really outgoing. I feel jealous and inferior, and embarrassed about how nervous I get. I wish you wanted to spend more time with me at the party so I didn't have to meet new people."

What are you noticing about the difference between being armored and being vulnerable in your requests?

First off, armored requests often don't sound like asking at all. Instead they appear as statements, observations, or criticisms. The underlying strategy is: You didn't do what I wanted you to do, so I'm going to criticize you and this will make you do it the way I want next time (without me having to ask).

Secondly, do you notice how short the armored requests are? They reveal almost nothing about the person speaking them. Hence, the word "armored". When armored, we can attempt to fulfill the goal of the Safety Police—to get what we want, including safety and love—without ever being vulnerable or experiencing pain.

There is a huge industry built on this premise, with people buying millions of dollars worth of books and training programs, teaching them how to "get the girl into bed" or "get the guy to put the ring on your finger" without having to be real or vulnerable. Just follow this system and script and you can stay in control and get the result you want without any risk of feeling pain. It's not real and it doesn't actually create healthy, lasting relationships, but it sure does sell. Why? Because so many people fear this kind of vulnerability.

But if we really want a life of extraordinary confidence, with rewards of deep friendship and connection, passion and purpose, and a lifelong relationship that keeps getting better, then we must master the art of vulnerability. Or at least get into the waters of vulnerability and flail around. You don't have to be that good at it for it to work incredibly well.

Notice how the vulnerable translations all revealed underlying feelings. Feelings that might not make you look great, like jealousy, anxiety, or inferiority. These are the ones we find most shameful or embarrassing and these are the ones we want to keep hidden.

We fear that if we reveal them, the other person will be completely turned off by our weakness, our neediness. They will see our imperfection and lose interest in being our friend, or no longer see us a lover or a desirable partner.

This, like all limiting beliefs, is actually the exact opposite of the truth. In reality, the more authentically and vulnerably we can reveal our underlying feelings, the more people are drawn to us. They respect the courage and confidence it takes to do something like that. And they feel a deep sense of love and connection with us because on some level they feel all of those feelings at times as well. They relate to your humanity and feel moved by it.

YOU WON'T GET WHAT YOU DON'T ASK FOR

This might seem pretty obvious, but we often don't operate as if it were true. Instead, we hint, we wait, we hope, we secretly get upset, we go quiet, we withdraw, and we sometimes punish the other person, hoping these approaches will somehow get us what we want. But they won't. And they suck.

Amira, a client of mine, was working with me to overcome decades of unassertiveness, self-doubt, and low confidence. As I helped her overcome her fears and become more outspoken in her work and with her friends, she grew in confidence. However, interacting with her mother was her biggest challenge: the area where she found it most difficult to be assertive. This is often the case. Assertiveness with family, especially parents, is often the top of the mountain, and something we are always working to become more skillful at.

She was telling me about a situation in which she was driving with her mother after a family dinner. Her mother was going on and on about her worries and concerns about each family member, which was her pastime. Amira was frustrated with the topic and preferred to discuss other things, but she rarely brought up things to talk about with her mother.

"Why not?" I asked during one of our phone sessions.

"Because whenever I bring something up, my mother criticizes me, or tells me to do it differently, or somehow makes me feel bad," she replied.

"I can see why you prefer to remain quiet," I said. Then I asked a question I love to ask. Because we're always so focused on what we don't like and what we don't want, we rarely stop to think about the opposite. So I asked her, "Amira, what *do* you want your mother to do when you share something you'd like to talk about?"

"Hmm," she paused as she really considered the question. "I want her to support me. To be curious and ask me questions. To listen to me and tell me that I'm doing a good job instead of pointing out all my mistakes."

She couldn't help but slip a little bit of what she didn't want in there, but that was fine. There was a ton of good stuff there.

"Great!" I said. "Could you ask her for that?"

She laughed. "No! I could never do that."

"Why not?" I asked.

"Because it would be so uncomfortable. And I don't know if she'd do it," she replied immediately.

Over years of doing this work, I've notice that people tend to answer faster when we get closer to them doing something they've never done before. Their safety police kicks into a higher gear and their answers become more frantic, defended, or otherwise focused on NOT doing the new and scary thing.

But I had an ace in my sleeve. Amira had mentioned in a previous session that her sister was much more assertive with everyone, including their mother. So I steered in that direction.

"How does your mother respond when your sister brings things up? Does she criticize her and tell her what she's doing wrong?"

"No," Amira replied. "She's different with my sister. Actually I asked my sister about this once. She said that mom does start by criticizing her, but my sister doesn't stop. Instead she tells mom what she wants. She'll say things like 'tell me I'm doing ok,' or 'can you tell me I'm a good person?'"

"Wow," I exclaimed. "That sounds pretty assertive. Does it work?"

"Yes, it does! I don't know how she does it. But my mother treats her differently. She doesn't even have to ask as much now."

"So she's trained your mother on how she wants to be treated," I observed. "Seems like you have a proven road map of what could help you get what you want."

Then, of course, we uncovered massive fear about asking her mother so vulnerably. We explored the times in the past when her mother couldn't give her what she wanted, and the pain and upset she was holding onto because of those times. As she healed these old wounds, she became more willing to try something new in the present. She was willing to take a risk now and see what actually happened when she asked her mother for what she wanted.

Another example is from my own life, where I use my strategy of trying to get what I want by pouting and leaving the room. It's a tried and true strategy and has a success rate of zero percent, yet I still use it on occasion.

Just recently, my wife was breastfeeding our second son in a rocking chair in the living room. Our older boy was asleep and I approached her to talk about the departure of Calvin. He was our family cat and we were giving him to a dear friend, because he was not thriving with two young children in the house. It was difficult and painful, but we eventually decided he would enjoy his life more at my friend's house. So I was going to transfer him with all his kitty stuff the next day.

I mentioned something to my wife about the details of the transfer. She nodded in agreement. I then said something about it sucking and me feeling sad about giving him away. "He's been my buddy for twelve years," I said, mournfully. She nodded again.

I felt a surge of pain and uncomfortable feelings. *Fine,* I thought, *I guess I'll just leave you and go deal with this on my own.* "Ok," I said curtly. "I'm going to bed." I walked towards the door, exuding as much pouting energy as I could.

As I reached the door, I paused for a moment. Because just that morning I'd been writing this chapter on asking. It would be ironic if I stormed out of the room without asking anything. It's a good thing I'm writing this book for me. I mean you. I mean us. So in that moment I paused and thought, *What do I want? And what am I not asking for?*

I turned around without thinking much and walked back to Candace. "Ok," I started. "I was walking off in a huff there but instead I thought I just needed to ask for something," I declared.

"Ok," she said with a smile, responding well to my honesty. "What do you need?"

I wasn't sure, so I took a few guesses. "Maybe to hear about your experience with Calvin, or hear empathy about my mine."

She responded sweetly. My beautiful wife—tired beyond reason—began to give even more. She described how difficult it must feel to lose a friend of so many years. I instantly felt a rush of relief and love. Wow, asking for what you want feels good.

You just have to do it. Realize it in the moment if you can and just get it over with. Fast. Usually the most direct, authentic, and often vulnerable way of asking is the best. It might feel the most uncomfortable at first, but soon you know good things will come after the initial discomfort.

So go do it. You can start with the best and most fun way to learn: a game.

THE NO GAME

"Can I get my bowl for free?" I asked with a twinkle in my eye.

"Uhh, why?" responded the woman behind the register. She had a puzzled look on her face.

That's as far as I'd planned. I had nothing else lined up. So I said the first thing that popped into my head.

"Because I'm so good looking?"

"Mmmm, no." She said with a laugh.

"It was worth a shot," I said as I reached for my money clip (that's right, I use a money clip because I think I'm a high roller).

It *was* worth a shot, wasn't it? Why not? Why not ask for what you want?

What happens when she says no? Nothing. I just turn around

and walk away. Nothing bad whatsoever happens. No one hits me. No one throws a drink in my face. The only thing that could happen is some uncomfortable feelings in my solar plexus or chest. And those are just created by believing the stories in my mind.

It's bad to ask.
That was rude.
I put her out.
Other people watching think I'm a jerk.
I didn't have a reason to do that.
I'm no good.

That last one is really interesting. It's just one of the default statements our mind can spit out in response to getting rejected. Even if we didn't really want the thing we were asking for. Even if we didn't really expect to get it. Even if we didn't really care. Still, there it is. That critic is just sitting up there, lounging around with his feet up on the desk, reading the newspaper. He's got his shoes off, his tie loosened, and he's really enjoying some time off.

Then all of a sudden he hears you got a "no" and he leaps up out of his chair. *What happened! What did I miss? Someone said no? About what? It doesn't matter. You're bad! You're bad! You're bad!*

Absurd, isn't it? I'll say. So here's what we do to break free. We collect nos. Collect them all over the place. Ask for shit all the time, everywhere you go. Make a game of it with your friends when you're out on the town. Who can get three nos first?

A little while back I was flying with a friend to San Jose, California. I was super thirsty before we took off, and I had forgotten to purchase a bottle of water at the airport before take off. As soon as we sat down I flagged down one of the flight attendants.

"I'm super thirsty, can I have some water before we take off?"

Oooh, bold! No, that's not the no game. That's a lame request. Of course she's going to say yes. The purpose of the game is to ask for something you think is going to get you a no.

Anyways, she says "Yes. I can get you a can of water." (That's not a typo. A can of water. Like a soda can but instead of soda inside its water. Strange. Have you ever seen that before? I'd never seen one before or since.)

So I said, "Can I have six cans of water?"

"No." She quickly replied. Stone-faced. Icy.

"Alright," I said. "How about three?"

There was a slightly long, slightly awkward pause...

"Ok, I can do that."

Oh shit, I was expecting her to say no again. I didn't actually want three cans of water, but there you go. You just might find you get more yeses than you think.

Do you see the value of this game? It's something I often have participants at my weekend intensives play. At a recent event I was out with several participants and we were playing the No Game near a row of food carts. As often happens, when we go out to play, one person out of the group of four hits it hard and just starts asking for nos. The other three breathe a sigh of relief because apparently he's going to get all the nos for them. Whew.

But that's good. Watching someone is valuable, because you see that nothing bad happens (and that they get a "yes" a surprising amount of the time), but it's not enough to set you free. You have to do it yourself. A lot.

I pointed to a nearby food cart and suggested one of the participants go to the vendor and ask for a free soda. He stared at me wide-eyed. Terror. Alright, I decided to demonstrate. I walked over to the Thai food cart and greeted the woman at the window.

"Hi there, can I have a can of soda for free?" I said in a warm, loud, cheerful tone.

She stared at me wide-eyed. Confused. Her husband came over from the back of the cart. They spoke briefly with each other in Thai in a hushed whisper. After their exchange he also seemed confused.

I simply watched them speaking, beaming positive energy with a bright smile on my face.

When I play this game I like to try my hardest to get a yes, even though I'm ultimately going for a no. The harder I try, the more uncomfortable I might get, thus getting the most liberation out of the game. Like squeezing every last drop out of an orange when turning it into juice.

He turned to me and said, "What do you want?"

"I want a free can of soda. My friend said I could get a free can of soda because I'm wearing a pink shirt," I said in a jovial tone.

He paused, staring at me. Then he waved his hand in a gesture that I can only assume means "What the fuck, I don't know, sure." He gave the green light and his lovely lady handed me an ice cold soda. I strolled back to where the participant was standing, sipping on my silver can of victory. He seemed shocked and amazed.

"They gave it to you? What did you say?"

I gave him a play-by-play rundown and he seemed inspired. He walked off to go create some mischief and perhaps get a "no" for himself.

As I stood there enjoying my soda and watching some of the participants interacting with strangers, a man approached to ask me a question. He was wearing filthy clothes, his hair was disheveled, his eyes were bloodshot and he was missing several teeth.

"Do you have any spare change? I'm trying to get enough to get something to eat."

Bold. I like it. What level of request was that? Probably a 3, right? He has no idea how I will respond.

"How about I just get you something?" I offered.

"Wow, sure," he said. He seemed genuinely pleased.

I knew just the place. We walked right back over to the Thai cart that had generously parted with their soda just a few moments earlier. The woman in the window seemed surprised and genuinely pleased to see me. Perhaps when we ask boldly people aren't offended and don't dislike us. Perhaps we become memorable, intriguing, and a presence that brightens their day.

I pointed to the menu of pictures on the front of the food cart. "What would you like?" I asked the man.

"Ummm..." He hesitated, seeming a little uncomfortable. It's sometimes hard to ask for what we want, and sometimes even harder to receive it. "How about this one?" He pointed to a small appetizer meal.

As I saw his discomfort in that moment, I decided to create a new experience for him. I don't know how long he's been homeless, or anything about his history, but I can imagine he's gotten a lot of rejections. People are probably regularly upset with him for asking. What if he is rewarded for what he asks for?

I had a banner up in the course room that read: THE WORLD IS A FRIENDLY PLACE. I use it to help remind all the participants that others are not so harsh, judgmental, and quick to criticize us as we think they are. What if I could help this guy feel that the world is a friendly place? Help him believe that life will give him what he asks of it?

"Anything else?" I asked.

"Uhh, how about this one?" He pointed to a full meal option.

"Great. Anything else?"

He paused. "Well, I would like to get food for a friend. This is for two people. It really is."

"Sure, what else would you like?"

He chose two more items off the menu. "Anything to drink?" I asked.

He chose a can of soda. We ordered and I told the Thai woman to give the food directly to him because I needed to get moving.

Sometimes we get a no. And sometimes life gives us more than we ever asked for.

As I walked back towards the hotel where we were holding the event, the participant who watched me get the soda jogged up beside me. In his hand was a bright red can of Coke.

"How did you get that?" I asked him, already knowing the answer.

He laughed. "They gave it to me at the first cart I asked for it."

This is the No Game.

I dare you to try it.

I bet you'll be nervous before you do it. Why? Because on some level we're all scared of rejection, scared of no. We are also full of stories about why it's bad to ask, how harmful and hurtful it is to those poor other people, how inappropriate and impolite we're being. Bullshit. Assuming you're not being hyper-aggressive or intimidating people, you're just making a simple request. You are doing it in quite a friendly and polite manner. And they have the ability to say no. You don't need to care-take and coddle people so much. They are strong, they are powerful.

Underneath all those stories is fear. And it will remain there until we extinguish it. The only way to do that is to run straight towards it until it vanishes into nothing. Into no fear. Into fearlessness. If you and I were hanging out, you could ask me to ask anyone anything, and guess what? I'll do it.

Anything.

And while getting a "no" for a silly request or getting a free can of soda might not seem that significant, the impact in your life can be astronomical. When you build this muscle of asking and getting nos through this game, you are conditioning yourself. You are in training.

Then, when it comes to game time, you are in much better shape to win. You want to ask a prospective customer to buy from you. You want to ask that incredible and attractive stranger out for a date. You want to ask your friend to listen to you and help you with a challenge in your life. This list could be endless. Every day we have opportunities to make bold requests, and to reap the rewards in our lives. The question is not "Will you ask?", it's "how boldly and how often?"

CHAPTER IX:

POWER

As you begin to identify the excuses and stories you used to tell yourself and see through them, you will encounter the fear that has always been lingering beneath these stories. And when you face the fear inside of yourself by feeling your feelings, and face the fear outside of yourself by taking action in the world, you will start to experience the results of doing so. These include feeling more confident, being more relaxed about money (and ultimately earning more), enjoying more love, and feeling more power. That's right, power.

This whole chapter is all about just that. Power is good. We want more of it, and the more we have, the better we feel. But there are some misconceptions about power; some limiting and fearful ideas that keep us from completely accessing and enjoying our full personal power. For many years you may have been keeping your power away, stuffing it down as far as it will go, into the bottom of your socks, and mistakenly seeing yourself as less powerful, or even powerless.

Prepare to liberate yourself from whatever is stopping you from having as much power as you want. Prepare to unleash the power to be who you want to be in the world, the power to act how you want to act, the power to say what you want to say, and the power to do what you're really here to do!

You just might find that once you have a taste of this, you'll never want to go back.

What Is Power?

When you hear the word power, who do you think of? Presidents, political leaders, CEOs, military generals, He-Man, Judge Dredd? Many people think of external power structures. They think of others who strongly influence large numbers of people. But that's only one kind of power and it's not the one I'm talking about.

I'm talking about personal power: your ability to choose your own direction, actions, and, ultimately, your own destiny. This may involve impacting or influencing others, but it's not about being officially elected or sanctioned to do so by some social or political structure. In fact, the power I'm talking about here is the freedom to do what you want, and the ability to make anything you want to happen in your life and in the world.

Do you want to pursue a certain career, earn a certain income, or create a certain business? Perhaps you want to move to a new city, pursue a higher degree, or find a new group of friends. Power is what allows you to do any or all of those things. And a lack of power prevents you from getting off the ground, or from continuing to see your vision through.

Personal power is also about being how you want to be in the world. This includes saying what you want to say, asking the questions you want to ask, and choosing the way you interact with others based on an internal compass. This is in direct contrast to the low power position of constantly looking to others to determine whether or not you are okay. Holding back, hesitating, and determining what to say or do based upon what you think others want is the opposite of power. It's submissive.

In my experience, living this way can feel extremely confining, limiting, and depressing. What is your experience with power? How powerful do you feel, both in this moment, and on a daily basis? Where in your life do you feel most powerful - at work, in your dating life, in relationships? Where do you feel least powerful? What situations do you feel completely powerless in?

Take a moment to do a quick personal power inventory. Be honest with yourself. There's no shame in not having as much power as you would like to have in one or more areas of your life. In fact, being real about what's actually happening in your life is exactly what is going to set you free. It in itself is an act of power.

Now let's help you release the brakes and leap over any obstacles to power in your path. Let's see how we can magnify your natural power, freedom, and feelings of certainty so that you can easily talk to anyone, speak up for yourself, go after what you want, and live from a place of extraordinary confidence.

Fear Of Power

We are all aware of the power-hungry dictators and despots lurking in the annals of history. Their legacy has taught us that people with great power can become crazed and self-serving. As the famous saying from 19th century baron, Lord Acton, goes, "Power tends to corrupt, and absolute power corrupts absolutely."

Every day we see another person on T.V. striving for more political power, or CEOs of large corporations maneuvering to become CEOs of a different, slightly larger corporations. As a result of this, we can conclude that everyone wants power and that everyone's trying to get more of it. But that's actually not the case.

The average person feels disempowered much of the time and is actually afraid of power. Especially their own personal power. And so, while we want the glory and the perks that can come from power, we often avoid cultivating and building it because we have an unconscious fear of our own power.

What are these unconscious fears? Well, you tell me. Imagine for a moment that you had unlimited power. You could create whatever you wanted, pursue any career or business endeavor, and earn any amount of money as a result. You could walk over to anyone and say anything you wanted. You could challenge and disagree with whomever you wanted, whenever you wanted. You could feel a sense of raw energy, strength, and physical power in your body. Nobody could mess with you, stand in your way, or keep you down.

As you imagine this, how do you feel? Excited? Nervous? Uncertain? Not much at all?

The excitement comes from sensing the truth about your power, which we'll talk more about in a moment. The nervousness or uncertainty comes from fears about what it means to have power, and how others would view you. And if you're not feeling much at all, you might have settled into a powerless state for so long that you won't even allow yourself to imagine that being powerful is a realistic option for you. If so, that's okay. Like we've identified with other new feelings so far in this book, these negative sensations are just layers of fear, excuses and stories getting in the way. And all of those can be removed in a heartbeat.

Here are some of the most common fears I've come across when it comes to personal power. I personally held many of these around me as a cage that prevented me from accessing more of my full power. Perhaps you are doing this, too:

10 Common Fears of Power

- If I am powerful and successful, it is somehow taking from others who are less so.

- If I am my full powerful self, I will be disliked, ridiculed, and condemned.

- If I boldly speak up and pursue what I want, I'll be persecuted or killed.

- Others will see my power as arrogance and dislike me.

- Others will feel jealous of me and dislike me.

- Power is oppressive. By being powerful I am marginalizing and oppressing others.

- If I am powerful, people will see me as power hungry or greedy and dislike me.

- If I am powerful, people will see me as a threat and want to fight me or keep me down.

- If I am my full powerful self, I won't be able to work at my job and they'll fire me for being too much.

- Power is bad. Wanting power is bad.

Which of these fears do you recognize in yourself? Which ones do you think are holding you back from claiming and living with more power? Are there any other fears you've noticed that could be getting in the way, slowing you down, or stopping you?

The most common ones all come down to two major fears:

1. People will dislike me.

2. I'll be hurting others somehow (which makes me a bad person).

These are, of course, complete hogwashery. Total nonsense. Distortions and misperceptions of what power actually is and who you'll actually be when you have more of it. But that's often what fear is, a misperception of the future, one which spooks us out of boldly moving towards it. And by often I mean always.

Forgetting Our Power

"You are infinitely powerful."
- Christian Mickelsen

Here's the thing about fearing your power and keeping it away. That strategy doesn't work. It can't. Because power is who you are. It is in you and it's in what you're here to do. It is infused into your cells and your breath and your movements. Power is unavoidable. It's already inside of you right now.

Of course you can stall it out. You can push it away and try to not make it so. But whenever you do, alarm bells go off in your head and heart. When you aren't pursuing what you really want—in your career, your love life, or even just interacting with people day to day—how do you feel? Crappy. Disengaged. Scared. Depressed.

And when you push away and deny your power around others

you feel even worse. You spend all your mental energy on pleasing others, currying favor, and hoping they'll like you. You worry incessantly about what others think of you, wondering if they'll keep liking you, and if you're good enough for them. You crave approval like a meth fiend who hasn't had a hit in three days. It's not pretty. And it's not you.

Because you are infinitely powerful. You, in your natural state, are completely free to create and go after whatever you want. You are free to say what you really think and feel, no matter who you are speaking to. Have you ever seen a little kid speaking with someone? He doesn't care how powerful they are, or what kind of shit they're wearing. He'll show them his toy car collection and then tell them not to touch his stuffed monkey without feeling any fear of their disapproval. That is power. And that is your natural state.

We just forget this. We lose sight of it. We believe the stories we hear from people who have also forgotten this and thus feel disempowered. And so they disparage and criticize others who seem more powerful than they are. They even unwittingly criticize or attack the freedom, confidence, and power present in their own children.

You would be surprised how many parents have a strong form of social anxiety about how people view them based on what their children do. Even as an expert on social anxiety, I didn't realize this until I had kids. Then I noticed that in some situations involving my children, other parents' reactions to my kids could be awkward. Am I supposed to control my kid here? Is he doing something inappropriate that bothers people?

I noticed that these situations gave me a fear of others' perception of me as a parent, and a desire to make my kid change, or at least say something out loud to him so that other people see that I'm a responsible parent. This is all approval-seeking nonsense. I saw it in myself immediately and decided I was not going to do that. I'm not going to do something based on what I imagine other people want to see. Especially if that involves criticizing my kid or teaching him something limiting and fear-based.

As I looked around, I started seeing this happen everywhere. Parents on airplanes being supremely apologetic because their nine-month-old infant was crying. Dude, your baby is nine months old. Of course he's going to cry in a pressurized metal tube flying through the sky. If someone gets upset about that, who's issue is that?

Dozens of times I've had kids come up and start interacting with me or with my kids. Then the other parent runs over, over-apologizes to me, and makes a show of telling their kid to "stop bothering them." They do this without even seeing what is actually happening: I am engaged, everyone is enjoying themselves, and no one is bothered at all... until the moment I notice what that other parent is doing, then I'm bothered by the parent.

So parents teach their kids to have low social power. Don't bother others. Be polite. And this instills the fear that to be powerful, bold, outspoken and free around others will bring on dislike, disapproval, and a loss of love. It's terribly limiting, unconsciously transmitted, and the complete opposite of the truth. Because, in reality, the more powerful, outspoken, bold, and authentic you can be, the more others will like, love, and adore you. The more powerful you are, the more loved you are. It's funny how our fears are often the exact opposite of what's really true.

And this idea that you are somehow taking others' power or hurting them by living powerfully yourself is also completely false. It's based on a misconception of what power actually is. When people see someone getting their way by taking it at others' expense, they say, "look at what power does—it hurts and corrupts." But that's not power, that's force. And it's not being powerful, it's being scared.

Many people are forcing their agenda all over the world. From the brutal dictator to the physically abusive husband, there are millions of examples of people controlling others through fear, intimidation, and force. This is not power. It might get a certain result in the short term, but it is harmful, highly toxic, and founded on fear and desperation.

These behaviors do not result from being powerful. These types of antisocial actions are not the monster that will come out of you when you stop people-pleasing and hiding from your power. In fact, that level of brutal force and endless hunger for power we see in the violence around us actually comes from a deep insecurity of feeling totally powerless, insignificant, and unlovable. To escape these pains, an abusive person overcompensates by controlling and manipulating others.

So let that fear of being abusive go. Any fears you have that you'll be perceived as forceful or manipulative are just your Safety Police trying to keep you in line and in the land of zero risk. It's time to shed these naive fears. It's time to stop acting powerless and blaming forces outside of yourself. It's time to step up and claim the power that's always been inside of you.

SOCIAL POWER

Social power is perhaps the most important form of power because all of the things you want to experience or create probably involve other humans. Whether it's a successful business, a happy marriage, or a thriving social life, it's going to involve interacting with other people. Hence no power is more important than our social power.

Social power is the ability to be your most powerful, bold, authentic self in as many situations as you can. It involves saying what you want to say, asking the questions you really want to ask, and spontaneously expressing yourself without heavy filters or inhibitions.

It includes being direct, clear, and honest about what you want and don't want. It requires you to be able to disagree, challenge, or otherwise speak your mind as needed. It allows you to speak to new people, powerful people, and attractive people without feeling less than or fearful about their perception of you. It gives you the ability to lead others, delegate tasks, and call people out when they aren't keeping their agreements. Basically, having social power means being a confident badass. Now let's help you get it.

Internal Verus External Frame

In order to access your full social power, you must make one fundamental shift. This is from an external frame of reference to an internal frame of reference. Let me explain.

A frequent claim many of my clients make is this: "I'm not good at telling stories or talking to people. I'm boring." At which point I say, "great!" which always confuses them. I'm mainly doing it to break the self-hypnosis of the story they're telling themselves. They've told themselves this story so many times it becomes a hypnotic trance and feels absolutely and undeniably true.

"How do you know you're boring?" I continue. "Is there a specific piece of evidence you can tell me about?"

"No one seems interested when I'm talking."

Well, that's not very specific. So I'll probe deeper, "Can you remember a specific instance where this happened?"

Sometimes they can, and sometimes they can't. The actual evidence may be lost in the data files. All they're left with is an idea about themselves. A big fat abstract concept. A word. One that is completely demoralizing yet feels absolutely true.

But when a specific moment can be recalled, it often goes something like this: "I was speaking with some colleagues last Monday and one of them asked how my weekend was. As I was telling him, he seemed disinterested and impatient."

"So because he seemed disinterested and impatient, that means you are a boring person? I ask.

"Yes. Yes it does."

This is a perfect example of living from an external frame.

We all have a frame of reference in any given situation, especially new situations, or any situation where we feel uncertain. This means we look for some kind of signal to determine how we should act, think, and feel.

Let's say you'd never been to a football game before (that's American football, not soccer for my international friends). Maybe you've never even seen one on TV. But a new friend of yours says you absolutely have to come experience live football and gifts you a ticket.

At the game, there is a ton of stuff happening you probably don't get at first, both on the field and in the stands. So, you look to your friend and the people around you for indications of how to react and how to interpret what's happening. When something happens on the field and everyone cheers, you cheer. When something else happens and your friend grabs his forehead in disgust, you grab your forehead, too. Because you don't know how to act in this situation, you look to your friend for guidance. You are looking outside of yourself. You have an external frame of reference.

This is how many people approach much of their lives. They are constantly looking to others to determine if what they are doing is okay, allowed, appropriate, normal, good, and right. Their entire frame of reference for how to act, think, and feel is largely external.

This is especially common in social situations. We look to others' reactions to see if we're dressed right, saying the right things, and being polite enough. Was that story you told interesting? Well, only if everyone seemed engaged. Am I a funny person? It depends on if my friends laughed at my joke. Am I attractive? It depends on if he smiled at me, or if she seemed interested in talking with me.

The external frame of reference is a powerless frame. When you are using it, you are giving all of your power away, sometimes to strangers and people you don't even know that well. I call this the Power Bleed and we'll talk about that more in just one second. For now, though, just stop it. Stop looking so much to others to determine what you should do, think, or feel. Stop looking outwards and start looking in.

An internal frame of reference comes from inside of you. You assess a situation and determine what feels right to you. You ask yourself questions like, *What do I want? How do I feel? What do I think about that? What do I really want to do?*

And then you act based upon the answers to those questions. You do what you want, even if not everyone approves. Even if no one gave you the green light. If you see a striking woman you want to meet, you simply walk over and ask her a question. If you see a handsome man who makes your breath catch, you walk up to him and smile. If you want to interrupt two colleagues talking in the hallway because you have an important question to ask one of them, you walk over and insert yourself. If you want to stand up at your friend's wedding and offer a toast on the spot without having prepared anything, you stand up and speak from your heart in front of the group.

You act based on what you want to do. You are guided by your own internal system. You are the leader of your own life. You are powerful.

But what if...?

What if it's the "wrong" thing to do?

How do you actually know if it's the wrong thing? Because someone doesn't respond well? Now we're back to an external frame. See how fast that happens? If you wanted to say it, or it felt important to you to do it, then stand behind it. Someone else might be upset. And that's ok. You won't die, and neither will they. Later in this chapter you'll learn powerful ways to quickly diffuse upset and how to stop worrying about upsetting others in general.

What if I do something bad or inappropriate? What if I'm totally out of line?

Like taking your pants off at a dinner party? What are you, two years old? Relax. Trust yourself a little more. You don't need that heavy policing of yourself to stay in line. You have a natural guidance system that makes you attentive, caring, loving, and good. You don't need to make it happen by fearing others' responses. Instead, trust your own feelings, thoughts, and desires. Trust your intuition and your gut. You have way more wisdom inside of you than you give yourself credit for.

Power Bleed

Most people lose much of their social power, not because it's taken from them, but because they hastily give it all away.

Before you enter a room—whether it's a business meeting, a cocktail party, or dinner with your spouse's friends—you are either accessing your power or bleeding it all away. Here's how most people do the latter (which is a fancy way of saying the second one).

Before entering the room, you think to yourself, *I hope this goes well, I'm not very good at meeting people, I hate speaking up in meetings, I hope I don't mess this up.* You may be imagining ways this scenario could go poorly. You might even be remembering similar past experiences where it did not go well.

You are forgetting your power, seeing yourself as less than you really are, and thinking you need something from these people, which is usually either approval or acceptance. Sometimes your goal is just to impress others (so they will like and love you). Now all the power is in their hands because, in seeking their approval or acceptance you've given it all away.

It's like the Nintendo game The Legend of Zelda, which I only played for the NES because I'm old school. In case you're not familiar with it, the premise of that game is there's a magical source of power called the Tri-Force. It's a glowing triangle, and it's badass. Anyway, apparently the evil elf Ganon has kidnapped the beautiful elfin princess Zelda. As Link, the hero of the tale, it is your quest to find the princess and defeat Ganon, thus ridding the land of his evil scourge. Getting nerdy enough yet? I'm just getting started.

As a pathetically untrained elfling with nothing but a wooden sword, you must first build up your power to even stand a chance against Ganon. And so you travel across the land, gaining experience by hacking apart forest monsters and claiming useful items from dungeons. You are also questing for the broken pieces of the Tri-Force, which has been shattered all across the land (no doubt due to Ganon's mischief). Each time you find a piece, you triumphantly hold it over your head, gaining more power and capability. Eventually, you find all the pieces, assemble the Tri-Force and murder the shit out of Ganon. I think. I'm not sure if I ever actually beat the game.

In any case, the Power Bleed is like shattering your Tri-Force all over the room. You enter the room in a powerless state, thinking you need to reclaim the broken shards from each person. Each interaction, each moment of the conversation, and believing that each person holds some power that you must get back. *If they like me, think I'm funny and interesting, see me as capable and smart, then I've recovered a piece of my self-worth.* But that's not enough. Even if one person approves of you, you're not done. Now you need to get the same from the next person, and the next, and the next. It's exhausting. And it's totally made up.

The Tri-Force isn't broken. It's right there inside of you, glowing orange and bright. Take a deep breath in, right into the center of your chest. Let it out now, and then take another deep breath in—as if you're breathing directly into your heart. Feel that sense of power, that knowing that you already are enough, that all you need is inside of you. You don't need a stranger to approve of you. You don't need everyone there to think you're brilliant. You don't need anything from anyone. Just let it go. Trust in yourself and know you are awesome, right now in this moment.

Why are you valuing others opinions so highly? You know who you are. You know your positive qualities, what you bring to others, what makes you unique and significant. You know the nature of your own heart and what a loving, confident, kind person you are underneath all that fear and self-doubt. Why are you putting another person's perspective above your own? Especially when that perspective belongs to a stranger or anyone who has never really spent time with you. It's crazy. They don't even really know you, and yet if they think you're boring or too quiet, then you automatically take that on as true about yourself.

The real issue here is how much *you* love and accept yourself. If you are "right in yourself," on your own side, and accepting of who you are, then you are connected with your power and no longer bleeding it away. The Power Bleed comes from not thinking much of yourself and therefore seeking external approval to help you feel like you're good enough. It's like you're constantly running from a worthiness deficit and the external approval temporarily brings you back to baseline.

But what if *you* were the source of power? What if *you* were the source of approval and love? The one who accepts other people, finds their greatness, and shares it with them?

It's amazing what can happen, and how quickly things can change, when we shift from getting to giving. Instead of getting this person to like me and approve of me, how can I give love and approval? How can I help this person feel at ease, know they are accepted, and help them see how awesome they are? When you ask yourself questions like that before entering a room, your entire world changes. Social anxiety and self-consciousness melt away as you focus outside of yourself. People respond completely differently. They listen to you more, seem more engaged, interested and intrigued. They want to talk with you, hire you, or date you. Because you have what everyone is seeking.

With What Moon Language

Admit something:
Everyone you see, you say to them, "Love me."
Of course you do not do this out loud; otherwise,
someone would call the cops.
Still, though, think about this, this great pull in us
to connect.
Why not become the one who lives with a full moon
in each eye that is always saying,
with that sweet moon language,
what every other eye in this world is dying to hear?

--Hafiz--
(translated by Daniel Ladinsky)

ASSERTIVENESS: HOW TO BOLDLY SPEAK UP FOR YOURSELF

A big part of social power and the ability to confidently and freely be yourself around anyone, in any situation, is being free to speak your mind. This is assertiveness. We spend so much time policing ourselves: second-guessing and double-checking what we should or shouldn't say. *Will they like it? Is that an appropriate thing to say? Is that too much? Is that too honest? What if they get upset? What if they don't like me for saying it?*

All these questions and all this filtering creates a dam in the river of ideas and thoughts inside of you. Feelings are meant to be felt and released. Your perspectives, ideas, and preferences are meant to be expressed and released, not held inside, stuffed down behind layers of fear and self-doubt. I did this for many years and it was bad news. Because of this, I experienced chronic tension in my solar plexus and ongoing problems with my guts. So much stuffed down emotion that couldn't get it out.

Fuck it. It's time to just start saying stuff. Seriously. Right now. Stop hiding, stop making excuses, stop finding reasons not to and just do it. Just say it. Say what you're really thinking, ask what you really want to ask. Just blurt it out. Release the dam and get into the flow. It's a lot less predictable, less controlled, less boring and a hell of a lot more fun.

From what I've seen over the years, most people want to have this freedom. They want to speak freely and boldly and care less about what others think. And yet they have a long-standing pattern of avoiding assertiveness out of fear. Of focusing on pleasing others rather than being real and authentically themselves.

This pattern of avoidance can be so habitual and so unconscious that you might not even know when you are doing it. Let's take a moment to reflect on it now. What are the main reasons you don't currently speak up as much as you want to? What excuses or stories do you tell yourself that allow you to stay quiet, small, and feeling powerless?

Here are some of the most common stories we tell ourselves to avoid being assertive.

If I speak up...

Others will get upset with me, dislike me, and stop wanting to be around me.

I will hurt other peoples' feelings and they will feel devastated and I will be a terrible person and feel guilty.

They will be disappointed and I couldn't do that to them.

They already have so much on their plate, I don't want to burden them with my desires or needs.

They are going to say no and then I'll feel embarrassed and ashamed for asking.

They will see me as dominating, controlling, demanding, or too needy.

Now is not the right time; I'll talk with them later when I'm not upset about it any more.

They will react with anger and attack or criticize me and I won't be able to handle it.

Actually that last part is unconsciously tacked on to every single one of these stories: I won't be able to handle it. That's the real fear. I won't be able to handle their upset, their anger, or my feelings of self-loathing or guilt.

What are you telling yourself you can't handle? Is that really true? Or would it just be unpleasant or uncomfortable? How do you imagine you'll ever get better at handling it if you constantly avoid it? Luck? Black magic?

The only way to gain this ability is to practice it. The only way to increase your social power is to build it, step-by-step. In each moment you have a choice. You can choose to avoid speaking up and stay in the Safety Police's land of certainty, or you can choose to blurt out what you really think, feel, and want and see what actually happens. One choice keeps you stuck, small, frustrated and resentful. Rarely getting what you want. The other builds your strength, generates power, and ultimately sets you free. As always, the choice is yours, from moment to moment.

Just Fucking Say It

Often when I'm working with clients on increasing their social power and confidence there will come a point when they are faced with the choice to speak-up or avoid. By now they are on board with the speak-up plan. They are sick and tired of living their lives in fear-based, people pleasing, Nice Personville. They are ready to do it. There's just one question...how?

They will ask me, "But how do I speak my mind in that situation? I'm so nervous. How do I do it?"

This is a time when a "how" question is bogus. Sometimes asking how to do something is great. For example, instead of asking, "Why don't I have anyone to date right now?" you can ask yourself "How can I meet and ask more people out?" This will get your mind out of giving you reasons why you suck and into providing active solutions. That's a great use of the "how" question.

A less great use of the "how" question is when we know exactly what we need to do, we just are scared to do it. In this case the "how" becomes a delay tactic, a clever way of convincing ourselves that we need more time, we need to figure something out before we do it. In fact, we want to have it all figured out before we take action so we can get it right and do it perfectly, thus avoiding all conflict, discomfort, and messiness.

At the end of the day though, there is no how. There is only do. It's the DO muscle from the ACTION chapter, remember?

Just fucking say it. That thing that comes to your mind. That response. That question. That joke. Stop waiting around. Stop rolling it around in your head for thirty seconds until the moment has passed. Just let it out. Now.

As you do, your conversations will turn from boring, stiff, scary interactions that you can't wait to make it through to fun, exciting explorations. The reason they're boring and stilted now is because you are prioritizing certainty above anything else. You know what will happen if you play small and stay quiet and nice. It's familiar and predictable.

But when you just blurt something out, you're immediately in the river of uncertainty. It's fast, spontaneous, and exciting. You don't know what's around the next corner. You can spend all day at the side of the river, wondering why you're scared to get in. *Does it come from my childhood?* Probably. Now jump in the water.

No, wait, I haven't figured out why I'm so scared yet. And besides, how do I jump in? I just don't know how to jump in yet.

What the hell are you talking about? You just jump in. You dive in, you fall in, it looks good, it looks awkward. It doesn't matter. Just get in the water. You'll figure the rest out later as you go, by necessity.

A while back I was at a hippie music and arts festival out in the woods in Oregon. My wife and I were lying in our tent, enjoying the early morning, warmly snuggled together. This is before we had two small children and could still spend hours just lying there doing nothing. Ahh, the luxury!

Outside the tent we could hear two young boys who were camped near us. They were probably four or five years old. One of them said to the other, "My dad knows your mom and so we all camped together. When we got here we found you guys. And then we played together yesterday and now we're friends."

"Wow," replied the other boy. "That's a really long story."

My wife and I laughed. What an awesome response. What freedom. The other boy didn't seem to care. They remained fast friends all weekend. No one got horribly offended, no one left in a huff and never came back, no one died.

Just fucking say it. Give yourself the permission and the freedom to be who you really are. How you naturally were as a young kid, when you were free to say what you really thought. Before all the layers of fear and doubt and approval-seeking got piled on. Just stand up and let all those layers fall to the ground, like a pile of blankets you no longer need.

Someone's talking and you are not engaged at all in what they're saying? Interrupt them. Abruptly change the subject. Or do it gracefully. Whichever, it doesn't matter. Just fucking say something.

When someone challenges you at work, implying you don't know what you're doing, fire back. Speak up. Ask them questions to find out why they're making that claim. Allow yourself to be louder, bolder, stronger, and more powerful. It's ok if you look upset or frustrated. You don't have to hide all that down in your guts. Those feelings are actually part of being a vibrant, alive, complete human.

You might think you need to hide everything unpleasant, keep everything smooth, and only speak up when you're certain it will be well received. You do this because you don't want people to dislike you and you hope that if they don't dislike you then by default they will like you. This actually isn't true. They might not dislike you, but they might not care that much about you either way. "Oh, that Aziz guy, yeah he's ok. Nice enough." That isn't exactly passionate.

The truth is, people will like you more when you speak up. When you just say what you're thinking, insert your opinion, or throw your two cents into the ring, people will like you more. That doesn't mean every single person is going to like you and be your friend. And it doesn't mean that no one will ever disagree with you. But life is not about getting everyone to approve of you and avoiding all conflict and friction and keeping everything smooth. That's a coward's life. That's a dismal life of fear and low self-esteem. You are not meant for that life.

Fuck it. Just say it. Just let it out. Let it be messy. Let it be uncertain. Trust that you will figure out more as you go. That once you are in the water you will learn how to swim. Perhaps awkwardly at first, but if you stay in the water, you will soon glide powerfully with skill and grace. But in order to to that, you first have to get in the water.

BEING SOCIALLY FEARLESS

If there is one place it is the easiest to be fearless, it's in social contexts. Being fearless jumping out of a plane, or in combat? A lot harder. Because you are in mortal danger. You could die.

But social fear? In comparison that's a piece of cake. You are not going to die. There is no threat to your safety or your life. Just endless worried thoughts that fabricate catastrophes of isolation and ruin. But those are completely made up. Bullets in combat? Those are not made up. I'm telling you, being socially fearless is easy. Here's how to do it.

First, assume everything is fine. Assume everything is okay until proven otherwise. Instead of having the default assumption that people are going to be upset with you, why not assume that everyone is going to be fine with what you're doing or saying?

So many people walk around assuming everything they do is impolite, inappropriate, and somehow upsetting or annoying to others. Their life is one big apology. They apologize for bumping shoulders, apologize for starting to talk at the same time as someone else, apologize for saying "no" to someone, and apologize even when something is not their fault. They even apologize when there's no problem and nothing to actually apologize for.

How many times per day do you say, "I'm sorry"? Unless you are making grievous errors that really warrant an apology to rebuild a relationship, I'd suggest cutting way back. If you gently bump shoulders as you walk past someone, that's not the time to apologize. That's you assuming others are going to be upset with you and you trying to dodge that upset with a hasty and automatic apology.

One client I worked with was so overly apologetic we decided to have him do an "apology fast." He was instructed to consciously not apologize for a week. He came back to the next session a week later and said he couldn't do it. He held back about fifty percent of the time, but in so many scenarios the apologies just poured out of him. First, I told him that changing any habit by fifty percent in one week is a huge and dramatic improvement, and almost nothing happens that quickly. Second, keep going!

And so he did. After a month he was apology-free, except for instances that really warranted a true apology. He told me that one amazing result of that experiment was he just felt more powerful wherever he went: at work, on the street, in the store. He was no longer seeing other people as these angry and scary figures who he had to keep appeasing lest they lash out at him. He reclaimed his power.

And so can you. Stop seeing strangers and everyone else as angry parents. You are not a child who is powerless and has to appease the big bad adults. Stand tall, breathe deep, keep your head on the horizon and your eyes looking right into the eyes of others, no matter if they're a colleague, an attractive man or woman, the company CEO, or a stranger. You are both powerful adults. Both equal.

From this place, assume that whatever you are going to say or do is fine. Assume that the world is a friendly place, that people want to help you get what you need, and that others are absorbed in their own lives and not judging you all the time.

Ask your question, interrupt the conversation, join into the discussion, share your opinion, say something is a bad idea, explain why you didn't like the movie, say what restaurant you want to go to, tell that person "no," ask that person why they said "no" to you, challenge others, say what you're really thinking. And assume that others will respond positively, openly, and warmly. And if they respond otherwise, you can handle it.

The world is not a reflection of what your parents did when you were growing up. If your mom got mad when you asked questions, that doesn't mean everyone is going to get mad at you for asking questions. If your dad got upset when you challenged him or didn't immediately and silently obey, that doesn't mean your boss will react the same way. That's a simplistic conclusion that comes from a lack of self-awareness and too much avoidance. You need to step up and take the risks and see what actually happens in the real world with lots of different people. Give people the chance to show you who they really are. This will give you a much more complex and accurate map of how people respond. It's time to upgrade from the one you created when you were six years old.

Instead of assuming they'll be upset, you can be surprised when someone's upset. "Oh, you didn't like me asking those questions? Interesting." "Oh, you didn't want me to share my opinion there? Huh! I'm surprised. And curious. Why not?"

When you can meet someone else's upset reaction with surprise and curiosity, there's nothing you can't handle. The essence of this approach is, "Oh, you're upset? Tell me more." We don't need to run from this stuff and hide under our beds. We can lean into it.

"I can't believe you said that in the meeting. That was absolutely ridiculous. We had them until you fucked it up." That would be a pretty uncomfortable thing to hear from a colleague, wouldn't it? Ooh, how about a boss? Freaky. At this point, most people would take one of three approaches. All ineffective. All safety-focused. All cowardly.

Option A: Hastily and profusely apologize.

"I'm so sorry. That was terrible. I don't know why I said that. I should have kept my mouth shut."

This might get your boss to stop criticizing you in the moment, or it might not. Either way, it won't actually be solving anything.

Option B: Defend, Blame, and Explain

"I can't believe they offered us such a low amount. It's insulting. The only reason I shared that info in there was because accounting told me those numbers. They are a mess over there."

Confuse, distract, derail. Whatever it takes to get the heat off of you. If it wasn't a boss, you might blame the other person directly. There's something wrong with me? No, sir, there is something wrong with you!

Option C: Limp Dead Horse

"..."

You just stay quiet and take it. You hang your head in shame and silently agree with everything your boss says. You hope by being quiet and just taking it that the upset will pass quickly.

Let's contrast these three wonderful strategies against something that actually works: being surprised and curious. Here is an example of how a conversation might go when you approach it in that way. Notice how it actually leads to a dialogue, whereas the other strategies are designed to end the conversation as quickly as possible.

Boss: I can't believe you said that in the meeting. That was absolutely ridiculous. We had them until you fucked it up.

You: Oh, you really didn't like me saying something in there. Tell me more. What specifically did I do that fucked it up?

Boss: Are you kidding? You don't know?

You: I can see you're really upset with me. I have a number of ideas about how that could have gone better. And I'm curious to hear more about what you were seeing.

Boss: Well, for starters you shared about our numbers from accounting. Why would you tell them that? Now they know exactly what we are able to do and they are going to turn the screws on us.

We can get them as a supplier but it's going to cost us way more.

You: Ah, so you are concerned that with the info about some of our numbers they're going to take advantage of us and raise up their prices.

Boss: Yes, that's exactly what they're going to do.

You: And what are you worried will happen as a result?

Boss: We're going to pay through the nose here and not have anything left to fund the Receiver project, which is what we need more than anything for the next five years.

You: Wow, I had no idea. So you're most worried about something interfering with the Receiver project.

Boss: You're damn right I am.

What did you notice about this exchange? What stands out to you?

At this point you can apologize, or explain your thinking. But notice how it's coming from a very different place. Not from fear and conflict avoidance, but in order to share your own perspective or to help your boss understand why you did what you did.

Notice how curiosity allows you to find out what's really going on. Whenever someone gets upset, instead of making it immediately about you and assuming it's your fault, slow down. Breathe. Become curious. I wonder what button got pushed in them? I wonder what they're scared of underneath and trying to get angry about to feel more powerful? What do they really need here? Certainty, security, to feel significant? Armed with this curiosity, you can deal with any conflict, regardless of whether it's with your spouse, a stranger, a customer, or your supervisor.

Reflect back to them what they are saying in order to gain clarity for yourself. Find out exactly what they're upset about, and why it bothers them. Get specific. The phrase "tell me more" is one of the most simple and powerful ways to head directly into upset in a way that opens the other person up.

Because, like all feelings, upset and anger just want to be heard and acknowledged. Once you hear and acknowledge the anger, you will almost always notice a marked shift in the other person. They will calm way down, be way more open, and actually seem to like you more. I've had people go from complete anger and either saying or implying "fuck you," to feeling happy, relaxed, and feeling quite positively towards me. "This guy here, he's great!"

All thanks to curiosity. So know that you can handle anything. Any upset, any conflict. There is no reason to constantly be on guard, trying to avoid it. Just do what you want to do, say want you want to say, and trust yourself. On the rare occasion that someone gets upset, know that you can handle it. The next time someone gets upset with you, get curious, and prepare to have a conversation unlike any other

The piece about sharing your perspective after being curious is quite important and one I used to overlook. It was my fear of direct contact and conflict that caused me to simply listen and empathize and not voice any countering perspective. But this, too, is an incomplete strategy. We must be able to speak our minds, share our opinions, and put our feelings out there or else we will leave feeling frustrated, resentful, and with unresolved questions.

Going back to the example above after you've heard your boss's opinions about your performance in the meeting, you might say: "From my perspective, it was important to share the numbers from accounting. If they see what our capacity is and what we're looking for, they are going to be more eager to supply us."

You don't need to make your boss sound wrong and get into an argument. You also don't need to shy away from sharing your reasoning and perception. This is incredibly important: your opinion matters. Your expertise, insight, and intuition are valuable. You might be seeing something that your boss isn't. He doesn't even have to agree with you. In fact, he might not. But that's not the point. The point is to value yourself and your opinion, to be a powerful person and a leader who can speak his or her mind, and to leave the situation feeling more at peace and resolved rather than full of pent-up, unspoken feelings.

The Path

Being socially fearless is less of a destination and more of an ongoing path that you continue to walk down. The more you practice fearlessness, the better you'll be at staying on the path. When you veer off, you'll notice it and learn to quickly get back to your power and what's really true.

Veering off feels like fear. Fear of what others will think, fear of others being upset with you, fear of imagined confrontation or conflict. It feels like pent-up emotion, frustration, and seething resentment. It can also feel like intense anger or rage that you experience as feeling and thoughts that you would never share. Whenever you notice any of these things, congratulations! You've just located where you are: off the path. Out in the woods somewhere.

To bring yourself back, start by pausing right where you are. One of my favorite teachers, Tara Brach, refers to this as a "sacred pause." Instead of blindly running through the underbrush, sobbing, slamming into branches and shrubs, just stop. Pause. Breathe. Feel the feelings of fear in your chest, or stomach, or throat. Notice the racing thoughts, the virtual argument in your head, or the imagined terrible scenario of someone hating you. Take five minutes and stop running from your feelings.

Just this morning, before I sat down to write this, I was disconnected from my power. My wife and I just had our second son. He is one week old, and he is asleep on my lap as I type this. I noticed I was having intense, repetitive fearful thoughts and feelings about a new client. His situation is complex and he was sending me many lengthy emails with dozens of concerns listed in each one. I felt a pressing need to answer everything in every email prior to our next session, afraid of setting boundaries around session times, and afraid of him being upset with me.

Off the path. Pause. Breathe. Feel. So, I did what I always do when I'm running from feelings and have a hard time turning and facing whatever's there. I snort a line of cocaine and keep running faster. No, I'm kidding. I set a countdown timer on my watch for twelve minutes. Twelve happens to be the day of the month I was born, the number on all my soccer jerseys as a kid, and my favorite number. It's also a solid length of time to spend feeling my feelings.

The first few minutes are always the hardest. Ugh, I don't want to feel this. There's a thrashing around inside, trying to get away. Compulsion to respond to a different email, or start working on this book. Do something, anything, rather than feel whatever's underneath. But, the timer helps. I know I'm not doing anything else until that sucker goes off. So I breathe deeper and I feel more. I go right into the center of that shaky, unsettled feeling square in the center of my chest.

After a few minutes, I feel a powerful shift. The feelings are still there, but my mind has stopped running. There is release and softness in my breath and body and I am open and curious about the uncomfortable feelings. I glance down at my watch—it's been seven minutes. This is usually the case for me: about five to seven minutes of thrashing resistance before I surrender. If I don't pause and set the timer, I can remain in thrashing resistance for hours. Or better yet, I'll keep running ahead of the feelings by staying perpetually busy with endless projects and activities.

As I relax, I remind myself: I don't need anything from this client. I don't need him to like me, to want to work with me, or to approve of me. I will serve him in the best way I can, and I am not responsible for his reactions, feelings, or desires. I remind myself there are many people who want to work with me, and only a small number I can take at any given time. I don't need to please him or worry about his upset. I can serve him powerfully, and I can be curious if he is upset with me.

As the anxiety about this client melts away, and as my body starts to relax, I feel an even more uncomfortable sensation in my chest. Oh dear. This one is way scarier, way worse. All of a sudden I realize the anxiety around the client was mostly a distraction from an even more uncomfortable feeling. The more you practice this, the more you will discover these kinds of subtle avoidance maneuvers. We will often avoid painful feelings like grief, hurt, or anger by becoming overly anxious or obsessively worried about some problem in our lives. It might be significant, or sometimes trivial, but we will feel an absorbing amount of anxiety about it and an intense urge to "figure it out," or do something to solve it right now. Time after time, with clients and with myself, I've seen that this is an elaborate way to avoid the feelings we don't want to feel. But for me in that moment, there was no avoiding it now, it was here and needed to be reckoned with.

As I looked down at my sleeping boy, barely a week in this world, my heart wrenched. He is so utterly vulnerable, and I am too. My heart is precariously placed inside of three people who are outside of me: my wife, our older son, and now this little dude. I am permanently linked to each of them. Should he get sick, or die, I will be crushed. Lousy fear of loss. Lousy vulnerability. I want to be a rock, an island. I want to be invincible to loss, to pain, to vulnerability. But alas, I don't think that's possible if I want to live fully and with an open heart, deeply connecting and loving others. It's the price of admission I'm afraid.

So I felt that heart wrenching feeling in my body. I felt it burn and twist and move all around my chest. I felt it turn and squeeze in my heart, as if it were stretching the edges to make it bigger so it could include this new little one.

All our fears are fears of feelings. Face the feelings and you can handle anything. All the fears about people being upset, about messing something up, about being disliked or rejected, are all just fears of uncomfortable feelings in your body. The feelings you don't want to feel in the future. But you're already feeling some version of them now. So just let yourself feel them. Go right into them with a bold willingness and courageous heart. No matter how intense or unpleasant, if you stay in your body and don't get lost in thinking about the feelings, you will make it to the other side. They will pass. And you will feel more open in your chest, more powerful, more clear, and more resourceful.

From this place, to get back on the path and make progress, you must go do the things you are afraid of. That means you assert yourself, speak up in the meeting, and challenge your colleagues when needed. You share more openly with friends and reveal your vulnerabilities to your spouse or lover. You get out in the world and face your fears directly.

As you do, you progress further and further along this path of social fearlessness. And many things that used to scare you will no longer impact you at all. Things that used to terrify you and keep you up at night may create minor anxiety that you can rapidly work through and let go of in minutes or an hour. Each time you face uncomfortable feelings in yourself or take actions out in the world, you grow in power. As your social power increases, so does your social fearlessness and sense of personal freedom.

MAKE SHIT HAPPEN POWER

In addition to social power, personal power also includes your ability to do things in the world. I like to call this Make Shit Happen Power. The earlier chapters in this book were designed to help you remove excuses and stories, face your fears, and get into massive action. These steps are essential to breaking free from stagnation and inaction into creating more and making things happen in the world. You transform from being an effect in life to a cause. You influence yourself and the world around you to go after what you want and design your life as you would like it to be.

While the previous chapters spring you into rapid forward motion to make shit happen in your life, there is one other aspect of this power that is incredibly important to master. This is how you make decisions.

The Power Of Decision

One of the best ways to build power in yourself and in your life is to decide. Decisions are good. Making decisions is good. In fact, you can decide right now to be more decisive.

Why are decisions so powerful? Because they direct action. They move you forward in life by giving you direction and momentum. Making them requires trust in yourself and creates trust in yourself. Trust strengthens you to make decisions. Especially big decisions about your future, your family, your money, or your life.

The other day I was speaking with a man who wanted to step up in his life. His boss, best friend, and ex-girlfriend all told him he needed more confidence. He needed to stop second-guessing himself, stop doubting himself. To just say what he thought and do what he wanted to do more. That's why he sought me out.

He had dreams of being a director in his company or even starting his own enterprise. He wanted to get over his fears about meeting women and being his authentic self with them so he could create an outstanding relationship. He wanted to transform his life.

Sounded good to me. I liked the guy. He was self-aware, intelligent, and had a good heart. So I decided. I decided which coaching proposal to offer him and did so. But he soon became tormented. He wanted to do it, but he couldn't pull the trigger. It wasn't the money;

he could afford it. It wasn't the motivation, because he really wanted the changes. It was his deep fear of making a strong decision in the moment.

I asked him if he wanted me to give him some coaching around that. He agreed and we explored his fears, what it would mean if he said yes, what others would think, and on and on. After about thirty minutes of this, I was pushing up against my next appointment and I told him I had to go.

He said he had to ask his friend. He wanted his friend to decide for him. And I knew then that he was too stuck for me to help him at this time.

We must make decisions in life. Yes or no. It doesn't matter. But make one. Do it now. You can start small, with what shirt to wear today or what meal you order at a restaurant. Give yourself ten seconds to scan the menu, pick something and decide. Close the menu. Next topic. The more decisions you make, and the bigger those decisions are, the more powerful you become. However, there are two major pitfalls that can trip you up on your decide-your-way-to-ultimate-power journey.

The Inner-Committee Method

I learned about this concept from Robert Glover, the author of *No More Mr. Nice Guy* (which is an awesome book for building personal power). Actually, I'd been using this method of decision making for years, I just didn't know what it was called. Basically, when faced with a decision, you imagine a bunch of different people and what they would say about it. You also imagine what they would think of you based on your decision.

The list could be small—you imagine your spouse, or a parent, or a close friend. *What would she say? What would he say? What would my friend think of me if I did this? How would everyone feel about it?*

Or the list could be large. You imagine your spouse, parents, friends, and co-workers. You imagine what the friend of your friend might think. You factor everyone you can think of into the decision. *What "should" I do so the highest number people would approve of what I'm doing? I don't want anyone to judge me or think less of me for any reason now…*

Ugh. It's painful just to write this section. It brings me right back to that place of people-pleasing unassertiveness that I spent many years of my life flailing around in. It makes me want to shout out: *Get out! Get out now!*

Drop the committee method. No one is in charge of your life for you. No one else's opinion is more fitting than your own when it comes to the decisions in your life. Step up and decide to use the Internal Decision Method from now on. That means you check with yourself first and foremost. Start with yourself. *What do I want? Why do I want that? What would that bring to my life? What do I NOT want?*

If you want to factor other people in, be specific and clear as to why you are choosing them. As in, "I want to consult with my dad about his thoughts on the financial aspect of this because he's been studying finances for thirty years." It's not about getting his approval, it's about getting some wisdom and tactical perspective. Of course, if the decision directly involves someone else, you can have a discussion with them about their desires. But still, you must ultimately decide. Internally. From the inside.

The more you use this method of internal decision-making, the more powerful you will become. You'll stop looking outside of yourself for certainty from someone else. Sure, they may temporarily give it to you, but deep down you will feel more uncertain and insecure because you know you are not in charge of your own life.

Pay attention over the next few days to the decisions you make, both small and large. Notice when the committee starts to speak up, and affirm in yourself that you can make decisions internally and for yourself. You can even discuss it with people and get their input, but you are still in charge of making the ultimate decision. And as you do this, notice how much more powerful you feel.

Maximizing

"The alternative to maximizing is to be a satisficer. To satisfice is to settle for something that is good enough and not worry about the possibility that there might be something better."
- Barry Schwartz

When my brother and I were teenagers we used to drive places in our parents' old car. I didn't have my license yet, so Tariq was in charge of driving (and therefore the radio). These were the rules he made up, and he was always better at debating than I was. Perhaps that's why he's a lawyer now.

Anyway, as we drove around town, he'd be pressing the buttons of the pre-programmed radio stations. When he found a song he liked on slot number 1, he would pause and say, "Ah, cool. I like this song." Then he'd rapidly press numbers 2 through 6, always to return back to his song on number 1.

"Why do you check the other stations when you like the song on the first one?" I asked one morning on the way to school.

"Because there could be something even better."

This is maximizing. It's a term I picked up from Barry Schwartz and his book, *Paradox of Choice: Why More Is Less*. Maximizing is the decision-making style where you want to check all your options. You want to price check ten different alternatives to make sure you are getting the best deal. You want to check thoroughly to make sure there's not something better, longer lasting, or somehow superior. While a small amount of due diligence seems good for bigger decisions, this approach often creates more indecision, confusion and suffering. Barry suggests that keeping too many options open seems to cost us emotionally and psychologically. That it does.

When we are maximizing we are operating with this flawed thinking: there is one option that we could pick that will bring all good things and no bad things. That we can know all possible outcomes and consequences of our decision and there is a clear "right" choice. All pleasure, no pain. This leads to confusion, indecision, anxiety, and stress. It also leads to regret and self-criticism after the fact, as we look back and say, "Ahh, if only I'd made the other choice…The *right* choice."

The alternative to maximizing is "satisficing." This means assessing your choices, weighing them for a brief time, and then making a decision. Bam. I'll go with that. Let's do it. This kind of decision-making involves letting go. Letting go of trying to be perfect, trying to avoid future discomfort, trying to only have pleasure and no pain in life. You let go of always trying to be right, and never making mistakes. You realize that there's a "good enough" choice, and it will bring pleasure and pain. It will have awesome benefits, and some unforeseen challenges. That's how all decisions work because that's how life works.

The key to switching from maximizing to satisficing is to see maximizing for what it is: a fear-based approach to decision making focused on avoiding all pain. As such, instead of indulging it, you can simply notice it and then switch to a different style.

For small decisions, start satisficing immediately. All over the place. Which route to take to work, which meal to order, which movie to watch. Make those decisions in seconds, and stick to them. Notice if you have a maximizing spasm afterwards of fear, regret, or FOMO (fear of missing out). Perhaps you longingly look at your friend's eggs benedict and think, *Why on earth did I order the breakfast burrito?* Let yourself be wracked by regret for a few minutes. That's just your maximizing pattern thrashing around as you work it out of your system. Keep going. Make it a habit to make small decisions quickly.

For bigger decisions, like directions for your business, making a large purchase, or beginning a work or personal relationship, you can assess a little more. But even then, gather what info you need, which can often be done in one or two days at the absolute most. Then, with that data, make a decision and do it. Yes or no. It doesn't matter. The decisiveness is what matters.

Trust in yourself. Know that there are no wrong decisions. Each path will lead to amazing gains, as well as problems and challenges. You can't avoid problems in life nor would you want to. Dealing with problems is what keeps you growing and strengthening yourself. Without problems you'd become a lethargic, atrophied, fragile lump of inert matter. You may think you don't want any problems, but trust me you want them. So invite them in. Hopefully they are higher quality problems than you faced a year ago, or five years ago.

Decide, and then boldly step down the path you've chosen. Own it. Work with whatever happens that you don't like. Enjoy the goodies along the way and take some time to feel grateful for them.

DECISION TIME

Once you've broken free of maximizing and the inner committee method, your decision-making will rapidly improve. You will make decisions with force, conviction, and swiftness. You will build more trust in yourself and your power will increase exponentially. And here's the best part: decisions lead to greater action. When you decide, you're no longer holding off, hesitating, or waiting to do or not do something. You just do it. Or if you decide to not do something, you're done with it and you move on to something else that you do decide to do. Thus with more decisions, comes more action. More action equals more learning, more progress, more results. This leads to career advancement, explosive growth in your business and income, better relationships, better health, more confidence, and a better life.

Ready to get out there and make some decisions?

Let's start right now. What is one decision you can make in this moment that will help you move forward in your life. It could be small or large. Something you've been bouncing back and forth on, or procrastinating about. Bring it to your mind right now. Stand up, take a deep breath in, and feel your feet on the floor, strong and firm. Tap into your own inner knowing. Forget what anyone else would think or say; you have all the answers you need inside of you now. Everything you need is inside of you right now. All the courage, power, confidence, and certainty you need is right there, right now. Breathe deep, feel that decisiveness and just choose. Right. Now.

Good. Now put it into practice. Go take action on that decision immediately. Send that email. Make that call. Schedule that appointment. Look up that person on the Internet. Get those running shoes on. Whatever it is you decided, do it now. The more you do this, the more power you generate, and the more confident you become.

The secret key is now. In fact, this is so important the entire next chapter is dedicated to it. So let's dive into that now, shall we?

CHAPTER X:

NOW

"When would now be a good time?"
- Tony Robbins

Here we are. Almost at the end of the book. You've learned more about confidence, overcoming fear, taking bold action, speaking up for yourself, asking for what you want, mastering money, and being the most powerful version of yourself than most people will learn in their entire lives. You are swimming in a vast pool of insight, understanding, awareness and information.

Perhaps you feel excited by the idea of liberation. You imagine what your life will be like when you are free from fear and self-doubt: when you are able to say and do what you want more freely. Perhaps the idea of maximizing your career and financial confidence so you can become truly wealthy—both in money and in gratitude—fills you with energy and inspiration. And maybe knowing that you can find and share love with many people, including that one special person, warms your heart and brings tears of relief to your eyes.

And yet, all of this is just hypothetical. It's potential energy. Potential transformation. None of it becomes real until you step through the doorway that is now open before you.

THE DOORWAY

Whenever we have a moment of insight, a doorway opens. We see something about ourselves, we decide we're going to change something, and we determine what our new action will be. In this moment, like any moment, there is an opportunity to take action and shift the course of our lives toward a positive direction. We are temporarily free from the negative stories and excuses that hold us back. We are inspired by our outcomes and our vision so that we have the motivation to face fear and break through to a life of confidence and action. We are ready. This is the doorway.

It's a doorway into a new life. A new way of being in the world that completely changes what the world around you looks like. This leads to new beliefs, new behaviors, and ultimately a new identity. It also changes the results you get in all areas of life and the responses you get from other people. Once you step through the door, you'll find yourself on a path towards your ultimate destination: where you truly want to go.

But this doorway doesn't permanently remain wide open. In fact, sometimes our motivation and hunger to make big changes is fairly short-lived. If you do not take action in the moment, right now, then the doorway tends to slowly close over time. When the stories and excuses are cleared, and we can so vividly see what we want, the only thing standing in the way is fear. And the longer you stand at fear's doorstep, hesitating and waiting to go in, the scarier crossing that threshold becomes. The more daunting, uncomfortable, and overwhelming it seems. The longer you wait, the harder it gets. This is true for almost everything.

Then, in that moment of hesitation, the stories and excuses rush back in to fill up the space your waiting has created. Your Safety Police reforms their squad, and now they are stronger than ever. Now they've got the additional ammo that you "tried something before and it didn't work." This, of course, is absurd because you didn't really try anything. You just read a book and maybe dabbled with an exercise or two. But that's good enough for the Safety Police's evidence file, and they will use it to thoroughly convince you that nothing will work, that it's not worth wasting your time and getting your hopes up, that you should just resign yourself to a mediocre life of safety.

That is, of course, unless you step through the doorway. Better yet, leap through it. If you can leap through and commit yourself to something on the other side, there's no going back. You've thrown your hat over the fence and now you have to climb over or else you'll never get it back.

This chapter is about helping you do just that. Because there is only one time to step through the doorway. Only one time to do anything, really. And that moment is the present moment—right now.

The Dream Killers

That sounds like it could be the name of a bad 80s band. But actually, The Dream Killers are the things we tell ourselves that prevent us from taking action right now to maximize our confidence and create the life we want. Dream killing might sound kind of extreme, but that's really what these stories do. It's not the dramatic Wild West shoot-out kind of killing that we've all come to know and love from movies and video games. It's actually the more sneaky, invisible, longer-term kind of killing, like drinking yourself to death, or eating heavily processed, sugary foods for most of your life.

Too grim? I'm afraid it has to be. Because these killers are no laughing matter. Stick with me, because we have to illuminate these sneaky saboteurs so that you can uproot them and step into the seat of all your power, which you can only access in the present moment.

THE MYTH OF "SOMEDAY"

"There are seven days of the week and "someday" is not one of them."
- Rita Chand

This one is so effective because it seems so plausible. Our Safety Police love to use this one because if they tell us never to do something, that can rouse suspicion in us. Never take action to break free and create the life I want? That's not good. But what if it says, "Oh, you totally will. Someday. Someday really soon. Like next month when things have calmed down. Or next year when you have more money to invest in figuring out the solution to this problem."

It not only sounds plausible, it even sounds reasonable. It's the sensible thing to do. Except it almost never is. Unless we're talking about blowing all your savings on a gigantic big screen TV, the time to take action is almost always now. I'm talking about the actions that you know will improve your life, like applying for that new job, stepping up at work and going after leadership roles, creating your own business, pursuing that person you find irresistibly attractive and amazing, going out after work to meet people instead of going home and being lonely, calling that acquaintance and turning them into a friend. That kind of action. The time for that kind of action is now. Always now.

Someday is a sneaky delay tactic designed to put off the discomfort of facing whatever fear accompanies the action you know you must take. Asking that person out? *I could get rejected and feel embarrassed and inadequate. I'll do it later.* Take that sales course to improve my performance and grow in my career? *Geez, that means I'll have to do more sales calls and rack up more nos. That sounds unpleasant. I ll wait until next year when I have the money to invest in that course. I just can't afford it right now.* And on, and on. We can easily do this in most of the areas of our lives that really matter.

Somewhere deep down we are secretly hoping that the problem

will just solve itself. Sometimes we have a semi-believable story, such as: *my social life will get better when I move to that bigger city so I'll worry about making new friends then.* But often we don't even have an idea or plan about how things will get better. It's just a strange form of denial that we use to tell ourselves that something in the future will somehow be different, even if we don't take any new action today.

The result of this is that we avoid discomfort, avoid risk, and avoid the unknown. We stay with what is familiar in the moment, even if it's disappointing or painful. At least it's familiar and safe, dammit! And the myth of "someday" allows us to stay in this holding pattern until that day arrives. Which, of course, it often doesn't.

So fuck someday. What are you putting off until next month, or next year? What stories are you telling yourself about why it's better to wait and do it later? Are they really true? Or are they just a clever way to dodge fear and stay in your comfort zone?

Whatever your reasons are for wanting more confidence in your life—more social freedom, more friendships and connections, amazing dates and a loving relationship, massive career success and a feeling of purpose and accomplishment—all of that is outside of your comfort zone and will only happen when you start taking action now.

Guess why? Because it will take a lot of action to get to any of those things. More than you probably realize. So you'd better get started right now. The sooner the better. Post haste. Forthwith. With great swiftness. Go. Do it. Right. Now.

THE MYTH OF SLOW CHANGE

This one is sticky like molasses. It makes your life feel like a slow novel that trudges through boring stuff till finally it stumbles onto a good moment. I personally don't have much patience for books like that. If I can't get into the plot within the first thirty pages, I usually move on to something else. Why waste my time with a boring story?

Many people hold the unconscious belief that change takes large amounts of time. That years and decades are required to create the shifts you want in yourself and your life circumstances (if they can even happen at all). This creates a heavy feeling around change, and slows down our actions to a snail's pace. Change is hard, it takes forever, and sometimes people can't change at all.

I had one client who loved to ask me this question. "Aziz," he'd say as he squinted his eyes and looked up towards the ceiling, "is it really possible for someone to change? I mean, can it *really* be done?"

I always wondered why he looked up in the sky as he said that. The first time he asked, I shared my thoughts about the subject.

"Yes." I said with absolutely certainty. "I've made these changes myself and I've personally seen hundreds of other people do it is well. You can absolutely make massive shifts in your confidence if you put in the energy and focus."

The second time he asked me this question, I became curious about what he might be feeling. "Are you asking because you doubt that you can change?"

But by the third, fourth and fifth times he asked, I started to realize this was not a real question. It was a delay tactic disguised as a legitimate philosophical inquiry. This pondering was a way to eat up our session times without focusing on his stories, excuses, or fears. It stopped us from getting to real actions he was going to take that week to transform his life. He subconsciously wanted to stay in the land of slow change, where change may or may not even be possible at all.

Yes, big, long-held patterns of social anxiety can take time to change. Reprogramming yourself from the passive, unassertive nice person into the bold, direct, leader that you really are will take practice over time. Getting skilled at speaking with people, engaging groups, approaching attractive strangers, being your most bold and authentic self on dates, and anything else you want to excel in will take time.

But the change happens in an instant, and that instant leads to a series of change-filled moments. The change begins the moment you open your mouth and say something different. The moment you make the joke, or take the risk to flirt, or raise your hand to speak up in a group. The change happens right now. It doesn't happen slowly over time. It occurs right as you do it. And then the next day, you do something like that again. You raise your hand again in the next class. You volunteer to lead the next team meeting. You walk up to the most inspiring and powerful person in the room and you introduce yourself and start a conversation with them. You challenge your colleague because you have a different perspective that you want to share, even though you feel intimated. You take action the next day, and the next, and the next.

In this way, your life is made up of a series of moments. Each moment is a choice to be bold and step outside of your comfort zone. Each is a fork in the road where you choose the path you are going to take. When you do this, and you consistently stay on the path of confidence, boldness, and courage, then the bigger changes in your life circumstances happen with great speed and swiftness. You achieve what you want faster than you ever imagined possible. All because you decided to change right now.

THE QUEST FOR WHY

The final dream killer I want to uproot is the quest for "why". This is the idea that we need to know why something is happening before we can change and solve it. It is actually the basis for much of the psychotherapy that is still practiced around the world, which is based on philosophies pioneered by Sigmund Freud and others. The idea is that if you just intellectually knew why you felt sad, or anxious, or upset, then these feelings would somehow magically disappear.

While there can sometimes be a sense of relief at being able to identify exactly what you're feeling in the moment, and guess as to where it might be coming from, this by no means resolves the feelings or helps you take immediate action to transform your life.

One client of mine was recently divorced and had spent many years of life in a dissatisfied marriage, feeling limited and stuck. Now he was free to explore, build his confidence, and find the perfect woman for him. Only he was terrified to approach and start a conversation with any woman, especially one he found attractive. He imagined she would reject him because he was not attractive, smooth, or otherwise good enough.

As we discussed his fears and I began to help him overcome them, he kept wanting to discover the big "why". "Why am I so scared of women in the first place? Why do I feel this fear?"

I don't know, perhaps two years of psychoanalysis would reveal that his mother did not treat him with enough warmth between the ages of two and three, and so now he is perpetually imagining all women are harsh rejecting people, just like he experienced his mother to be during those formative years. And maybe that would bring a surge of confidence and he could easily start conversations with women and ask them out. But probably not. And I've actually worked with many people who have gone through therapy, sometimes as much as five years of it. They come out the other side with the same problems. Same limitations. Same stories. Tons more insight, but no dates. No action. No substantial change.

I'm much more interested in doing whatever works, and preferably as quickly as possible. So I said this to him, "Going over to a woman you find attractive and starting a conversation with her is like jumping into a swimming pool. It can be scary to just jump in the water—what if it's cold, what if it hurts when I hit the water? We could sit on the side of the pool and theorize as to why you might be afraid to jump in the water in the first place, but I don't see how that will make it any easier to get in there."

So instead we focused on how to manage that sensation of fear in his body, and how to stop running from it. I taught him how to meet it with self-acceptance and compassion instead of frustration and impatience. He then practiced facing that fear inside of his own body regularly. Soon he began by getting in the shallow end. He said "hi" to women as he walked by them on a busy street. He gave occasional compliments to women as they walked by. But he never stopped and talked with them. This was the shallow end of the pool, low-risk type stuff. But it was immediate change.

Feel the feelings, face your fears, and take action. This is how you will transform. Sometimes reflecting on painful experiences from our past, making sense of them, and healing old emotional wounds is incredibly liberating and necessary. But in my experience that process is less focused on figuring out the "why" and much more focused on releasing painful feelings and negative beliefs.

Having a detailed story about why you are afraid to do something is the booby prize. It might be satisfying, but it doesn't automatically create the freedom you want. That is just your mind hoping for an easy way out. *Maybe I can just figure all of this out in my brain and then I won't have to feel any uncomfortable sensations or face any fears!*

Nope. The only way out is through. And the only time to go through is now.

LEAPING THROUGH

An extraordinary life awaits you when you step through your fears and into the unknown. Prior to meeting me, one of my clients had lived his life afraid of taking any steps into the unknown. She did not even have a clear sense of what unfortunate and painful experiences lurked in shadows beyond that door. She just felt fear, dread, and panic about making the leap out of her safe place.

One day in a session I asked her, "What do you imagine will happen if you take a risk? What are you most afraid of?"

"I don't really know," she replied. "I feel like I would just fall into an endless abyss. A scary, dark place that I couldn't get out of."

"It's true," I agreed. "You could fall when you take a leap into the unknown, towards what you really want."

She nodded.

"And," I added, "it's about a three foot fall."

She paused for a moment, lost in her reverie until my words sunk in. "What?" she asked.

"It's about a three foot fall. Into some mud."

She looked at me, confused.

"We think it's an endless abyss. A pain that will swallow us up and never end. But that's not how risks—or life—work. The reality is that when we fail, or fall short of our goal, we fall down into some messy, unpleasant mud. Then we thrash around until we can figure things out enough to lurch forward through the muck. This rough patch of being in the mud lasts an hour, a day, or a week, and then we are back up on dry land. Things get easier again, and you make it through."

She had a thoughtful expression on her face and was nodding slightly. I could see it was landing well, so I continued.

"And, now you have a sense of confidence that you can handle the fall. That you can navigate the mud. This gives you more courage and willingness to leap the next time. And if you are growing and moving towards what you really want there will be a next time. And a time after that. One doorway into the unknown after another."

Then her mind was blown and she went on to earn forty-nine billion dollars the next year. No, I'm kidding. But she did make a fundamental shift in our work together, where she stopped sliding through life, attempting to dodge all risk. Instead she began putting herself out there, step-by-step: at work, in her romantic life, and in all of her interactions. This lead to becoming a leader in her field, and thriving in her romantic life, which was something that had eluded her for many years.

What doorway can you leap through? More precisely, in order

to get what you want, and to create an extraordinary life that fills you with excitement, pride, and fulfillment, what doorway *must* you leap through? Right now, in this very moment, you know what it is. Perhaps you need to start being more direct, honest, and assertive. Perhaps you need to let your guard down, reveal more of yourself to others, and be more vulnerable. Perhaps you need to create your own business, change jobs, apply for a new position, or even change careers. Only you know what that leap is.

What's on the other side of the door excites you, inspires you, and makes you feel alive. The jump scares you, feels big, overwhelming, or downright terrifying. I don't know what your leap is, but I do know one thing. The time is now.

You Can't Get Out Alive

A teacher and hero of mine, Les Brown, likes to remind audiences at his talks of this simple fact about life: "You can't get out alive!"

You are going to die. For reals. So are your parents, your friends, your colleagues, your customers, your kids, and your pets. Everyone you know right now will one day be dead. We hope that death comes sequentially, to those who are oldest first, but we all know it doesn't always work that way.

The maternity ward where my wife birthed both of our sons is on the seventh floor of a children's hospital in Portland, Oregon. In the floors below us were sick children, recovering children, and dying children. Floor three is the children's cancer treatment ward. I accidentally got off there one day when I was trying to get back to our room on the top floor. Yikes.

We all know this, but we often don't act like we know this. We act as if we have forever. We have tomorrow. We have "someday". Maybe we do. But maybe we don't. Today might be the last day you see your kids. This morning might be the last time you say goodbye to your husband.

An acquaintance of my wife lives in a nice neighborhood in Portland, with very little crime. A month ago her husband went to the store to pick up a few groceries. As he was exiting the store and returning to his car, he was assaulted by two men and one woman. They shot him, killing him on the spot, and drove off in his vehicle.

My purpose in sharing this is not to be morbid, or to induce some sort of "You have the live every moment like it's your last!" frenzy. That level of pressure can be exhausting. Instead, we just want to be jolted out of our illusion that we are guaranteed so much time that we can put everything that is important off to another day.

Sooner or later, you are going to die. Even if you attempt to avoid all risk, play it safe, and minimize failure and rejection, you are still going to die. Given this inevitable end, how do you want to play the game? What kind of life do you want to lead? Do you want your time here to be an adventure, an epic tale of love and loss, triumph and defeat? The journey of a hero?

Across all cultures, everyone loves heroes. They go after great things, fight for noble causes, and face danger head on. Can you imagine a movie or novel in which the main character considered doing something epic, then decided it was too scary and stayed inside to watch TV instead? Then he thought about it again, felt nervous and full of self-doubt, and decided it was just too much work. And then he hung out in his house and stayed small and safe all month and all year. And that was the entire book. I mean, that was the entire book. Not much of a bestseller blockbuster there. Maybe an indie film that you'd walk away from in a sort of hazy stupor…

In any case, you are the director of your life my friend. You are the writer, the producer, and the dude who holds the boom mic. You are in charge of the entire show and you control your destiny. Do you want to find true love and create a lifelong relationship that just keeps getting better? You can do that. Do you want to make friends with amazing, successful people who inspire you? You can do that as well. Do you want to earn great amounts of wealth and enjoy more free time? Also yours for the creating.

It's your movie. Design it how you will. Cast who you want in it. And if you are determined to do whatever it takes, you will get there. Once you remove the layers of excuses and stories, the only thing stopping you is fear. And if you take bold action in the face of fear, then fear will soon have no power over you. Then it's just pure action, learning, growing, making mistakes, and learning some more. An inevitable path to success.

And one thing that accelerates this path is having a fire under your ass.

Healthy Urgency

The sooner you get started, the sooner you'll reach your destination. I know, it sounds pretty stupid-obvious, but we often don't act based on this fact. Let's say you wanted to drive across the United States from New York to Los Angeles. Why you wouldn't want to fly and be done with it in five hours, I have no idea. But let's say you had to drive for some reason. Maybe you're moving all your worldly possessions in a sole U-Haul truck.

Assuming you're not on speed and looking to break the record of twenty-nine hours, it will take you about four days to travel from coast to coast. So there you are, sitting in your packed up apartment in New York, about to set off into the unknown. If today was Monday and you left right away, you'd get there by Thursday. But what if you waited for two days and left on Wednesday? Then you'd arrive by Saturday, two days later. What if you waited until next week?

Why would I sit around in my empty apartment waiting? I'd just get on the road already! Exactly. This is the kind of energy you want behind taking action towards your goals and dreams. *Now* is the time. Not next Thursday, not next year, and good Lord not "someday." This is a healthy sense of urgency. When something is urgent, it means that it is important and requires swift action. We must move forward now.

One client of mine was a highly intelligent, successful doctor. He worked as a hospitalist and was very capable and confident in his career. However, he was not satisfied. He knew his real passion was in the world of business. His hero was Elon Musk. He had dozens of entrepreneurial ideas for products or programs that could serve the medical industry and beyond. He had the intelligence, the skill, and the knowledge of the field. He was ready. But he just sat in his empty apartment in NYC, surrounded by boxes, waiting.

Whenever he came close to diving in, committing himself, and taking action, he'd shrink back with one of these stories or excuses: "Now is not the right time. Later. Soon. When I move to Seattle. After I get married. When I have a better idea." All of these translated into one extremely limiting phrase that he never said directly: "I'll do it some time vaguely in the future."

Our work together was primarily focused on gaining confidence in dating and creating lasting relationships. When he did bring up his business ideas, I was intrigued and engaged. I was excited to hear his ideas and discuss an action plan so he could begin implementing right away. After the second time we spoke about it, however, I realized it was not a current project. It was a "someday" affair.

Highly successful people have this sense of urgency, this sense of "let's take action on this now." It's the opposite of the extended committee meeting that spends the entire two hours determining what they will talk about in their next meeting. It's about getting into action right now, in this very moment. Move the needle. Roll the ball. Whatever metaphor you prefer, just get moving!

There is so much I want to do. I want to write more, create more, record more. I want to teach more people, improve the programs and workshops I lead. I want to spend more time with my wife and two small children. I want to train with the world's most intelligent and successful people. I want to travel, learn, grow, and have adventures. My days are full. If there is an important project, I want to work on it today. Now, if possible.

Can you feel the energy, power, and motivation that comes from urgency? It can fuel you, drive you, and inspire you to move forward faster. It gives you the energy you need to take massive action in the world, and the strength to get back up when you fall down.

I describe this as "healthy urgency" because there is an unhealthy sense of urgency that we can feel from being stressed out. This happens when we have more that we want to do than there is time to do it in. And we are demanding it all get done now, and if it doesn't something terrible will happen. This leads to stress, impatience, irritability, and burnout.

You can hold your goals and dreams with urgency and still live a relaxed, spacious life. The key is to create structure and routines that give you space to slow down and think. On every work day I take forty minutes to either go for a walk or a run. This gives me time to reflect, feel my feelings, look at the bigger picture, and just breathe some fresh air. The days I practice this ritual I experience a healthy sense of urgency to make the most out of this precious life. The days I skip the ritual, I feel myself sliding into agitation, impatience, or unhealthy urgency. *If I don't get all this done now, everything's going to implode!*

What can you focus on to create that sense of healthy urgency for yourself? What would you need to remind yourself of each day? And what daily ritual can you practice to help you stay relaxed and grounded as you crush it in life?

MISSION AND PURPOSE

It appears that all humans want to experience a sense of purpose in their lives. Other animals don't seem to have this gnawing desire, but we sure do. If our lives and activities don't feel guided toward something meaningful to us, we soon begin to lose interest, passion, and hope.

Some people deal with this by trying to numb themselves. After working all day at a boring job they don't like, they immerse themselves in alcohol, video games, or television. Others become bitter or cynical, ridiculing anyone or anything that seems to be vibrant, alive, and hopeful. And still others look for a way out, but are afraid to take any risks, so they view the freedom and purpose of others through a thick wall of glass, aching with desire and envy for the things they cannot touch or be a part of. And some people step up.

I had a conversation with a man one time who was struggling to find a sense of purpose in his life. He was successful in his career, but it didn't challenge to him enough. His marriage was crumbling and he was on the fast track to divorce. "I spend hours thinking about it," he said to me. "I just have no idea what my purpose is. I don't know why I'm here, ya know?"

Why we are here is a big mystery that I would not be so presumptuous as to have a simple answer to. We are barely skimming the surface of the massive universe of galaxies all around us, as well as the infinite microscopic world of particles. It is a vast, expansive, grand mystery.

But I do know that we as individuals need to feel some sense of meaning or purpose. A sense of purpose is essential to feeling energized, alive, and optimistic. So I asked him, "What have you come up with in your inquiry?"

"That's the thing," he sighed, as if he'd said this many times before, "I just don't know. I thought about travelling and just exploring the world. I thought about helping people like you do. I even thought about starting my own company. I have so many ideas. I just don't know which one is my purpose. Which one I'm supposed to do."

Supposed to? **Sounds** like an external frame to me. As if there is someone out there who knows what the "right" thing is for this man. He was hoping for a simple answer, for someone to just tell him so he could relax and be done with it. I did no such thing.

"It sounds like you have a lot of good ideas," I began. "A number of things that you are drawn to. And you seem like you are waiting to get some sign about which one is the right choice."

"Exactly." He said, seemingly relieved that someone understood his predicament.

"Well it seems natural for you to be questioning your purpose in life after the end of your marriage. That is a common form of grieving, letting go, and growing.

"I personally don't believe we have a single purpose. We are far too complex creatures for that. Instead, I believe we have multiple purposes at different times in our lives. Different missions we are here to carry out.

"For example one of my purposes is Mass Liberation. I'm here to help as many people as possible liberate themselves from fear, self-doubt, and any other anxiety that stops them from being their authentic, free, powerful selves. I'm also here to be a loving and present father to my two sons. To support them, guide them, learn from them, and teach them as they grow into powerful leaders themselves. I have other missions too."

"Hmm," he said, taking it all in. "But how did you know those were your purposes?"

"That's another myth that trips people up. It's this idea that we are somehow supposed to know our purpose from the beginning and just move right toward it. Perhaps some people are that way—they know at age six that they are going to be a mechanic, or a surgeon—and they follow that path their entire life.

"I certainly wasn't that way. I think it's a much messier process of step-by-step exploration. Each step of the way, I moved towards what made me feel more alive and engaged. This often involved taking a risk or stepping through my fears. Back in college I switched from studying computer science to psychology. I was two-and-a-half years into my bachelor of science when I decided to switch. My computer science buddies at the time were shocked. 'But you've put so much time in,' they exclaimed. 'What will you do?'

"I didn't know. I just knew I was not prepared to spend my life in a cubicle. I knew it wasn't right for me. So I took a big, scary step into the unknown. And I fumbled around for a while, feeling like I was falling, trying different things. *Geography. That's interesting, maybe I'll try that.* So I sat in on an upper level Geography class. There, in an overly warm, under-ventilated room I stared at an ancient projector showing slides of city zoning grids. Good God. Geography wasn't it.

"I kept exploring until I stumbled into an introductory Psychology course. It was fascinating. I loved learning about all the experiments, the way people thought, and the earliest forms of marketing psychology. I had no idea what I would do with a humanities major, but I felt engaged and alive, so I took that step."

To discover your purpose(s), you must take action. You must let go of old, familiar, safe, and stifling situations and step into the unknown. Try something out for a while, see how it affects you. Do you feel more alive, and more energized as you move towards it? If so, take the next step. If not, move on to something else.

If you are unsure, take a day and reflect on all the options you are considering. Go for a long walk and hold each option in your mind, noticing how you feel about it. We are guided by our emotions more than anything else. Decide. Then take action. If you want to travel, begin making a list of places you want to visit and things you want to experience. Hell, maybe even pick the time, put it on your calendar, and book a flight. If helping people is your goal, then think about how you would like to do that. Be guided by what sounds inspiring and makes you feel alive. Maybe it's helping kids, or mentoring someone at work, or volunteering for some cause you care about. Then sign up for something, schedule something, *do* something.

Your unique purposes are like bright red apples growing on a tree. You are a little inchworm beginning your trek to the apples at the trunk. You work your way up to where all the branches fork out in different directions. Which one has an apple at the end? You don't know. So you pick one and start inching down it. Step-by-step. Soon you will hit another fork, then another, as the branch gets smaller and smaller. You won't know until you get there if there's an apple at the end of the path you've chosen. If not, that's ok. You have all the time in the world. So you inch back and choose a different path. Sometimes the apple is the reward, and sometimes it just feels good to be making progress down a path and eliminating options.

What are you here to do? What paths can you explore to increase your sense of mission and purpose?

Sometimes we think purpose comes from a dramatic shift. We have to leave our jobs, end relationships, or move to a different city. While that might be the case, they're by no means the first options I would consider. Instead, I'd be curious about what situations you are shying away from right now in your current world. Where are you avoiding, playing small, and hiding? If you were going to play bigger, be bolder, and love more fully, what would you do?

Many times, experiencing a lack of purpose in your career or a relationship is not the result of being on the wrong path. Instead, it's usually the result of questing for comfort along that path, which has strangled the joy and excitement right out of it.

What would scare you in your career? What goal or project makes your stomach lurch? What seems impossible or unreasonable? What conversation would make you uncomfortable in your relationship? What do you avoid talking about because it's scary? What do you really want to ask, to share with, and to reveal to your partner? If you're feeling nervous, you're on the right track.

Because fear and purpose go hand in hand. Your mission involves facing those perceived dangers, and taking those risks. Being as safe as possible and minimizing all discomfort is not a mission. It will not lead to a sense of purpose, passion, confidence, or fulfillment. Let fear guide you. Let it be an invitation. Take a bold step into the unknown.

THIS MOMENT

Regardless of what your missions are, how successful you might be, and how much love you have in your life, there is one thing that determines how confident and fulfilled you feel: this moment.

All of your actions are going to occur in this moment. All of your feelings and thoughts and desires are happening right now. Everything you are experiencing is happening right now.

We can spend so much time mentally time travelling to the past or the future, that we forget those mental experiences are not real. They are movies we play in our minds, much like the blockbusters you see in the cinema. As you watch those films, you are not in outer space, or the desert, or wherever else the movie is taking place. You are right there in the seat, shoving handfuls of your wife's homemade popcorn that you snuck in because it tastes way better than that dry theater junk.

The same is true for our mental projections, except we often forget this. We imagine a painful moment in the future, when something bad happens, or we experience an inconvenience or rejection, and we fully buy into it. It's as if we scream in the theater, "Oh my God! There are aliens in here!"

We tense up, flood our body with stress hormones, and prepare to deal with the painful events. We live them out, feeling all the pain, fear, and distress of that moment. Only it's not real. It's a prediction. It's a fantasy.

Extraordinary confidence resides in this moment right now. Planning and envisioning an inspiring future can be great. Reflecting on past times and old memories can bring depth and meaning in our lives. But the habitual, and addictive obsession with events in the future, and the repetitive re-livings of the past, do not serve us. They rob us of confidence and joy, leaving us stressed and depressed, even if this very moment is beautiful.

When you notice your mind is in the future, buzzing like a fly hitting its head against the window, smile. Take a breath in and feel it. Feel your feet on the floor. Bring your awareness to your senses, the colors you see, and the sounds you hear. This is what is happening now. You can handle now. When you get to any event in the future, it will be now, and you can handle that too.

Most of the time we flit off to revisit the past or imagine the future to avoid some uncomfortable feeling or sensation in the present. Whether it's a stressful workload, physical pain, or the ache of loss, our minds would much rather watch a future movie, even if it's scary. Hell, the scarier the better, because then it's absorbing enough to distract us from those damned uncomfortable feelings.

Slow down. Breathe. It's okay to feel. You can handle any feeling if you don't fight it, don't analyze how to get rid of it, and don't resist it. Just surrender to it. Let it move and expand and grow inside you. Let it twist and churn and burn. Let it move and flow and burn itself out.

And there you are. Watching it the whole time. Loving it. Noticing your breathing, your feet on the floor, the world around you. Right here in this slow, rhythmic, eternal *now*. Feelings arise, peak, and subside. Situations and events begin, peak, and end. Relationships start, continue, then conclude. People are born, they love, they die.

Whatever it is you want to achieve or experience in your life, think about it now. Success, adventures, money, relationships, love, power, material possessions. Whatever it is you want, bring it to mind now. Now imagine getting it, experiencing it, achieving it. You did it! You found the love of your life. You became a manager or an executive. You created your own successful business. You earned a million dollars, purchased a house, and bought your mom a car. You did it.

How would you feel after? Proud? Victorious? Like a success? Worthy? Able to finally relax? Feel what it would feel like to achieve everything you wanted. Let yourself bask in this victory.

You already are all of these things. You can feel proud, victorious, and successful in this moment. You are worthy. You are enough. Can you feel the relief that comes from knowing you are already there? You don't need to do anything, achieve anything, or get anything to feel worthy, lovable, valuable, and significant. You matter because you exist. You are lovable because you are alive. All you need is within you now. I love you.

THIS GIFT

Life is a gift.

Yes, it's hard. It's full of pain. Each of us will experience physical pain, sickness, loss, and the death of those we love.

Last night I was up forty-two times because our two young children were sick and would alternate waking up, screaming (I got off easy, my wife woke up 814 times). They were experiencing so much physical pain. I was experiencing emotional pain and fatigue. It was hard. Life is full of these hard moments.

And it's a gift.

From who knows where and who knows how, you exist on this planet. You have eyes that see and ears that hear. You are surrounded by green, blue, and white: forest, clouds, and sky. You have the most advanced and complex supercomputer in the known universe operating between your ears. You can run, dance, sing, and shimmy. You are a spark of life, of energy.

What a crazy, mysterious game we find ourselves in. The rules are vague, the outcome uncertain. How do you want to play? What do you want to create? How much love do you want to give? How much do you want to let in?

This gift is not like free passes to the movies, or a bag of your favorite candy. Rather, it's more like a guitar or a skateboard. The former provides instant entertainment and pleasure. Nothing to do on your part but sit down, open your mouth and enjoy. No effort, no discomfort. Easy. The latter is exciting when you first receive it, but then you soon find it's not so easy or immediately pleasurable. When you first learn to play the guitar, it's difficult, uncomfortable, and sounds pretty bad. I have yet to learn how to skateboard, but the few times I tried, I fell off and landed on pavement. Also hard.

But what happens when we stick with it and keep persisting, despite the challenge of learning something new, of making mistakes, and of falling? Pushing through the discomfort, we experience a new world of beauty and joy. The sweet melody of the guitar fills our hearts, and it is that much sweeter because it is our fingers plucking the strings that make the music. The rush of skating down a hill and feeling the wind in your face as you fly past cars and lawns fills you with excitement and elation. You earned these pleasures.

Life is the kind of gift that requires effort to enjoy. To live an extraordinary life requires a commitment to mastery of all areas that are important to you: health, relationships, love, finances, career, family, and anything else that really matters. Once you've made this commitment and choose to go down this path, your life is never the same again.

My brother is an avid backpacker. He is continually drawn to the mountains and rivers of the Sierras, finding a sense of peace and solace in the vast expanses of untamed wilderness. I have been out to the mountains a number of times with him, and he has a saying that I've always found profound, even though it's not meant to be. When we are hiking down a trail and there is a fork, and we are unable to determine which way to go based on our maps or any other forms of guidance, we must make a choice. In those instances he likes to say, "When there's a fork in the road, take the path that goes uphill."

A life of extraordinary confidence is the uphill path. It challenges you, tests you, scares you, and forces you to grow. As you climb higher and higher, you are rewarded with experiences, relationships, opportunities, wealth, power, and love. You are able to see more and more of the world around you, liberated from painful fear, limitation, and self-loathing. The higher you climb, the better it gets.

I, of course, am at the peak of the highest mountain– the beacon of unlimited confidence. No, I'm kidding, I don't know where the hell I am. Somewhere on that path, just like you, taking one step at a time. I do know that I can recognize others who are climbing as well. There is a vibrancy, an energy, an aliveness to them. They are engaged in life; their eyes are wide with all there is to see.

If you are reading this book and you have made it all the way to the end, you are most certainly on this path. Even more likely, you have been growing for years and will continue to do so for the rest of your life.

One day I hope to meet you on the trail. We might stop and talk, or simply share a nod of recognition between one extraordinary human being and another.

ABOUT THE AUTHOR

Dr. Aziz is a psychologist, author, and coach who is internationally known as the world's leading expert on confidence. Through his coaching, books, videos, and online media, he has helped thousands of people break through shyness, social anxiety, and self-doubt to create richer, happier, more confident lives.

What is most remarkable about Dr. Aziz is his own personal struggle with self-doubt and social anxiety. After reaching a low point in his own life, he made a powerful decision to do whatever it would take to get the confidence he always wanted. This lead to a passionate pursuit of studying confidence from every source, including books, audio programs, seminars, and a doctorate degree in clinical psychology from Stanford and Palo Alto Universities.

Dr. Aziz is the author of the best selling book, *The Solution To Social Anxiety*, as well as over a dozen e-books, including *5 Steps To Unleash Your Inner Confidence*. He is the host of the podcast, "Shrink For The Shy Guy", and the YouTube show, "The Art Of Extraordinary Confidence". Dr. Aziz is most passionate about his direct work with individuals and groups in coaching programs and weekend seminars. To find out more about all of the resources Dr. Aziz offers, go to, http://SocialConfidenceCenter.com.

Dr. Aziz lives in Portland, Oregon with his wife and two boys. To find out more about his personal story and inspiring journey to confidence, visit the About section of the website listed above.

ADDITIONAL RESOURCES

Books

5 Steps To Unleash Your Inner Confidence

This e-book contains powerful and proven techniques used by the world's top psychologists and coaches to help you overcome your fears and self-doubts. Whatever area your lack of confidence is impacting, this e-book can help you. It gives you the basic tools and strategies you need to start mastering your confidence today.

To download your free copy today, go to,

http://SocialConfidenceCenter.com

The Solution To Social Anxiety

In this inspiring, breakthrough book, Dr. Aziz guides you on the path out of social anxiety into lasting confidence. You will discover why you feel anxious around others, and the exact steps you need to take to develop social confidence in all areas of your life.

To get your copy today, visit, http://SocialAnxietySolution.com

Confidence Training Programs

The Confidence Unleashed System
In Dr. Aziz's complete confidence system you will discover the world's most powerful tools for overcoming fear and anxiety, eliminating self-doubt, and taking bold action in the world. Discover how to boldly speak up at work, confidently approach attractive strangers, and be the most powerful and confident version of yourself in dating, business, and your social life.
To learn more, visit, http://ConfidenceUnleashedNow.com

The Confidence Code
In this program, you will discover exactly how to unlock your social skills and conversation mastery. Learn how to feel relaxed talking with anyone, always know what to say next, create engaging and memorable conversations, and join group conversations. The more you master conversations, the more successful you can become.
To learn more, visit, http://YourConfidenceCode.com

30 Days To Dating Mastery
This step-by-step program will help you take you from feeling stuck and shy with women to a place of bold confidence and freedom. Through daily Strategy Sessions you will discover how to see yourself as attractive, overcome approach anxiety, confidently ask women out and get dates, and really enjoy dating and connecting with women. Each day you have a specific Mission which helps you take action and rapidly build confidence so you can start getting dates and attract the woman you've always wanted.
To learn more, visit, http://30DaysToDatingMastery.com

Coaching Programs and LIVE Seminars

Unstoppable Confidence Mastermind Program

This is an exclusive 1-year program that is limited to a small number of people. It includes weekly group coaching calls with Dr. Aziz, private 1-on-1 sessions, access to Dr. Aziz's Confidence Library, and VIP passes to all his LIVE seminars.

To learn more, visit,
http://ConfidenceUnleashedNow.com/mastermind

Supremely Confident Conversation Master Weekend Intensive

In this 3-day event you will master your ability to comfortably and confidently talk with anyone. You will discover how to easily start conversations with anyone in a completely relaxed way, always know what to say next to keep the conversation going, and become more dynamic, charismatic and engaging. Most importantly, you will learn how to comfortably be your authentic self so you can enjoy connecting with others at work, in dating, relationships, and life.

To learn more, visit, http://SocialConfidenceCenter.com/Events

Unlimited Dating Confidence Bootcamp

In this 3-day immersion event, join with Dr. Aziz to radically increase your confidence in your dating life. Through exercises, coaching, and taking action in the world, you will discover how to confidently approach women, start conversations, and get numbers and dates. You will also learn how to eliminate your fear of rejection and create fun, exciting relationships by being your authentic self (without any weird "pick-up artists" tricks).

To learn more, visit, http://SocialConfidenceCenter.com/Events

The Ultimate Confidence Breakthrough Weekend Intensive
Join Dr. Aziz in a life-changing 3-day LIVE event where you will discover how to instantly activate feelings of power and confidence so you can handle any situation in your life. You will also learn how to rapidly eliminate fear, social anxiety, and self-doubt so you feel comfortable in your own skin no matter what, and finally stop worrying about what others think of you once and for all. People leave this event feeling more bold, free, and powerful than ever before.
To learn more, visit http://SocialConfidenceCenter.com/Events

Printed in Great Britain
by Amazon